Ken Yeager

Trailblazers
Profiles of America's Gay and Lesbian Elected Officials

*Pre-publication
REVIEWS,
COMMENTARIES,
EVALUATIONS . . .*

"**F**inally, a book that treats the new phenomena of openly queer elected officials with light instead of the usual heat. These case studies in our changing political climate should open the door to a new focus of academic research."

Jonathan Katz
Chair, Gay/Lesbian/Bisexual
Studies Department,
San Francisco City College

"**K**en Yeager is uniquely qualified to write about our struggle for a place at the table. This compelling book is another important piece in preserving our history, telling our story, and inspiring future generations."

David Mixner
Author of *Stranger Among Friends;*
President of DBM Associates,
West Hollywood, CA

The Haworth Press, Inc.

Trailblazers
Profiles of America's Gay and Lesbian Elected Officials

HAWORTH Gay & Lesbian Studies
John P. De Cecco, PhD
Editor in Chief

Trailblazers
Profiles of America's Gay and Lesbian Elected Officials

Ken Yeager

The Haworth Press
New York • London

The Haworth Press, Inc., 10 Alice Street, Binghamton, NY 13904-1580

Softcover edition published 2000.

Cover design by Marylouise E. Doyle.

The Library of Congress has cataloged the hardcover edition of this book as:

Yeager, Ken.
    Trailblazers : profiles of America's gay and lesbian elected officials / Ken Yeager.
       p.   cm.
    Includes bibliographical references and index.
    ISBN 0-7890-0299-X (alk. paper)
    1. Legislators—United States—Biography. 2. Gay politicians—United States—Biography.
I. Title.
E840.6.Y43 1998
306.76′6′092273—dc21
[B]
                                         98-26320
                                              CIP

ISBN 1-56023-920-4 (pbk.)

To Terry Christensen, who has given support and encouragement
to my endless wild ideas—the good ones as well
as the questionable ones—for the past twenty-three years.

ABOUT THE AUTHOR

Ken Yeager, PhD, was the first openly gay elected official in the Silicon Valley, having been elected to the Community College Board in 1992 and reelected in 1996. In 1984, Dr. Yeager co-founded one of the largest gay and lesbian political organizations in the San Francisco South Bay area. With over twenty years of experience in electoral politics, he is an expert at managing campaigns and has worked as a congressional press secretary in Washington, DC. Currently, Dr. Yeager teaches political science at San Jose State University and specializes in state and local government and gay and lesbian studies.

CONTENTS

Acknowledgments

As I wrote this book, I learned what authors before me have discovered: no book is written without the support and help of many people. Some friends I would like to thank who made time in their busy lives to read these profiles and to offer sound advice are Jean McCorquodale, Paul Morrell, Terry Christensen, and Carolyn F. Yeager. I am indebted to my pal, Leslee Hamilton, for her loving help in all aspects of the book. I am grateful to John DeCecco for recommending to The Haworth Press that they publish the book.

Other people who provided invaluable assistance along the way are Dave Fleischer, Kathleen DeBold, Mary Acheson, Steve Van Beek, John Latimer, John Laird, Ruth Bernstein, Fanny Rinn, Rick Sajor, Tim Cole, Perry Dean, John Hassell, Sally Clark, Dick Papich, Dale Herron, Darren Deffner, Roy Christman, Dan Dusterberg, Fran Solomon, Michael Marr, Linda Dunn, Brian Bond, Dan Divittorio, Aleta Fenceroy, and Jean Mayberry.

There were many travel expenses involved with the interviews, and I am grateful for the grants I received from the College of Social Sciences and the Department of Political Science of San Jose State University, which helped cover the costs.

Lastly, I would like to thank Michael Haberecht, who made my last six months of working on this project more fun than they would have otherwise been.

Introduction

*PROFILE OF AMERICA'S OPENLY
GAY AND LESBIAN ELECTED OFFICIALS*

It seems that with each election cycle come historic firsts. For example, in the November 1997 elections, Cathy Woolard won a seat on the Atlanta City Council. In doing so, she became not only the first openly gay official in Atlanta but in the entire state of Georgia. When Jay Fisette won a seat on the Arlington County Board, he became the first openly gay person to hold office anywhere in Virginia. Mary Wiseman earned a place in history as the first openly gay person to win election in Ohio when she won a seat on the Dayton City Commission. David Catania made headlines as a white Republican who became the first openly gay person elected to the Washington, DC, City Council. Annise Parker went into the history books when she was elected to the Houston City Council. And in the waning days of 1997, the newest person to join the list of gay elected officials was Pam Cuthbert of the Ypsilanti, Michigan, City Council when she came out as a lesbian.

These are just six of the estimated 124 openly gay and lesbian elected officials currently serving on school boards, city councils, county commissions, the judiciary, in state houses, and in Congress. They are singled out merely because they are the gay people who took office most recently. Just as easily I could have mentioned Vermont State Auditor Ed Flanagan, the first openly gay person elected to statewide office in the country. There is Margo Fraiser, an elected lesbian sheriff in Austin, Texas. Or Diane Sands, who serves in the Montana legislature. Or Tim Mains, who has served on the Rochester City Council for twelve years and was just elected to another four-year term. Or Tom Ammiano, a former schoolteacher and stand-up comedian who sits on the San Francisco Board of Supervisors. Or Jeff Horton, who works to improve the education of hundreds of thousands of school children as a trustee of the Los Angeles Unified School Board. Then there are the four lesbians who decided to run for Congress in 1998: Wisconsin State Representative Tammy Baldwin, San Diego City Councilwoman Christine Kehoe, former Massachusetts legislator Susan Tracy, and retired Army Colonel Margarethe Cammermeyer—each vying to become the first person to serve in Congress who was out before being elected.

That there are only 124 openly gay people out of 455,000 elected officials nationwide means that, statistically speaking, they are an insignificant number. In my view, this makes them all the more worthy of study because they beat the political odds by getting elected. Who are these trailblazers? What unique political and personal traits do they possess that allowed them to be trusted enough by voters to elect them? For historical and political reasons, I felt it was important to learn more about these men and women who succeeded in an occupation where the words "heterosexuals only" might as well be stamped in big letters.

*   *   *

Perhaps it is not surprising that so little is known about gay elected officials. Scant information is known about gay people in general. As an academic, I am aware of how few studies are done on or about gays and lesbians. Colleges and universities continue to be among the more homophobic institutions in the country. But the fact that hardly any information is available on gay and lesbian elected officials surprised even me.

My interest in learning more about gay officials goes well beyond the academic, however. As a gay person involved in politics myself, I wanted to learn as much as I could about these officeholders as people and as politicians. I was curious about how they were able to get elected where so many had failed or had not even tried. Did they always desire to run for office? What sort of planning did they do in advance? How out were they when they ran? Were they attacked by their opponents for being gay? What are their legislative agendas? How have their lives changed since being elected?

After I decided to write the book, I was faced with the challenge of choosing whom to include. I wanted a representative sample of women and men, Democrats and Republicans, people from big cities and small towns from all regions of the country, and officials from different ethnic and racial backgrounds who served at all levels of government. Plus, I wanted each to have a unique story to tell so the book would keep a reader's attention.

Choosing the people was difficult. I had attended two conferences of the International Network of Gay and Lesbian Officials (INGLO), so I already knew several people on an informal basis. Others were chosen after reading newspaper articles about them or talking with Dave Fleischer and Kathleen DeBold of the Gay and Lesbian Victory Fund. My friend John Laird, the former mayor of Santa Cruz, had some suggestions too. Although any of the 124 elected officials would have made good copy, I had to keep demographics in mind. There was room for only so many people from one geographical area, from one size of city, from one level of elected office.

All of the interviews were conducted in person. After making advance arrangements, I flew into the city where the person lived and stayed several days. With the exception of two people, I met with everyone at least twice, generally for an hour or more each session. When possible, I attended events with them or sat in on meetings. I went to the library and read articles about them. To gain additional insight, I talked to people who knew them well. I tried to make the profiles as accurate as possible, but if an elected official chose not to include all the circumstances surrounding a certain event, I had no way of knowing it.

The following are the people whose lives are profiled in this book:

- **Minnesota State Senator Allan Spear:** Spear is the longest-serving openly gay official in the United States. Much of his profile concentrates on changes he has seen over his twenty-five years in office and how he and fellow Minnesota State Representative Karen Clark fought to pass a statewide gay rights bill.
- **Judge Victoria Sigler, Dade County, Florida:** Sigler's profile begins with the story of Anita Bryant and the defeat of the Dade County nondiscrimination ordinance that led to the first national backlash against gay rights. Sigler discusses how she

is able to survive in Dade County's conservative political climate.

- **Mayor Bill Crews, Melbourne, Iowa:** Melbourne is a town of 700 people in the heart of Iowa, and Crews has been its mayor since 1984. He came out publicly at the 1993 March on Washington. Discussed in the piece is the vandalism done to his house, as well as what it is like to be gay in a small town.
- **Seattle City Councilwoman Tina Podlodowski:** As the co-parent of two children, Podlodowski is part of the lesbian baby boom. She and her partner are on the front lines of gay parenting and children issues.
- **San Diego City Councilwoman Christine Kehoe:** Kehoe is an excellent example of someone who was a foot soldier for many years and who discovered one day that she could be a candidate. The focus of this profile is Kehoe's first campaign and how the gay community rallied behind her.
- **New York City Councilman Tom Duane:** The emphasis of this piece is Duane's life as the country's first self-disclosed HIV-positive elected official. Discussed is Duane's decision to reveal his HIV status in his city council campaign and what the reaction was to the news.
- **Dallas School Board Member José Plata:** Plata is one of the country's few gay Hispanic elected officials. For anyone who thought that political life was glamorous, this profile details how contentious and mean-spirited life on an elected board can be.
- **California Assemblywoman Carole Migden:** This profile covers Migden's work as chair of the important Assembly Appropriations Committee, as well as her background in local, state, and national Democratic Party politics.
- **Mayor Neil Giuliano, Tempe, Arizona:** A month after Arizona Republican Congressman Jim Kolbe came out before being outed by the gay left, the Republican mayor of Tempe announced he was gay before being outed by the religious right. This profile covers the events leading up to Giuliano's announcement and how his life changed afterward.
- **U.S. Shadow Representative Sabrina Sojourner:** Sojourner is a lesbian African American who is a shadow congresswom-

an from Washington, DC. The story discusses her activities in the early days of the feminist movement in California, her struggle to resolve emotional family issues, and her views on race and diversity in the gay and lesbian movement.

- **Profile of the City of West Hollywood:** When West Hollywood was formed in 1984, it was dubbed "gay Camelot." The chapter traces the city's early history, the campaign for cityhood, its innovative policies, and whether the city has lived up to its expectations. Included in the profile are interviews with the three elected officials who constitute the only gay city council majority in America—John Heilman, Steve Martin, and Jeff Prang—as well as the country's only openly gay city manager.
- **Victory Fund Founder William Waybourn:** Although not an elected official, Waybourn is a founder of an organization whose sole purpose is to elect gays and lesbians to public office. His profile traces his own political life, details how the Victory Fund was created, and includes discussion of several historical policy issues, such as gays in the military.

The last profile is my own. I have been involved in San Jose politics for many years and was elected to the local college board in 1992. Although it is generally a wise policy never to hold oneself as representative of anything, I decided to include it in the book because it offers a more detailed discussion of the mechanics of running a campaign than the others. It also tells the story of what happens when an opponent sends out a vicious hit piece attacking someone's sexual orientation.

Besides telling readers who America's gay and lesbian elected officials are, these profiles provide a gay political and historical travelogue. Although this was not my original intention, when I was on a flight home from Miami, it occurred to me how the lives of my interviewees were rich with history. Their political lives covered a period from 1972 to the present. Some of the events discussed are the Stonewall Riots, Anita Bryant's Save the Children crusade, the overturn of St. Paul's gay rights ordinance, AIDS, California's AIDS quarantine initiative, the 1993 March on Washington, gays and the military, the Defense of Marriage Act (DOMA), child custody issues, and the lesbian baby boom.

*   *   *

My study of America's gay and lesbian elected officials had two parts. The first involved conducting personal interviews. The following are some of my observations about the officials.

- It is interesting to note that not all fourteen officeholders were totally out when they ran for office; for some it was an evolution. For example, when Iowa's Bill Crews was appointed mayor of Melbourne, he was not out. When he later ran for state senate, there were widespread rumors that he was gay. In 1993, he publicly declared his homosexuality in an editorial in the *Des Moines Register.* When he ran for reelection as mayor in 1995, he had his first opponent in years. He won, but it was a tight race. Tempe's Neil Giuliano was not out when he ran for city council in 1990. By the time he ran for mayor in 1994, there was innuendo about his sexual orientation. In 1996, he came out publicly rather than being outed by fundamentalists. Dallas's José Plata never officially came out during his 1995 campaign, although there were articles in the Dallas newspapers discussing rumors about his sexual orientation. He now speaks frankly about being gay. Minnesota's Allan Spear was not out when he ran for state senate in 1972, but then no elected official was. Spear's friends knew he was gay, but the general public did not. Spear came out publicly in 1974 and has been reelected ever since.

  The remaining officials were definitely out. Seattle's Tina Podlodowski, New York's Tom Duane, and San Francisco's Carole Migden are three of the most out politicians, but they come from cities with a history of gay political visibility. Same with John Heilman, Steve Martin, and Jeff Prang from West Hollywood. For gay candidates to win office in their city where between 35 and 40 percent of the population is gay and lesbian, they must have a long track record of political activism in the gay community. Christine Kehoe's sexual orientation was well known to voters because San Diego newspapers always mentioned she was gay. Dade County's Victoria Sigler was out to the legal community, but because she was unopposed in her race for judge, little media attention was paid to her. Washington, DC's, Sabrina Sojourner's election was never in doubt—she was a Democrat running against a Republican in a city where 85 percent of the voters are Democratic—so she received little coverage. As for myself, I had been involved in gay politics for many years and was well known in the community.

- The fact that not all gay candidates are totally out to the voting public when they first run for office demonstrates the difficulty that they face in knowing how best to represent themselves. As several of my interviewees discussed, the line between being a gay candidate and a candidate who happens to be gay can be difficult to walk. And while the gay label may not be a liability in cities with a large liberal voting constituency, elsewhere it may be best not to highlight it.

- Most of the officials were naturally inclined toward politics. Six were active in high school and/or college, four had some involvement, and the remaining four became interested in political matters after college. That ten of the fourteen had an early interest in politics shows that the seeds of public service are planted early. In college, most majored in the humanities; only five were political science majors.

- Most worked their way up the political ladder. Except for two people, all had previous campaign experience, either with helping to elect a candidate or opposing an antigay ballot measure. Four were former staff aides to elected officials, and several participated in political party activities. Two were involved with the early feminist movement. This reinforces the common wisdom that anyone thinking of running for public office must first pay his or her dues.

- Most were involved in their local gay communities. Nine officials said they were actively engaged in gay politics prior to running, two answered that they were moderately involved, and three said they were not at all active. This involvement seems necessary, especially if a candidate is looking to gays and lesbians for money and volunteers.

- Three were the target of an antigay mail piece, while two were targeted in subsequent campaigns. Three experienced a low level of attack, and six had no attack. Although a higher percentage of these fourteen officials were targets of hit pieces than were gay officials as a whole, it does demonstrate that such antigay attacks still occur and that gay candidates must be prepared for them.
- There is a good electoral fit between candidate and constituency. At one end of the political spectrum is Tempe's Neil Giuliano, a white, moderate Republican who is mayor of a city where 80 percent of its residents are white and 55 percent are Republican. On the other end is Sabrina Sojourner, an African-American Democrat who is a U.S. shadow representative from Washington, DC, a city where 65 percent of the residents are African American and 85 percent are Democrats. Five of the most politically outspoken gay officeholders come from cities where gay activism is almost a requirement—San Francisco, New York City, and West Hollywood. Others come from places where it is best to have moderate politics, as is the case in San Diego, Dallas, and Dade County. Two of the officials, Minnesota's Allan Spear and myself, were elected from districts that included a large university with which we were associated. Bill Crews grew up in a small Iowa town that is not dissimilar to the type of town where he is now the mayor. Seattle, with all its software engineers, elected Tina Podlodowski, a former Microsoft manager.
- Nine of the fourteen officeholders have longtime companions. All five lesbians are in relationships, but only four of the nine men. Interestingly, four of the five women (but none of the men) were previously married, with several calling themselves "late bloomers" when it came to their homosexuality. One woman has a child from her marriage; another has two children with her lesbian partner. Most officials bring their partners to political events, helping to reinforce the image of gay people being in long-term, committed relationships.

* * *

A second part of the project was to gather more information about the country's 124 openly gay and lesbian elected officials by sending them a questionnaire in the summer of 1997. Ninety-four officials filled out the questionnaire, which is a 76 percent response rate, a figure regarded as high in quantitative research methodology. The following material is only a small portion of the data collected, but it gives a good overview of gay and lesbian elected officials. The survey also confirms my belief that the eleven people profiled in the book are fairly representative of the group as a whole.

To begin, gay and lesbian officials serve at all levels of government. As with women and minorities, their greatest numbers are at the city level, where it is often easier to make inroads and to run low-cost campaigns. Here are the levels of government and the number of officials in each:

- U.S. Congress—2
- State level—17
- County level—10
- City level—40
- School board or community college—15
- Judges—10

Two-thirds (67 percent) of the ninety-four elected officials are men, one-third women. That there are so many more men than women should not be surprising. This gender gap exists in legislative bodies from city halls to the U.S. Capitol.

They are well educated. Twenty-three have a BA, thirty-three have a JD, twenty-six have a master's, and seven have a PhD.

Politically, 46 percent of gay and lesbian elected officials considered themselves progressive, 24 percent liberal, and 25 percent moderate. Only 2 percent said they were conservative, with another 2 percent saying radical.

Almost all (93 percent) of the gay officials who responded are Caucasian. That such a large percentage of gay officials are Caucasian is understandable, given that the struggle for gay and lesbian civil rights has largely been a white, middle-class movement. Of the remaining respondents, three were African American, two Hispanic, and one Asian American. To my knowledge, these are the same overall numbers for the 124 officials except for Asian Americans, of which there are two.

The constituents of these officeholders are largely Caucasian too. Almost two-thirds of the officeholders have districts that are over 46 percent Caucasian. African Americans, Asian Americans, and Hispanics make up only 10 percent or fewer of nearly two-thirds of the officials' districts.

Gay officials are overwhelmingly Democrats. Eighty of the respondents (93 percent) are registered with that party. Five are Republican, and one is "no party." Just as the officeholders are Democrats, so are their voters. Over two-thirds of the officials are elected from districts with over 50 percent Democratic registration.

Contrary to what many people may think, their districts are not overwhelmingly gay and lesbian. The following are the percentages of gay constituents in their districts:

percentage gay constituents	percentage of districts
1 to 10	65
11 to 20	24
21 to 30	9
31 to 40	1

As with the eleven people profiled, most (80 percent) were actively involved in gay politics before their elections. This involvement usually was with the local gay and lesbian political organization (67 percent of all respondents). Forty-seven percent worked with a local AIDS organization; 40 percent said they worked on a campaign for a gay or lesbian candidate; and 34 percent worked on an antigay ballot measure.

Gay officeholders are often accused of being single-issue. To see if this is true, I asked how much time in a given month they spent on legislative issues of concern to the gay and lesbian community. Here are the percentages they gave:

- Less than 5%—55% of respondents
- 5 to 10%—18% of respondents
- 11 to 20%—18% of respondents
- 21 to 30%—9% of respondents

This means that 73 percent of the respondents spent 10 percent or less of their time on issues directly related to the gay community. This low percentage makes sense, given how few issues at the local, state, or federal level directly involve sexual orientation.

This does not imply that no significant inroads have been made while they are in office. Asked which policies had been approved by their governing boards, 30 percent said domestic partner benefits; 34 percent said nondiscrimination laws or ordinances; 16 percent said AIDS nondiscrimination laws or ordinances; 27 percent said funding for gay and lesbian organizations or events; and 6 percent checked "other."

As far as their positions on current political issues, given that almost half of the officeholders consider themselves progressive, the answers are not too surprising. These gay and lesbian elected officials, regardless of gender and political party, are overwhelmingly civil libertarians who believe in equal rights for all groups. Excluding judges who wrote that the canons of judicial behavior prohibited them from commenting, here is how they responded:

- Support a woman's right to choose an abortion—98%
- Support same-gender marriages—98%
- Support affirmative action laws—95%
- Support limitations on amount of money that can be donated to campaigns—80%
- Support the right of public workers to strike—78%

The results of the survey demonstrate that gay and lesbian elected officials are different from other officials in a number of important and substantial ways. Yet, when research is conducted on politicians, gay officials have not been analyzed separately as a group. This oversight may lead to an inaccurate assessment by researchers of what is occurring politically and legislatively.

For example, studies consistently show that male officeholders are far more conservative than women officeholders. However, if researchers include a category for sexual orientation, they would discover that not all males hold similar views. As noted, gay male officeholders are much more liberal than men and women, with lesbians being even more so. Thus, to ensure that research findings are as accurate as possible, when appropriate, it is necessary to include sexual orientation as a variable.

Studies on minority and women officeholders have increased our knowledge of how minority and women politicians have entered the political process and their impact upon it. Such information is absent regarding gay and lesbian officials. It is hoped that further studies are conducted on these elected leaders so their contribution to the electoral process can be better understood and fully appreciated.

*   *   *

The focus of this book is on individual politicians rather than on the communities that helped elect them. But as the survey and the interviews reveal, openly gay and lesbian officials do not succeed in a vacuum. They have a lot of help along the way. They are the beneficiaries of the work done by those who created local organizations where they gained the necessary experience and made vital contacts. Also, they relied on scores of volunteers to carry their message to the voters. In return, the next generation of gay leaders received valuable campaign training. Gay activism begets more activism.

This same principle applies on a nonpolitical, individual level. I remember when Ellen DeGeneres and her TV character, Ellen Morgan, both came out. Although gay people saw DeGeneres as a courageous role model, I think many failed to appreciate how they themselves were responsible for creating the atmosphere that allowed her to make her announcement. It was because hundreds of thousands of gays and lesbians had discussed their sexual orientation with family, friends, and co-workers over the past thirty years that America and Hollywood were ready for a lesbian lead character in a sitcom. Likewise, DeGeneres's actions make it easier for others to now come out.

Currently, openly gay people have been elected in only twenty-four states. That number will rise as (1) qualified gay people realize they can be out and run for office, and (2) voters come to appreciate the contributions gay and lesbian officeholders make in the political arena. It is my hope that this book will speed up both processes so the talents of more gay and lesbian elected officials can be used to solve the pressing problems facing our local communities and our nation.

Chapter 1

The Longest-Serving Openly Gay Elected Official in America: Minnesota State Senator Allan Spear

Wednesday, March 26, 1997. It was down to the wire. Only three days were left for all bills to be approved by any committee if they were to remain alive in the 1997-1998 Minnesota legislative session. All eyes were on the Defense of Marriage Act (DOMA), a bill that would ban same-gender marriages. In 1996, the U.S. Congress had passed a federal DOMA bill, and numerous states had approved a similar version. Now it was Minnesota's turn to debate the issue.

The outlook for blocking DOMA was bleak. The Minnesota House of Representatives had attached it as an amendment to a Health and Human Services spending bill. Now the state senate had to contend with the matter. So far, opponents had succeeded in stalling it, due to the strategic skills of the senate's President and Chief Presiding Officer Allan Spear. As the longest-serving openly gay elected official in the United States—and the world—Spear was prepared to use whatever legislative measures necessary to stop the DOMA juggernaut.

Much of his strategy was already set in motion. As planned, the bill languished in the senate's Judiciary Committee where the committee chair, a good friend of Spear's, refused to hear it. If no hearing were to be scheduled by Friday, it would be dead as a free-standing bill.

To maneuver around Spear, the bill's senate sponsor had one course of action left: a parliamentary procedure called Rule 40. Rule 40 permits a bill to be heard on the floor of the senate without first being heard in committee if a majority of the senators consent. Although the Democrat-Farmer-Labor (DFL) Party held a majority in the sixty-seven-person senate, some conservative DFLers appeared willing to side with Republicans. It was an ominous sign that thirty-four senators—a majority—signed a letter asking the senate majority leader to hear the bill. Eleven of the signers were DFLers. Spear and the Democratic leadership knew there was support for DOMA; if a vote was taken, DOMA would pass.

Spear understood the best way to deflect Rule 40 was to frame the issue as procedural, not political. As president of the senate, Spear was in an ideal position to do this. He and an aide to the majority leader went to the DFLers who had signed the letter and pointed out that the motion by a Republican senator was a challenge to the DFL majority's ability to set the agenda. On the senate floor that day, DFL Senate Majority Leader Roger Moe emphasized the procedural nature of Rule 40, stressing it was not a vote on DOMA.

The Republicans took the bait. Recounted Spear after the vote, "The Republican leader scolded the DFLers for not taking Republican bills seriously and even suggested, preposterously, that every bill introduced should be heard by a committee. As a result of the Republican leader's speech, the vote was a party-line procedural vote. A couple of people on each side abstained from voting, but no DFLer voted for it, no Republican against it. It was a perfectly deployed strategy." The crisis had been adverted. For now, DOMA was dead in the senate.

In the end, however, not even as skillful a legislator as Spear could stop DOMA. Political support was too strong. Because the house version of the Health and Human Services bill contained amendments that the senate bill did not, a ten-member house-senate conference committee had to agree on a single version. Not only did the house bill contain the DOMA provision, but it had language that prevented any public agency from granting domestic partner benefits. Despite the efforts of three conference committee members to remove the objectionable language, DOMA stayed in the bill, although the domestic partner ban was removed. The revised bill went back to the house and the senate for a final vote.

Over the years, Spear has learned to live with many legislative defeats. Only once was he really bitter about a vote, which was in 1977 when the senate failed to pass a gay and lesbian civil rights bill. While losing DOMA would be a defeat, "it would not be the end of the world," he stated.

On the day of the DOMA vote, Spear left the podium where he presided over the senate and returned to his seat. In an impassioned speech, he said to his fellow senators, "Why is this called the Defense of Marriage Act? It seems to me that insofar as gay and lesbian couples want to be married, they're not attacking marriage, they're embracing marriage. They are essentially saying that marriage is a desirable state. Marriage is something that provides benefits, that provides emotional stability, that provides the kind of recognition that all people in society want."

Spear then explained why some gay and lesbian people would like to have the benefits of marriage. "Part of it simply involves the financial security that marriage helps bring about—employee benefits for spouses, the benefits of the inheritance tax, practical benefits that unmarried couples are not able to enjoy. Some of it involves the security that marriage can bring in times of trauma—when a partner dies, when a partner is mortally ill. It's extraordinarily wrenching in those times for gay or lesbian partners, for example, to have to try to gain admittance to the hospital room because they're not members of the family or to worry about what might happen to their joint property if one should die intestate."

Then there is the importance of community acknowledgment of same-gender relationships. "I have been in a relationship with another man now for fifteen years, and I would venture to say that it is not much different from the relationship that most of you who are married have with your spouses. We share a home, we share our lives, we do most everything together, we plan to be with each other for the rest of our lives. Why should our relationship not get the same recognition and the same respect as any other relationship?"

Spear, who is a history professor, could not help but see similarities between the African-American civil rights movement and the gay and lesbian civil rights movement. "There will come a time when people will look back on this law and see it in much the same way as we see Jim Crow laws today—as a relic of an era when there was irrational fear, where there were irrational concerns that simply had no basis in reality."

Then, Spear said he was forced to take a rare action: oppose the entire bill because of one bad amendment. "I don't usually vote against omnibus bills because of one provision. But this is symbolically very negative to gay and lesbian people who are trying to live stable and responsible lives. The State of Minnesota is saying, 'We do not recognize and we do not respect the relationships that you have developed with one another.' "

It was an argument he could not win. The Health and Human Services bill with its DOMA provision overwhelmingly passed in both chambers and was signed shortly thereafter by Republican Governor Arne Carslon, making Minnesota the fourteenth state at the time to pass such legislation.

*   *   *

Of the estimated 124 openly gay and lesbian elected officials in the United States in 1997, Allan Spear has served by far the longest. Elected to the Minnesota Senate in 1972 and reelected seven times since then, he came out publicly as a gay man in December 1974, a month after Elaine Noble became the first openly gay person ever elected to office by winning a seat in the Massachusetts House of Representatives. Of the twenty-three gay elected officials serving in state legislatures across the country in 1997, Spear has the distinction of being one of two in a state senate. In 1994, he was elected president of the Minnesota Senate, making him the highest ranking gay person in any state or federal legislative body.

Standing 5'6", the sixty-year-old Spear has a small paunch, and the brown hair on his head is thinning. He wears thick-framed glasses and, when at the Capitol, prefers plain clothes, conservative ties, and comfortable street shoes. He was born in Michigan City, Indiana, an industrial town of 35,000 people an hour's drive from Chicago. Growing up in the 1940s and 1950s, he was aware of his outsider status, not only for his sexual orientation but because he is Jewish. "The other kids went to church on Sunday and we went on Friday night," he said. "We always had to explain at school why we weren't there on Yom Kippur and Rosh Hashanah. I can't remember any deep-seated anti-Semitism, just this kind of 'Yeah, he's Jewish; he does things differently.' And kids don't like to be different."

At fifteen, he became aware that he was not noticing girls the way other guys were. "In a small Midwestern town in the 1950s, you just didn't stroll in to your parents or school counselor and say you're gay," he stated. "So, I went to the library and looked up homosexuality. And when you open the card catalog to the 'H's,' that's OK—there's a lot of words that begin with 'H.' But by the time you're at 'Ho,' you're nervous and hope it's an open stack library. And by the time you're at 'Homo,' you're a wreck. And then you find the definition, only to read you are, quote, 'Krafft-Ebbing psychosexual, constitutional psychopathic inferior.'"

Spear attended Oberlin College in Ohio in the mid-1950s. Because of the fear of communism that was sweeping the country, life wasn't much better for him as a gay person than it was in Michigan City. Spear, who gave the 1997 commencement speech at Oberlin, tried to explain to the graduates what life was like forty years ago. "McCarthyism was a crusade not only for political conformity but also for sexual conformity. Communism and homosexuality, we were told, worked hand in hand to undermine the American way of life. Being gay at Oberlin in the 1950s was little different from being gay elsewhere—you stayed in the closet or else. There was no openly gay or lesbian life. Liaisons were furtive and the subject of whispered rumors." It would be more than a decade after Spear left Oberlin that he would come to terms with his sexuality.

It was while attending graduate school at Yale that Spear began to see a psychiatrist in the hopes of being "cured." He remembers the doctor saying that his problem stemmed from his poor relationships with women. "He told me, 'You relate to people too intellectually; you are unable to relate to them emotionally, unable to let down your guard, especially with women. Why don't you try letting those barriers down with women? Those homosexual fantasies of yours will go away.'" As with other gay people before him, Spear soon discovered that those fantasies didn't fade.

While at Oberlin, Spear began to study African-American history and later became active in the civil rights movement. He did his doctoral dissertation on the black community in Chicago. As to why African-American studies, Spear explained, "Being gay, I've always felt alienated, an outsider in society, and in the 1950s the most visible outsiders were blacks. I got involved in black history in graduate school because of my undergraduate activities in the civil rights movement. One interest naturally led to another."

In 1964, Spear accepted a teaching position in the University of Minnesota history department. A year later, President Johnson ordered the bombing of Vietnam. This event was a turning point in his life and started him on the road of electoral politics. He organized antiwar teach-ins at the university and campaigned vigorously for Eugene McCarthy's presidential candidacy in 1968. "Then I really got into it," he said. At the legislative endorsing convention in 1968, someone suggested he run for the legislature. He won the party's endorsement but lost to the incumbent in the general election.

The 1972 redistricting of the legislature created a seat that surrounded the University of Minnesota, making it ideal for Spear. With no incumbent, this time Spear entered the race as the frontrunner on the DFL ticket. On a personal level, Spear was becoming more comfortable with his sexual orientation and was telling more friends that he was gay. Although there were rumors about Spear being gay in the campaign, the issue was never directly raised by his Republican opponent. Spear won the race with 53 percent of the vote.

The following year, Spear came out to his parents. He remembered that they were shocked and upset, but the first thing they told him was that they still loved him and that it made no difference. Spear referred to this memory in his Oberlin commencement speech when he said, "For a gay man or a lesbian to come out to parents and family, friends and associates is, on the one hand, wrenchingly personal, yet at the same time the most important political decision one can ever make. Those who know that a family member or loved one is gay or lesbian or bisexual can never again see gay people as the dreaded 'other,' as nameless, faceless adversaries of all that is good and holy. Coming out is both a statement of personal identity and a reaching out to others to build a bridge of common humanity. It allows for honesty in our relationships with those we hold most dear."

It was during Spear's first year in office that a bill was introduced in Minnesota to protect gays and lesbians from discrimination. After giving advice to the bill's sponsor on how to frame the issue, Spear was asked point-blank by the senator if he was gay. "I told him I was," said Spear. "I expected him to say that I should keep it quiet and not ruin my political career. Instead, he said that if I ever chose to come out, his wife was a reporter at the *Minneapolis Star* and would love to do an article."

One of Spear's biggest concerns about coming out would prove to be the same for many elected officials following in his footsteps: being pegged as single-issue. Spear worried that he would be labeled as "gay first and foremost rather than as a DFLer, a senator, a liberal, or any of the other things I am." So, he delayed the announcement, choosing instead to work behind the scenes on gay issues. The turning point came when Elaine Noble was elected. "When she won, it made me feel a little less lonely," Spear stated. Now, he was ready to talk to a reporter.

Spear's announcement was front-page news. "State Sen. Allan Spear Declares He's Homosexual," read the headline in the *Minneapolis Star* on December 9, 1974.[1] The story appeared in *The New York Times* and was carried by all by the wire services. From a 1997 perspective, Spear's "declaration" may not seem so monumental, but it was a radical act in 1974. The Stonewall Riots in New York had happened only five years earlier. Harvey Milk was still running his camera shop on Castro Street; it would not be until 1975 that he would first run for office, and not until November 1977 that he would finally win. It was not until Gerry Studds acknowledged he was gay in 1983 that Congress had its first openly gay member. For public figures, coming out continues to be sensational news, as Ellen DeGeneres found out.

In the *Star* article, Spear discussed three reasons for going public. First, he wanted to "stop the tittering" that surrounded his being gay. "There's nothing I'm ashamed of. Nobody should have to talk about it on the back stairways." Second, he wanted to be free to speak as a gay person on gay rights issues without any ambivalence. Third, he felt an obligation to other people to reveal his homosexuality. "It's a time when gay people are beginning to emerge from their closets," he told the reporter. "Gay people are not confined to the classic gay professions. They're in politics, in teaching, in business, in everything you can imagine. It's important for gay people struggling with their own identities. They need all kinds of role models." He then added, "There's a critical job to be done in getting gay people not to hate themselves."

Spear also mentioned two political issues of concern to him. What is extraordinary is that these same issues would still be debated twenty-three years later during the Minnesota 1997-1998 legislative session: repeal of the state's sodomy laws and gay marriages—reinforcing the adage that when it comes to social change, it is necessary to take the long view.

Some of Spear's colleagues were uncomfortable with his announcement, although in general there was not much controversy. One of the more homophobic reactions came from a senator who introduced a resolution to appropriate $300 to pay for counseling for homosexual legislators. The resolution quickly died. Nor did Spear's announcement hurt him in his liberal district in his 1976 reelection campaign. Spear easily won with 69 percent of the vote.

Over the years, Spear put in his time, paid his dues, and climbed the seniority ladder rung by rung. Ten years after his election, he became chair of the Judiciary Committee, the first nonlawyer to do so. He chose the committee because of his commitment to civil rights and First Amendment issues. Over the years, he has become a leading expert on criminal law, civil law, and criminal procedure. He currently chairs the Crime Prevention Committee.

In 1992, the senate's president chose not to run for another term, creating a rare vacancy in a leadership position. Although the post does not automatically go to the person with the most seniority, many years in office are needed to make someone a credible candidate. Even after twenty years in office, Spear was still only fourth in seniority. A senator with several more years of service was the most conservative member of the DFL caucus. "He was wildly antiabortion," Spear stated. "This made him the number one target of feminists. Mention his name to them and they'd go into a rage. He was also rabidly antigay in a mean and nasty way."

Spear won the caucus vote, twenty-five to twenty. Because the position is one of the whole senate and not of one political party, the person needed to be approved by the entire body. With forty-five members, the DFL caucus had enough of the sixty-seven votes to elect their candidate if they voted as a block. On a strict party vote with four of the most conservative DFL members abstaining, Spear won, forty-one to twenty-two. When the DFL majority leader was asked by a reporter if Spear's being gay was a factor in the vote, he said, "It's a nonissue. Senator Spear was elected by virtue of the fact that he is one of the most respected members of the senate. He is eminently fair." Said Spear after his election, "It shows that it's possible now for gay and lesbian people who are able to work efficiently within the system to rise on the basis of merit."

*   *   *

"Fair," "inclusive," and "nonpartisan" are words that are often used to describe Spear's legislative style. Scott Dibble, a Minneapolis council aide, explained that Spear is known as a consensus builder whose moderating skills help to shepherd through compromise. Mark Wallem, Spear's aide, observed that whenever necessary, Spear tries to be inclusive of conservatives and Republicans. Spear himself admitted to not being a fierce partisan. "I'm a Democrat, but I work with Republicans. I don't always consider them the enemy. I think a lot of partisanship is silly and counterproductive."

As a veteran legislator, Spear knows how to pass controversial legislation, particularly as it relates to minority rights, women's rights, and criminal justice reform. It all begins with personal relationships. "It's important not to permanently alienate people," said Spear. "You don't want to get into a situation where people say, 'Oh, that's his bill. I'm going to vote against it; there must be something wrong with it.' You want to develop a sense where they respect you even if they disagree with you so you can work with them another time. The other thing about my style is that I'm a process person. I really believe you do better when you stick to the process, even when the process goes against you. As president of the senate, I try to interpret the rules, no matter where the chips fall."

The person who spoke these words is far different from the firebrand who was elected in 1972. As Spear admitted, "I'm a lot more moderate in style than when I first got into the legislature. Like many people of my generation, I started out as a 1960s radical who was active in the antiwar movement. I was involved in not only civil rights groups, but white groups that supported the Black Panthers. I said some very intemperate things at the time. I had to learn to discipline myself in what I said."

Spear echoed this thought during his Oberlin speech when he tried to explain to the graduates what the world of politics is really like: "The compromises and adjustments that I've been forced to make in my twenty-five years in public office have perhaps tempered my idealism but haven't destroyed it. Practical politics is a necessary counterpoint to the politics of commitment. It is as important to understand what *can* be done as it is to know what *should* be done."

When he was first elected, Spear knew what legislation he wanted to sponsor, but only later did he realize he was not certain how to get it passed. The best example of this occurred in 1977 when he sponsored a bill making it illegal to discriminate against gays and lesbians in employment, housing, public accommodations, credit, and education. After the senate's preliminary approval of the bill, the local newspaper carried a front-page story on the action. "All hell broke out," remembered Spear. "This was still far-out legislation. In 1977, no state had yet passed a gay civil rights law. Right-wing groups organized against it, and I began to lose votes. It was really crushing. I ended up not even bringing it up for a final vote. That was the closest I've come to giving a bitter speech attacking the opposition for what they'd done." Spear acknowledged that the experience was a low point in his legislative career.

Another major setback occurred in 1978 when Anita Bryant's antigay crusade descended on St. Paul. As had happened in Dade County, Florida, St. Paul's gay rights ordinance was overturned by a referendum. Spear, like gays and lesbians in the Twin Cities area, was devastated by the loss. The vote made it impossible for Spear's nondiscrimination bill to get even a hearing in a senate committee

~that year and doomed its chances for passage throughout the mid-1980s.

By the late 1980s, concern grew over whether the bill would ever win approval. It was then that Spear, openly lesbian Minnesota House of Representatives member Karen Clark, and other leaders began to devise a long-term strategy. The story of how Minnesota became the eighth state in the nation to pass a nondiscrimination law reveals two important ingredients required for winning a major gay-rights legislative battle: (1) someone is needed on the inside who knows what legislative steps need to be taken and when; and (2) hundreds of people are needed on the outside to coordinate activities and lobby for the bill.

One of the first steps was to counter critics' arguments that the bill was not needed. To that end, in 1989 Spear and others asked the governor to appoint a commission to document discrimination faced by gays and lesbians. The commission held hearings throughout the state. When commissioners traveled to some communities, they received a hostile reaction from people opposed to the commission's investigation. One hearing was so bad that the police had to be called to control the crowd. Spear, who served on the commission, said, "We soon discovered that most gay and lesbian people in these communities would not come out and testify. They said they didn't dare attend the public meetings and talk about their lives, so we began to meet with people in the mornings after the night meetings." Many of the commissioners were appalled by the tales of discrimination they heard. Stories were told about harassment on the job, death threats, and physical assaults. Gays and lesbians testified about being denied medical care and credit, being unable to buy houses, being asked to leave apartments, and losing their jobs. "This gave us evidence to go against the notion that we didn't need the bill."

A second step was to create an ongoing gay and lesbian organization devoted to the bill's passage. Up until then, all the work was done by ad hoc groups that disbanded after the bill's defeat, making it hard to sustain any momentum. To coordinate the work, a statewide campaign, "It's Time Minnesota," was established. The organization was in charge of all aspects of the effort, from raising money to hiring a coordinator, organizing volunteers, and lobbying legislators. Part of their charge was to build coalitions with other groups, a task they did successfully. Groups that endorsed the measure included the League of Women Voters, Minnesota Bar Association, Minnesota Medical Association, Minnesota Catholic Conference, Joint Religious Legislative Coalition, the Teamsters, AFL-CIO, American Federation of State, County, and Municipal Employees, and the Minnesota Association of Realtors.

Spear, Clark, and others understood that, to win a majority of votes, support was needed from politicians in suburban and rural areas. Thus, a large part of It's Time Minnesota's efforts were to find allies in these towns who would call or write their legislators. But, as the commission had found, many gays and lesbians in rural communities were living such fearful lives that they couldn't be expected to come forward. Members of other groups became invaluable in this regard, particularly realtors. "The leadership of the realtors was very sympathetic," noted Spear. "Plus, there are a lot of gay realtors. These realtors not only took a stand, but they called other people to get them to call their legislators."

A third step was obtaining the governor's support. Weary legislators, especially Republicans, could not be expected to take the political heat of voting for the bill only to have the governor veto it. Spear and others were able to secure Governor Carlson's promise that he would sign the bill. This turned out to be critical because Republican votes were needed for passage—votes that would have been hard to get without the assurance of the governor's endorsement.

A fourth step was convincing legislators that the public favored such a bill. As it so happened, there was evidence to support this contention. Throughout the 1980s, a majority of the St. Paul City Council wanted to pass a second nondiscrimination ordinance, but they worried about another referendum. To avoid a repeat of the 1977 defeat, they placed a measure on the ballot to amend the city charter to forbid referendums on human rights issues. This failed. Having run out of options, they proceeded to pass the ordinance. As expected, the opposition organized and put a referendum on the 1991 ballot. Everybody, including Spear, thought the ordinance would be overturned again, but this time it won, 53 to 47 percent. "For the first time in Minnesota, we won a popular vote on a gay rights issue," he said. "This really helped strengthen our argument with legislators that they could vote for the bill and not lose their next election."

By the time of the vote, several key amendments were added to the bill, amendments that Spear didn't like but knew were needed to obtain key support. The bill now contained certain exemptions for religious and youth organizations and for the rental of an owner-occupied duplex or single-family home. It also stated that it did not call for quotas or affirmative action requirements, the promotion of homosexuality in schools, or the recognition of same-gender mar-riages. Several amendments were offered during the debate that would have gutted the bill of much of its intent, such as exempting anyone who came in contact with children in any setting, including schools, and stripping the bill of all protections except in public services. These were both defeated.

Critical to the measure's success was that Spear worked with colleagues in the senate, while Clark did the same in the house of representatives. As Anne DeGroot, executive director of the Com-munity Action Council, a Minneapolis community-based gay and lesbian service organization, observed, "They were key players because they were able to influence the timing of votes and the actions of the committee chairs. They were able to use the clout they had built up over time to get reluctant legislators to support the bill."

The hard work and long hours put in by Spear, Clark, and every-one associated with It's Time Minnesota paid off when the bill passed both the house and senate. It was a triumphant moment. With the vote, Minnesota became the eighth state to pass such a law. Since then three others have joined the list. The ten other states are California, Connecticut, Hawaii, Maine, Massachusetts, New Hampshire, New Jersey, Rhode Island, Vermont, and Wisconsin.

Standing in the wings on the day of the vote was Steve Endean, one of the early pioneers of the gay rights movement in Minnesota. Endean founded the first gay organization in the state, the Minneso-ta Committee for Gay Rights. In 1974 he lobbied to get the St. Paul and Minneapolis city councils to pass their nondiscrimination laws. The 1978 St. Paul referendum defeat so dispirited him that he moved to Washington, DC, where he became the first director of the

Gay Rights National Lobby, which later evolved into the Human Rights Campaign. Passage of the bill was a poignant moment because Endean was dying of AIDS. "We passed that law just before he died," Spear stated. "He came out for the vote, even though he was really sick at the time. We passed the bill in the senate in the morning and it was taken to the house that afternoon. Steve was able to be here for both votes. He said that he would die happy seeing this happen."

Looking back on the twenty years of struggle it took to pass the bill, Spear said with the wisdom of an old warrior, "You always have to remember that there is going to be another day and another fight. No loss is the end of the world. I learned that on this bill where we lost it, and lost it, and lost it, and lost it. There were times I was close to despair, but I always had to say, there will be another day, just stick with it. When you lose something, you don't ever want to say or do things that are so bitter or have so much finality that it's going to compromise your ability to do something on the same issue some other time."

*   *   *

Spear's relationship, which he stressed in his DOMA speech, has brought balance and stability to his life. Until they met, Spear never had a long-term partner. The relationship has allowed Spear to create a life that is not totally dominated by politics. Spear's partner runs a beauty shop and is not involved in politics.

Before Spear was with his partner, he would work all week being a legislator, then spend Friday night, Saturday, and Sundays going to fund-raisers. This hectic schedule was curtailed when his relationship began. "It's easy for elected officials to develop a lifestyle where everything is centered on politics and little else," Spear explained. "All the parties you go to are political fund-raisers. Your social life is in the framework of the political world. When Steve Endean was here he couldn't possibly conceive of a party that wasn't a fund-raiser. He said, 'Why waste a party that isn't going to be a fund-raiser?'" Now, whenever possible, Spear tries to keep his weekends and evenings free. When the legislature is out of session and he teaches full-time, he is able to be home at a regular hour to prepare dinner.

Curtailing his public appearances has resulted in some people getting the wrong impression of Spear. "I think people respect me," he said, "but they see me as somewhat aloof because I don't go to all the events. My partner tells me that I should go to the bars more. But I hate the bars. I used to go years ago when I was single, but I tell him, I don't have any reason to go. All that smoke! I can't stand the smoke. I don't like to dance. That loud pulsating music drives me nuts. Besides, I'm a private person. My favorite social evenings are when we invite a few couples over for dinner or go over to someone else's house for good food, wine, and conversation."

Nor is Spear particularly social with his senate colleagues. Observed his aide, Mark Wallem, "Allan is not a back-slapper. He doesn't hang out at the Capitol from early morning to late at night. He has great insight into what is important and what is not. This means he doesn't have to meet with lobbyists and legislators just to do it. If he needs to talk with them, then he talks business. He's a friendly person, but he doesn't spend time in idle chatter."

There remains a small minority of people who wish that Spear were more radical about being gay, but he has learned to take the criticism in stride. "There are people in the gay community who disapprove of the kind of model that I have been, saying that I am an assimilationist—that although I'm out as a gay man, I have not sufficiently emphasized my gayness, and that I'm too mainstream. If other people want to develop different models, I don't have any problems with that. This is who I am. I am not comfortable in the role of the flaming queen or the flamboyant homosexual that some, including a few elected officials with different personalities, have chosen to play."

Spear, who people describe as modest, is not one to brag about his numerous accomplishments. While seen by others as an historical giant in Minnesota and national politics, Spear is apt to downplay the impact he has had. "The major part I've played in changing public opinion is being accepted to the point where my gayness now is almost a secondary part of my life and career," he reflected. "If people watch me while I'm presiding over the senate, they will probably not be seeing anything gay. They'll just see a senior legislator, who is president of the senate, chairing the legislative body. This means people have accepted me as a person. When it's appropriate, I bring up my sexual orientation, but a majority of the time it's just there, not commented on or particularly noted. A number of straight people around the Capitol have mentioned to me how they've switched their views on homosexuality because they've watched me and have seen that I was just a person doing my job. A number of gay people have told me the same thing. Watching me gives them a sense of what they can do."

Spear's twenty-five years in politics almost spans the entire period from the Stonewall Riots to the present, a claim that no other elected official can make. This gives him a unique vantage point from which to observe the distance the gay and lesbian rights movement has come. When asked what changes he has seen in his lifetime, Spear paused for a few moments and then said, "In the 1970s, I thought we were going to move more quickly. We made so much progress from 1971 to 1977 that I thought it would be continual. Then we hit that backlash with Anita Bryant's crusade and the emergence of Jerry Falwell. It was then I realized how long term and tough it was going to be, and that we would have to be in it for the long haul." But Spear is heartened by where the movement is headed. "Even though we had setbacks and progress seemed slow at times, there have been huge changes," he stated. "The very fact that domestic partners has emerged across the country as a genuine issue is an example of this. The notion of health benefits and legal recognition of gay relationships would have been wildly far-out in the 1970s. Now it's pretty mainstream. It just shows how the whole climate and the center of gravity has changed for gays and lesbians in my lifetime."

Chapter 2

Triumph in a County Where Defeat Is the Norm: Dade County Judge Victoria Sigler

There are several historic dates in the U.S. gay, lesbian, and bisexual movement over the last thirty years. Perhaps the most important is Friday, June 27, 1969, the first of two nights of rioting by drag queens fed up with the continuous harassment of New York City police in a Greenwich Village gay bar named The Stonewall Inn. It is the anniversary of those riots that is celebrated in June at Gay Pride events around the country. Another historic event is the 1974 election of the first openly gay candidate, Elaine Noble, to a seat in the Massachusetts House of Representatives. November 27, 1978, is the day that Harvey Milk was assassinated. On July 3, 1981, *The New York Times* ran its first article on AIDS, titled "Rare Cancer Seen in 41 Homosexuals."[1] One important date that is often overlooked is June 7, 1977. That is the day when the voters of Dade County, which includes the cities of Miami, Miami Beach, Coral Gables, and Key Biscayne, denied gays and lesbians their rights. The vote is viewed by gay historians as the first major backlash against the gay rights movement.

The first city in the country to formally adopt a policy banning discrimination based on sexual orientation was East Lansing, Michigan, home of Michigan State University, in 1972. Two months later, San Francisco became the second city to approve legal protections. Of the first cities to support these measures, most were university communities.

Although twenty-eight cities had adopted nondiscrimination laws by 1977, several had them repealed at the voting booth. But the real beginning of the backlash against these laws occurred when singer and Miss America runner-up Anita Bryant appeared before the Dade County Commission in January 1977 and stated that the proposed gay rights ordinance was a threat to the rights of county residents. Unable to persuade the commission to reverse their vote, Bryant promptly formed her Save Our Children group and began collecting 10,000 signatures to force a referendum on the June ballot. Because Bryant was the spokesperson for Florida orange juice, gays and lesbians throughout the country boycotted Florida oranges. No self-respecting gay person could be seen drinking a screwdriver in a bar.

In a campaign that foreshadowed the way that the religious right would frame the debate against gays and lesbians for the next twenty years (and be successful more often than not), Bryant called the ordinance a religious abomination and a license for gays to molest children. She asserted that homosexuals could not reproduce so they must recruit. Bryant was able to persuade the National Association of Evangelicals and other conservative religious groups to join her cause. The gay community in South Florida was caught off guard by the intensity of the opposition. The ordinance was repealed in a lopsided two-to-one vote. Said gay historian John D'Emilio, "The battle of Dade County let gay activists know that they wouldn't be fighting just the encrusted homophobia of the past. They were really encountering a new social movement that was coalescing around an opposition to gay rights."[2]

The victory launched Anita Bryant's national antigay crusade. Soon voters in Eugene, St. Paul, and Wichita repealed their ordinances. In many cities, the religious right used the issue to create new and powerful political organizations. In city after city, gays and lesbians had to counter the charge that they could not be trusted around children and that they were a threat to family values. The religious right put the focus on whether people approved of the gay lifestyle, rather than on if gays and lesbians needed protection from discrimination.

Almost twenty years later, as the anniversary of the Dade County vote approached, *Miami Herald* gay columnist Eugene J. Patron wrote in his column how stories related to Miami's 1996 centennial excluded the 1977 gay rights battle. Patron wondered how Dade County would commemorate this embarrassing episode. Patron believed that this is an important question because, contrary to popular thought, gays still are not accepted by local residents. "The success of South Beach as a gay nightlife and tourist mecca is often mistakenly used as a barometer of Miami's supposed openness and tolerance of gays and lesbians," Patron stated.[3]

In his column's conclusion, Patron told his readers what must occur next: "The task before the gay and lesbian community today is not to simply mark what happened in 1977, but to do something about what didn't happen and reach out to the people of Dade County to whom we are apparently not only invisible when it comes to protection under the law, but even when it comes to the recording of history."

It does not appear that gays and lesbians have reached out to their straight neighbors over the last twenty years or built political coalitions with other minority communities. That is the only conclusion that can be drawn from the nothing-less-than-astounding defeat in June 1997 of an attempt to have the Dade County commissioners pass a new ordinance protecting gays and lesbians from discrimination. Proponents wanted the vote to be taken on the twentieth anniversary of the defeat to show how far the county had come. Despite (or because of) the boom of South Beach as a new, trendy gay resort, Dade County had not moved an inch.

According to an account in the *Miami Herald*,[4] supporters assumed that the first vote on the ordinance would be, as is customary, perfunctory. Since all ordinances need a second vote or reading before becoming law, debate and public testimony are heard at the second reading of the ordinance. The first vote merely moves the issue along. That is why the gay group in favor of the ordinance made no plans to be at the meeting until later that day, and why they had not met with individual commissioners beforehand. Their lobbying efforts were to occur after the first vote.

Christian advocates took a more aggressive strategy. They gathered 5,000 signatures on a petition urging a "no" vote and had 600 people attend the meeting at 9 a.m. As an opponent of the ordinance was quoted in the paper as saying, "Let's do something unusual. Let's treat the first reading like a public hearing and show our disgust to special rights for homosexuals from the onset."[5] Because of the large number of people in the audience, the chair of the commission—and a supporter of the ordinance—decided to take up the issue out of order. Since it was not the second reading, there was no discussion among commissioners and no public testimony. To the shock of supporters, the commissioners then voted to defeat the ordinance, seven to five.

Herald columnist Carl Hiaasen, in a piece titled, "Old-Fashioned Discrimination Back in Vogue," summed it up best when he wrote, "Twenty years later, Anita's gone but the tune remains the same. Commissioners who killed the ordinance said they did so because they were morally opposed to homosexuality."[6] With biting satire, Hiaasen said it took courage for the commissioners to vote as they did, "to rise up and declare to millions of potential visitors: We don't like your kind." He also found it "inspiring" how black and Hispanic commissioners—a veritable rainbow coalition of prejudice—"put aside their differences and joined together in a common goal of keeping gays in their place."

By the end of his piece, the disdain he showed for the commissioners was thick enough to scrape off the page. "Heck, money isn't everything. Surely there'll be other tourists to fill the hotel rooms left empty by the ones we're running off. You know, the good kind. Heterosexuals."

*   *   *

For an out lesbian to succeed politically in an environment such as that of Dade County takes someone with unique characteristics and skills: a strong sense of self, good sense of humor, feisty enough to challenge the status quo while not creating enemies needlessly, and able to earn the respect of others. This describes Victoria Sigler and explains why she has flourished in South Florida since moving there in 1974. Hers is a story of triumph in a county where defeat is the norm for lesbians and gay men.

Sigler, who still considers herself "a Western gal," was born in Albuquerque, New Mexico, in 1951. She was seven when she moved with her mother and brother to Carmichael, California, a suburb of Sacramento. Her introduction to politics came when she was twelve. A friend of her mother's married a state legislator, and Sigler was allowed to hang out in his office. In high school, she volunteered in a legislative staff office that wrote bills for state lawmakers.

In junior high school she went to a job fair. Looking around at the various booths, she thought she might be interested in being a lawyer. She approached an older, white-haired man sitting behind the booth and told him that she wanted some literature. "Well, young lady," he said in a deep, paternal voice, "here is some information on legal secretaries and on court stenographers, but you should know that men are lawyers and women are secretaries and stenographers." The defiant side of her instantly emerged. "I thought to myself, I'm going to become a lawyer and come back to Sacramento and try cases against you. It really tweaked me that he said that."

Because generations of Sigler's relatives have lived in Colorado, she chose to attend college at Colorado State University at Fort Collins, earning a BA and an MA in political science. She also came from a long line of Republicans. However, at age twenty-one her nonconformist nature kicked in when it was time to register to vote. "What better thing to do to irritate your parents than to register as a Democrat?" she chuckled.

Sigler's father was working as a dean at the Miami-Dade Community College when he told her about a job teaching social science. Thinking it would be fun to teach for a while, Sigler moved to the South. She still remembers seeing signs at a public restroom designating use by "white" and "colored." "It blew me away," she said. As an indication of her ability to successfully juggle numerous tasks, Sigler attended Nova (later renamed Nova Southeastern) University Law School while still teaching. She clerked for private attorneys and was the law review editor of the *Nova Law Journal*.

It was not until she was thirty that Sigler realized she was a lesbian. Before that bolt of lightning struck, she was involved with a man whom she later married. Her first case as a lawyer was her own divorce. It was not until years later that she saw her ex-husband. "He had gone bald and gotten real fat," she chuckled. "That's when I suspected that God was a woman."

Sigler is a naturally gifted athlete. Today, problems with her knees restrict much of her physical activities, but when she was younger she competed nationally in downhill skiing, giant slalom, judo, and sailing. In 1990, she coached a softball team at the Gay Games in Vancouver, which won third place in the B division. In the 1994 Gay Games in New York, she lost the mixed doubles badminton match for the bronze medal. The victor: Her life partner, Sharon Unen, whom she had met on a blind date in 1990.

After graduating from law school, Sigler was hired by the Office of Public Defender as a trial attorney in the juvenile division. From there, she rose to the felony division where she supervised three trial divisions of felony attorneys and represented defendants charged with capital offenses. During her years as an assistant public defender, Sigler tried over 200 nonjury and more than 100 felony jury trials, including first and second degree murders, armed robbery, kidnapping, sexual battery, and drug trafficking cases. By the time she left the office, she was the executive assistant public defender, supervising 70,000 cases and 175 attorneys.

Sigler was blessed with many half brothers and stepbrothers due to her father's three marriages. As a daughter of her father's first marriage, she was old enough to help raise these "little brothers," as she refers to them. In 1985, one of her brothers died suddenly at the age of twenty-one. Although the exact cause of death is unknown, doctors believe it was from heart failure. A year and a half later, her father died. But it was the death of her twenty-four-year-old stepbrother, Patrick Gettings, in a 1990 hit-and-run accident that was the most painful and which radicalized her views on victim family rights. His death also led to her decision to run for judge.

Although they were stepsiblings and had not met until Sigler was twenty-three years old, Sigler's relationship with Gettings was like an older sister to a younger brother. They were buddies who hung out together and took long bike rides. They must have made an odd pair; he was 6'4" and 230 pounds, while she was a sliver of a person at 5'2" and 110 pounds with hazel eyes and blond hair.

"I'd Tom Sawyer him all the time," she recalled fondly. "He'd paint the house and I'd sit in the shade and drink tea and talk to him."

When telling the story of Gettings's death, Sigler often took deep breaths and her voice cracked. The passage of time has barely diminished her sorrow.

This is what is known about the accident. In the early morning hours of December 1990, Gettings was struck by a car as he was riding his bike. The woman who owned the vehicle that killed Gettings was known to be a heavy drinker. She lived alone and was the only known driver of the car. Approximately eight minutes after Gettings was run down, a neighbor witnessed the woman washing her car at 3 a.m. in 50-degree weather. Investigators later found the heavily damaged car with bits of his body embedded in the hood and windshield and pieces of his bike wedged underneath the car.

What followed is a frustrating tale that many victims' family members experience when dealing with the legal system. For Sigler, though, it was particularly hard because she had worked in the criminal justice system for fifteen years.

Shortly after the accident, Sigler became concerned at how slowly the Dade County State Attorney's Office was conducting the investigation. "I called a friend in the State Attorney's Office and said I needed help with the case. Even though I was a public defender and it was my job to litigate against the state, I had a good reputation. I never did anything dirty and was always a straight, stand-up lawyer. But when I tried pulling strings, I couldn't get anyone to move. My stepmother had been on the grand jury and was friends with Janet Reno, but she couldn't get the office to move either. A young, barely-qualified-to-do-homicide-work prosecutor was assigned to the investigation, and he fell on his face. We hired a private attorney who engaged an investigator to develop all the leads we could. We were told that the investigator located witnesses who could place the woman in a bar down the street from where he was killed. We were told that the witnesses saw her leave the bar and drive away only minutes before his body was found by police. We had a tight circumstantial case. But the state's office didn't interview anybody for a year. Memories get old and fuzzy. It was very frustrating."

To Sigler's disbelief, prosecutors decided that, based on the circumstantial evidence they had, they could not prove that the woman was the driver of the car, even though they knew it was her car that struck Gettings. Thus, prosecutors decided that there was not enough evidence to ask for a homicide or manslaughter conviction. "They filed a charge of tampering with physical evidence, which is a third-degree felony charge carrying a maximum penalty of five years," Sigler explained with a trace of resentment in her voice. Convicted of that crime, the woman received a sentence of a year in the county jail, many hours of community service, and five years probation, during which time she was required, on the anniversary of the accident, to work in a hospital emergency room where trauma victims are treated.

"Bubkes. Bubkes for a human life," said Sigler, using the Yiddish word for "nothing." She took a deep breath before continuing. "Nevertheless, it was a pretty stiff penalty for what she was convicted of. After the verdict was read, members of the jury stopped by where our family was and asked, 'How come she wasn't tried for murder? We know she killed him. Why couldn't we vote on murder?' We listened to that with tears streaming down our faces."

As an assistant public defender, it was part of Sigler's job to argue against the death penalty for her clients. Gettings's death forced her to examine her position on opposing the death penalty in every homicide case. "When the trial was over, I went back to my office and thought about resigning because I didn't feel I could continue being a go-for-the-jugular, hard-nosed trial lawyer. I understood for the first time in my life why people want the death penalty. It has nothing to do with logic or justice. It has everything to do with revenge. I think there are some people who commit crimes who are so heinous or evil that they have forfeited their right to live." Sigler believes that it would have been inappropriate to ask for the death penalty for the woman whom she suspects struck and killed her younger brother, primarily because she believes the woman was under the influence of alcohol at the time.

Sigler underwent a period of introspection. While not losing all faith in the criminal justice system, she did develop an empathy for victims that she did not have before. "I always felt bad for crime victims, their survivors and family members. I could feel their pain, although I hate that expression. So I wasn't totally stone-cold about it. When I became a victim family member myself, I began to see what these people were always talking about. They were saying that the system wasn't responsive and that the wheels of justice moved too slowly. Many prosecutors don't care about the victim or the victim's family. They think it's their case, not yours."

Voicing what many people feel when they confront the criminal justice system, Sigler said, "There is a certain insensitivity toward the victim. I don't think it is malicious, but when you work in the system for a long time you develop a shell; you become callous. I don't think victims understand that callousness, nor do I think that those of us in the profession see how the callousness makes us appear uncaring to people going through the system for the first time.

"Once I decided that I didn't want to be a homicide trial attorney anymore, I knew I couldn't return to child sexual molestation cases or step down another level and do home burglary and armed robberies. I had done what I considered to be the top of my profession, and I just couldn't do a less challenging level of litigation. So it was time to move on."

After several months of grieving, Sigler decided to become more involved with the South Florida Gay and Lesbian Law Alliance (GALLA). She made the decision when she realized that although she had spent most of her adult life fighting for the rights of students, minorities, and criminal defendants, and had supported women's liberation and protested against the Vietnam War, the group she identified with most was the one she had done the least for: lesbians and gay men. "I had stood up for others," she said poignantly, "but never for myself."

*   *   *

Sigler had never thought about running for public office until, at a GALLA meeting, a colleague put forth a challenge that Sigler couldn't resist. "This lawyer said he didn't think a gay person could run for office, be out, and win. I wasn't so sure about that, so I decided to test that theory."

Once she decided to run, Sigler knew she did not want to hide her sexual orientation. "Early in the process, I thought that I probably won't win anyway. I didn't have much money, I didn't go to Ivy League schools, I didn't run with the big downtown boys, I was a public defender, and I'm a woman. As long as I was going to do this thing, I was going to run as an out lesbian."

Sigler believed that her knowledge of citizens' fundamental constitutional rights and her belief that the legal system has to prosecute people who break the law would make her a good judge. "I had developed a sensitivity for both positions. Also, Patrick's death gave me a balance in how I looked at crime. Before, I think I would have been too liberal of a judge and too concerned with defendants' rights at the expense of the victims."

In Florida, as in other states, when candidates decide to run for office, they must file a declaration of candidacy. Most candidates complete this paperwork shortly before the official filing period begins as set forth in the election code. Filing such papers two years in advance could be viewed as excessive. Yet, that is how much notice Sigler gave the Dade County legal and political community when, in 1992, she filed papers to run for an open seat on the county court bench in the 1994 election.

The forty-one county court judges in Dade County handle civil lawsuits up to $15,000, uncontested dissolution of family matters, and criminal misdemeanors like battery, petty theft, and traffic violations. Conversely, circuit court judges do criminal cases and civil lawsuits above $15,000. Even though the judgeships are nonpartisan, lately they are becoming more partisan and more electorally competitive. A contested race can cost up to $150,000. The primary is held in July, and if no candidate receives 50 percent of the vote, a runoff is held in November.

Political campaigns were new to Sigler, and she was unsure about raising money, hiring a staff, and creating a message. She attended a training session for candidates sponsored by the Victory Fund and led by veteran campaign expert Dave Fleischer. At the training, she was encouraged to talk about the impact of her brother's death and the subsequent trial in her campaign. When Sigler announced her candidacy, she was emotionally ready to deal with the issue. "I've been in court and personally felt the way that the judicial system was not responsive to the family of a crime victim. We need to give all sides the opportunity to be heard," read her press release. She also was ready to talk about drunk driving. "We need to take the drunk out of drunk driving. The current system of merely taking away a drunk driver's license doesn't work. Repeat offenders go right out of the courtroom and drive away—no license, no problem. We need to be more creative with sentencing."

Sigler was told by a good friend that she should quit all her activities—especially her sports—if she ran for office. Half jokingly, the friend also advised her to leave her partner in order to have more time to give to the campaign. Sigler followed all her friend's advice religiously except for leaving Unen.

As with everything she has undertaken in life, Sigler quickly learned what she had to do and then gave it everything she had. She proved to be a tireless campaigner and fund-raiser, raising $100,000 before the primary. A week before filing closed, she had only one opponent who had filed papers. Then Sigler heard that another county court judge had decided to run for circuit court judge, creating a vacancy. Quickly, Sigler filed for that seat. When the clock struck twelve on the last day of filing, Sigler had no opposition. Because she spent little money during her campaign, most of it remains in the bank. She hopes it will keep future opponents at bay when she is up for reelection in 1998.

Since then, Mark King Leban, an openly gay man, was appointed by the governor to the Dade County bench. He subsequently was elected to the post, also unopposed. There are other ripple effects. More gay and lesbian lawyers are creeping out of the closet. Even a judge is starting to go to events with his male partner. Certainly with their elections, Sigler and Leban disproved the theory that an openly gay person could not win office in Dade County.

*   *   *

The legions of gay and lesbian lawyers notwithstanding, the judicial system is viewed in the gay community as homophobic. Judges such as Victoria Sigler and Mark King Leban do what they can to change the culture, but progress is slow. They are simply outnumbered by older, more conservative judges who have a narrow perspective on the world. Also, the judiciary itself is very closeted. Sigler estimates that 10 to 15 percent of the judges in Dade County are gay, yet only two are out. Most gay and lesbian lawyers are not out, either.

Florida is unrelenting in its bigotry against gays and lesbians. Gay people have virtually no protection when it comes to discrimination. Unlikely though it is, one place where gays have some protection is inside the courtroom. This is because the Florida Bar and the Florida Supreme Court added sexual orientation to their nondiscrimination ethics rule. Sigler tells the story of how it came about.

"I was at a GALLA meeting where we discussed who was going to go before the state Bar and present the case of adding sexual orientation," she said with her usual good nature. "None of the other members wanted to do it. All the guys thought it would be better if it came from a woman. Here were eighty lawyers and not one was willing to fight for our rights. I got so damn mad that I just said, 'I'll do it.'"

At the meeting of the Board of Governors of the Florida Bar, Sigler talked about how proud she was to be a lawyer and how much she respected the legal profession. She wanted the board to know, however, that many times while sitting in court she had to listen to her colleagues and judges make crude and embarrassing remarks about gays and lesbians. She told them, "I had to sit there and be insulted, keeping secret that I was a lesbian, afraid to speak out for fear that it would bring discredit or wrath upon my client. If you feel it is OK to say offensive things in front of someone that you respect as much as you respect me as a trial lawyer, then maybe you shouldn't pass the sexual orientation rule, but if you think it isn't fair for someone who has litigated as hard and as well as I have to stand there and take the abuse, then you should pass the rule." The room became quiet when she finished. Then committee members and people in the audience began to stand and applaud. "That really surprised the heck out of me," she said. "My heart was going a thousand beats a minute. I had never spoken about being gay in public before."

The following week the *Florida Board News* had a front-page story about Sigler's testimony and the affirmative vote by the Board of Governors to add sexual orientation to the ethics rule. Included in the story was a picture of Sigler, along with her new title, "Lesbian Lawyer."

Sigler and Leban make inroads in the legal system whenever possible. For example, at a statewide judicial conference, they both brought their spouses. As Sigler relates the story, when they entered the ballroom for dinner with their spouses, you could hear a pin drop. Although their intention was not to offend their fellow judges, Sigler and Leban felt it was important for others to see gays and lesbians not as sexually loose people or sexual predators but as people in a stable relationships who were "walking proud, looking good" with their partners. In her down-home, Western-style speech, Sigler said, "Some folks went out of their way to sidle up and talk to us. Just by chattin' with us, they were saying this is cool with me. However, I saw some judges giving us disapproving looks throughout the evening."

There have been incidences of bigotry against gays and lesbians in Sigler's courtroom. One of her court-appointed translators thought that two Hispanic women were lesbians, and said to her, "Judge, I refuse to stay in the room with these kinds of people." Because the two women spoke English, Sigler dismissed the translator, not wanting to reprimand her in open court. At the end of the day, she asked the translator what she meant by her comment. "She thought they were disgusting," stated Sigler. "So, I said to her, 'Well, let me ask you, how do you think I'm doing at this job?' 'Oh, you're just great,' she said. 'I'm asking you because I think you should know that I'm gay; I'm a lesbian, too,'" Sigler replied. "There are a couple things I want to tell you. On a personal level, your comments are insulting to me, but I respect your right to have your opinions. I know you're a deeply religious person. However, on a professional level, there is a sexual orientation ethics rule, and as a judge, I have an obligation to make sure that no one discriminates in my courtroom on the basis of sex, religion, ethnic background, or sexual orientation." Over time, Sigler and the translator became friends. When the translator would bring her children into the courtroom, they would run up and hug Sigler.

Sigler understands that courtrooms often are hostile places for gays and lesbians, with gays getting a disproportionate share of unkind remarks in court. As a way to avoid the justice system altogether, more gay people are using gay or gay-friendly mediators to resolve civil cases. But problems remain in criminal cases. Sigler believes that all too often when someone assaults a gay man or lesbian, the system is not willing to prosecute the assailant because the victim is gay. Judges rationalize that if the person had not been looking so queer in the first place, then he or she would not have been attacked.

An example of this was a case in West Palm Beach. Two men viciously beat and killed a gay man in the parking lot. In sentencing the men, the judge stated that it was the victim's fault because if he had not led a gay lifestyle, then he would not have been in the parking lot where gays hang out. In another case, the Miami police department did not even write a report when a gay man was assaulted. Again, authorities thought the gay man had brought it upon himself.

Florida is one of two states (New Hampshire being the other) where the legislature passed a law forbidding gays and lesbians to adopt children. This meant that the law automatically assumes gays and lesbians are unfit to be parents, so they cannot even be given an application to be judged on their merits. In contrast, drug abusers and felons who want to adopt can at least apply.

Winning custody of their children is difficult for gay and lesbian parents. In a well-publicized 1995 case, a Pensacola judge took a child's custody away from her lesbian mother and gave it to her father, even though the father had served eight years in prison for second-degree murder in a 1974 shooting of his first wife during a custody dispute over another child. The judge said that the girl should not be led into a lesbian relationship "before she has a full opportunity to know that she can live another lifestyle." In February 1997, the lawyer for the mother filed a judicial ethics complaint against the judge, citing the ethics rule saying that the judge showed bias and prejudice based on sexual orientation.

Despite all the evidence to the contrary, Sigler believes that gay parents must still prove that they are fit parents and that the child will not be harmed by living in a gay household. Explained Sigler,

"Over and over, plaintiffs have to spend a lot of time and money on experts to prove that there isn't a correlation between having gay parents and bad things happening to children. It's an extraordinary financial cost, which the straight parent doesn't have to be concerned with."

One way to minimize the problem is to educate all judges at the same time on the irrelevance of a parent's sexual orientation in child rearing. GALLA has prepared a curriculum for the training, but the judges have not agreed to hold the seminar.

* * *

After Sigler was elected, she asked the county's presiding judge to assign her to cases involving driving under the influence or driving with a suspended license (DUI/DWSL). Because she believes that taking a license away from a person does very little, she has been focusing her attention on the drinking part of the drunk driver equation. In addition to serving on a statewide DUI review board to determine the effectiveness of DUI programs, she works with a special county project that deals with drug and alcohol recidivism. Also, she tries to make sure any probation officer assigned to one of her cases understands issues involving addiction and drug use so they will have greater awareness of their client's problems. It has been her practice since being on the bench never to accept pleas at arraignment in either battery cases or traffic accident cases unless the victims are contacted first to express their opinions.

When in the courtroom, Sigler makes a conscious effort not to reinforce people's stereotypes about lesbians. "I try very hard to make sure that my hair is combed, my lipstick is on, and I'm in nice, soft feminine-looking attire. I do this because people know I'm gay, and I like to try to stretch the stereotypes," she explained. "Frankly, I'm most comfortable in gym clothes, or in jeans and cowboy boots. I'm a Western gal. Give me a flannel shirt and some moccasins, and I feel at home." Sigler knows that she can no longer go to the hardware store in grubby clothes. "People expect judges to sleep in their robe and eat breakfast in their robe," she said laughing. "In fact, the only time people think judges take the robe off is when they take a shower."

As a county court judge, Sigler deals with a mind-boggling case load. Each Monday and Wednesday she has approximately sixty DUI/DWSL cases. Tuesdays she handles misdemeanor cases. Thursdays is the motion calendar. Friday is for arraignments and violations of probation.

It was fascinating to watch Sigler deal with each DUI/DWSL case. Not a minute was wasted. If there was a delay in one case because of misplaced paperwork or because a lawyer had to consult with a client, she quickly called up another case. With numerous cases happening at once, it was impressive that Sigler never lost track of them.

Most DUI cases that Sigler heard were open-and-shut. The state legislature has determined minimum sentences for first offenses. The main issue is whether the defendant wants to plead no contest or not guilty. If not guilty, then the case is decided by a jury. Sigler handles all the nonjury cases first, then returns to those in which a trial by jury may occur. Some cases turn into a bluffing game, with the defendant's lawyer trying to see if the prosecution's case will fall apart.

Although Sigler always tells each defendant that he or she has an absolute right to a trial, she knows that in many cases a trial would be a waste of the court's time because the evidence against the defendant is so overwhelming. Often the defendant's lawyer knows that, too. One lawyer even asked Sigler to try to persuade his client not to go to trial. Approaching the bench, he said, "Perhaps you can talk to him. It may be more persuasive coming from you." With the good-natured banter that she typically uses in the courtroom, she responded, "I don't know why you say that. I've always found you persuasive." The lawyer smiled. Then, with flawless timing, Sigler added, "The verdicts notwithstanding." Everyone laughed. The client, who had a blood-alcohol count of .16, decided to plead no contest.

*   *   *

As a Westerner at heart, Sigler is surprised that she has remained in the South as long as she has. "I still can't explain why I've been here for twenty-five years," she said, shrugging. "I went to school, I got my license to practice law, and I forgot to leave."

Whenever they can, Sigler and Unen travel to Colorado where they enjoy camping, hiking, and white-water rafting. They also work on their three acres of mountaintop property with the intent of one day building a cabin. Not long ago, Sigler was admitted to the Colorado Bar. Eventually, she would like to spend half of the year in Colorado, the other half in Florida.

One activity that Sigler continues to enjoy and finds to be a great tension-releaser is coaching a women's softball team. The name of her team is the Furies. Appropriately enough, the number on her jersey is "1." The games, which are played at Flamingo Park in South Beach, give her a chance to "hang out with the girls, to spit, and to yell." Sigler described the games in South Florida as "a little hotter, steamier, and louder because of the weather and the Cuban and other Latin players." When asked if she ever misses playing, she responded with a soft, one-word reply: "Yes."

Wendy Rosen, a player on the Furies, has a great deal of respect for Sigler as a coach. "She has a great mind," she said with admiration. "She's not just thinking about now; she's thinking three steps ahead. She knows the strategy of the game because she's played it. And she's a great motivator because she's fair. She lets any team member play who comes to practice, shows up on time for the game, and who really tries. Not all coaches do that. Many just play their star players." If the team continues to play as well as it has at the beginning of the season, Sigler hopes to enter them in the 1998 Gay Games in Amsterdam.

Just as she learned from her stepbrother's death that there are no guarantees that she would have all the time in the world to run for public office, Sigler knows that rapidly changing demographics in South Florida may limit the number of terms she might serve as a judge. "Today, Dade County is 52 percent Hispanic, mainly Cuban, Catholic, and Republican. As an Anglo, that makes me a walkin', talkin' target with a big red mark on my forehead," she said. "I'm not complaining about it; I'm just facing facts. Soon I'll be an anachronism. At that point, it'll be time to move on."

In a moment of self-reflection at the end of a long day, Sigler, in her down-home way, said, "All of us are ordinary people. Every once in a while, life gives us an opportunity, and if we handle it in a responsible way and rise to the occasion, we can do something quite magnificent. One metaphor that works for me is this: Let's say you've been asked to step up to the plate. Usually you'll hit a grounder to the pitcher, but another time you might hit a home run. I played baseball for twelve years, and I only hit one home run, but I remember it like yesterday. If we keep at it, all of us are capable of accomplishing something quite remarkable."

Chapter 3

On This Six to Eight Inches of Topsoil:
Mayor Bill Crews, Melbourne, Iowa

Bill Crews knew his commentary in the opinion section of the *Des Moines Register* might have repercussions forty miles away in the small Iowa town where he is mayor. That is why before boarding a plane for Washington, DC, with his partner, Steve Kehoe, he sent a letter of warning to friends and family.

"On Sunday, Steve and I will join up to a million other Americans in the 1993 March on Washington for Gay, Lesbian, and Bi Equal Rights and Liberation," read the letter. "This expression of hope for justice greatly affects me because I am gay." Crews stated that the editorial he enclosed would appear in the paper. "I submitted this knowing that this must be my contribution toward understanding and individual acceptance."

It was Crews's coming-out statement. Although he had been mayor of Melbourne, Iowa (pop. 700+) for nine years, few knew—although many suspected—that he was gay. At age forty, the 6′1″,

185-pound, blue-eyed Crews had come to the point in his life where he no longer wanted to hide his sexual orientation. Crews, no novice to politics, was media-savvy enough to know that his piece would be newsworthy. After all, Crews had figured out how to get his name in the newspaper dozens of times. But as he flew from Des Moines to Washington, DC, he could not have foreseen the publicity his editorial would attract, or because of it that, four years later, aftershocks would still rumble through his life.

After landing in DC the Thursday before the march, Crews, who resembles Donald Sutherland with his big build, blond hair, and light skin coloring, spent Friday with other Iowans lobbying politicians. He and Kehoe then hosted a reception at their hotel for fellow Iowans participating in the march. Saturday they attended a brunch for gay and lesbian elected officials sponsored by the Victory Fund. There he was introduced as the newest "out" elected official and received a standing ovation from his new colleagues. Sunday was the march, which turned out to be one of the most spiritually affirming and politically successful gatherings of gay men and lesbians ever held. People who attended still get misty-eyed when recalling the hope and unity that filled each of the estimated one million people as they marched down the Capitol Mall.

If it was Crews's intention to bring the march home to Iowa with his editorial in the newspaper, he succeeded. The piece dominated the front page of the opinion section. "The Face of Gay America" blared the headline in three-quarter-inch bold type, with the headline beneath it reading: "Why an Iowa mayor will be in the 1993 March on Washington."[1] Below his byline was the customary postage-stamp-size photo of the author, but the graphic that overwhelmed the page was a 10-inch by 3-column drawing of a clean-cut, corn-fed American youth with short hair, chiseled nose, and high cheekbones, whose eyes gaze off into the future. Superimposed on the drawing are outlines of various states of the Union, with Iowa drawn smack on his forehead. Is this the face of gay America? It is unclear what the message is. In any case, central Iowa subscribers would have had a hard time missing the layout, regardless of how fast they were turning the pages that morning of April 25. The editors of the *Des Moines Register* understood the news value of what they had.

Sounding like a cross between Thomas Paine and Harvey Milk, Crews wrote in his well-crafted article that he was marching "to petition my government to provide liberty and justice for all. And I am marching to show those who would deny us our human dignity and civil rights that we will not be silenced."

Crews covered a lot of ground in the piece. As a way to make himself a sort of Every Iowan, he revealed details about his life, including the fact that he was in a fourteen-year relationship. He also touched on what he had done as Melbourne's mayor. He said he never made a big deal about being gay because he didn't think it mattered whether one was gay or straight. As gays and lesbians became more visible, however, opponents had risen up to "deny us this part of our identity and the full participation in society we deserve." It was the backlash that made him finally speak out.

As if anticipating comments by people who question the need for gay people to broadcast their sexuality, Crews wrote, "Make no mistake about it, a person's sexual orientation is part of that person's identity. Affirming that identity or 'coming out of the closet' must be seen as a fundamental aspect of our individual liberty—the freedom to be who we are."

After briefly discussing how the current antigay crusade tries to dehumanize gays and lesbians in the same way that the Nazis dehumanized the Jews, Crews took aim at religious fundamentalism, which he called dangerous because "it cannot accept ambiguity and diversity and is therefore inherently intolerant." Such intolerance destroys what it cannot convert. "Just as Adolf Hitler led the Glorious Aryan Race, so do Jerry Falwell, Pat Buchanan, and Pat Robertson lead a campaign for their self-styled family values."

In his conclusion, Crews hoped that his actions will help people who are struggling with accepting a gay or lesbian loved one, help stop the pain and hurt felt by many gays and lesbians, and teach others that gays are no different from anyone else. What is most important is that "gay men, lesbians, and especially straight folks continue to stand up against prejudice and hate. Help make it so," he pleaded.

In the following Monday's *Des Moines Register*, a front-page article reported that 300 Iowans took part in the march, and it named Crews the unofficial leader of the delegation.[2] In a quote that probably did not endear him to members of fraternal service organizations, Crews said of the marchers, "It looks like America out here today. People of all ages and all interests are here in this crowd. Yes, we have some who are a little flamboyant, but that makes us like the Shriners." And just to show that you can take an Iowan out of Iowa but not the Iowa out of an Iowan, Crews led the delegation in a cheer (give me an "I"), afterward thrusting his fist into the air and yelling, "Go, Hawks!"

Because of his commentary and the news story, Crews expected the usual antigay reception to greet him when he got home, such as letters to the editor denouncing him and disapproving looks from some townspeople. Returning home Tuesday night, Crews and Kehoe experienced a far more severe repercussion from coming out. There on the steel siding of their home, spray-painted with large black letters, were, verbatim, the following obscenities: Get the Fuck out; You ass Fucker; Queers aRe't Welcome; No Faggots; Melbourne Hates Gays; Get Out!!! Also, a fire extinguisher had been stuck through a broken window and discharged inside the family room.

Across the country, there were marchers who experienced similar antigay homecomings. *Time Magazine* reported that Tampa Bay resident Darlene DeBerry came back to find her trailer home burned by an arsonist.[3] A few days before leaving for Washington, she had received a phone call telling her that if she went to the march her house would be torched.

Sergeant José Zuniga, who served as a medic in the Persian Gulf War and was the Army's Soldier of the Year, had come out at a reception by the National Gay and Lesbian Task Force. When he returned home, the military initiated the paperwork to administratively discharge him from the service.

*   *   *

The town of Melbourne is located near the center of Iowa in Marshall County. It is fifteen miles from Marshalltown, the county seat, and about an hour's drive from the state capital, Des Moines. Founded in 1882 when the railroads came through, it was named after a man who worked for the railroads, although history doesn't seem to record why he was so honored. The town's unofficial motto is "Not down under, but right on top," which, Crews noted, has nothing to do with sexual proclivities. The town seal was brought back after Crews and Kehoe traveled to Melbourne's better-known counterpart in Australia. If you look closely at the seal, you can see kangaroos.

Approximately 40 percent of the town's residents are retired farmers or farm widows who moved in from the country. About 60 percent are working families in which at least one person commutes either to Marshalltown or Des Moines. For all practical purposes, the town is 100 percent white. The only exceptions are the one or two Mexicans who, from time to time, live in the trailer court.

If an inventory were made of the town, the following items would be on the list: one bar, two grain elevators, one bank, two churches (St. John's United Church of Christ and a United Methodist Church), a post office, fire station, library, city hall, a former airplane hanger that was converted into a recreational center, one outdoor swimming pool that was an indoor pool until a tornado struck in 1981 and blew off the roof, one insurance agent, two used farm machinery dealers, and four school buses.

Absent from the list: a grocery store (it's a fifteen-minute drive to the nearest supermarket), a school (the grade school shut down seventeen years ago), a gas station, a restaurant, or, for that matter, retail stores of any kind.

If Melbourne's one-story brick city hall looks remarkably like a fire station, it's because the building originally functioned as a fire station. No attempt was made to alter its exterior when it became a city hall except to add "Melbourne City Hall" above the three roll-up garage doors. The city council meets in an attached room and deliberates around two long folding metal tables.

As is common in the Midwest, Melbourne has a mayor-council form of government, meaning the mayor has no vote on the five-member council and can only sign or veto council actions. For his duties, Crews is paid $20 a meeting. On the city's payroll are a public works director and his assistant, a part-time clerk, two part-time librarians, and a part-time policeman who is also a deputy sheriff. The town has an all-volunteer fire department, whose fire engines are housed in the new fire station directly across the street from City Hall, which Crews played the key leadership role in getting built.

An example of a typical Melbourne council meeting was the one held on March 13, 1997. Agenda items included discussion of the progress of building a new library, renewal of a beer and liquor license for Clark's Bar, an announcement that the landfill's tire amnesty is scheduled in conjunction with cleanup day, and acceptance of a contract for renovation of the city's water storage tank. Other items included a request that the recreation board have a written procedure stating how the pool should be managed, and reports from the public works director about a water main break on Main Street.

Cost of housing in Melbourne varies, but the average price for a single family home is around $50,000. Crews and Kehoe live in the newer part of town, a subdivision called College Hill, although Crews is quick to point out that the town has neither a college nor a hill. Their split-level, wood-framed ranch-style house has steel siding that Crews likes because he hates to paint. It was on this siding that the graffiti was sprayed. When newspaper photographers took photos of the vandalism, Crews refused to be in the pictures. He made it clear that he did not want readers to associate gay people with antigay obscenities.

No one has been charged with the crime. As usually occurs in such vandalism cases, the perpetrator or perpetrators brag about the deed until word gets back to the police. But as Marshall County Sheriff Ted Kamatchus said, the case was more difficult to solve because "when you're dealing with this type of thing, people are more closed-mouth about it."[4]

As to the town's reaction to Crews, Jim Perin, the town's part-time marshal, said that Crews's public comments incensed residents who hate homosexuals. "It has gotten some people mad and upset that the town's name was being used, and he being the mayor. But a lot of people don't care. In fact, I would say a majority don't."[5]

Writing letters to the editor seems to be a favorite pastime in Iowa. Any time there is a controversy surrounding Crews, dozens of letters appear in the *Des Moines Register* and the *Marshalltown Times-Republican*. Religious fundamentalists were especially enraged over Crews's interpretation of the Bible, and Crews's supporters saw the vandalism as a validation of the long-suspected hatred of gay men and lesbians. The following are two typical letters written by fundamentalists.

From Harold Denton of Des Moines: "Mr. Crews states that he is on his church board. Does he believe what the Bible says, or does he translate to accommodate the lifestyle he chooses to live? Has he not read of Sodom and Gomorrah and the other Bible verses condemning homosexuals and likening them to kidnappers, liars, murderers, thieves, fornicators, adulterers, drunkards, and swindlers?"[6]

From Laanui Johnston of Marshalltown: "If God had created Adam and John, the world today would not exist. It would have ended with just the two. Homosexuality goes against God but also against reason and nature. It cannot reproduce, expand or multiply. There would have been no need for progress, to grow and build cities because eventually they all would have died without offspring to continue the generations."[7]

An example of an opposing view comes from Wanda Button of Conrad: "As a Christian, I am ashamed to acknowledge that much of the discrimination against and suffering of homosexuals has been directly or indirectly perpetrated by people who call themselves Christian. There is something terribly wrong with any form of religion that fosters prejudice, fear, hatred and intolerance, and condones injustice."[8]

Even Kehoe jumped into the fray, responding to Laanui Johnston with his own letter.[9] He wrote that her claim that gay people cannot reproduce was "ridiculous," stating that "nearly half of the gay people that I have met are either married with children or formerly married with children." He then joins the debate over the Bible, arguing how none of the original Hebrew books refer to homosexuality as sinful. He adds that the "account of Sodom and Gomorrah had nothing to do with homosexuality. Rather, the sin committed was one of inhospitality. Visitors were basically mugged and raped when they tried to seek refuge in these cities."

Crews and Kehoe's house has not been the target of any further acts of vandalism. Occasionally, however, they are awakened in the middle of the night by a drive-by yelling.

*   *   *

Crews and Kehoe moved to Melbourne in 1984 for the same reasons that other working couples do: location. At the time, Crews worked in Des Moines as the governor's representative on river management. Kehoe, an Iowa native with dark blue eyes and brown hair, continues to work in Marshalltown as a design drafter for Fisher Controls International, a manufacturer of valves and regulators. There was nothing remarkable about the tiny hamlet except that it was midway between the two cities. They found a nice, moderately priced house on a quiet street lined with silver maples and ash trees and moved in.

Shortly after Crews arrived, a councilman asked him if he wanted to be appointed mayor. Seems the current mayor had just resigned to take a job elsewhere. Although Crews originally declined, he accepted when asked a month later. His ego would not let him say no, even though he hardly knew anybody. He was unopposed in a special 1985 mayoral election to fill the vacancy, winning all fifty-seven votes cast. In 1987 and 1991, he was reelected without opposition.

In many ways, the offer of the mayorship was like a gift from above. Always interested in politics, Crews began early to lay the foundation for a life in government. In high school, he was a page for the Iowa Senate. He also became involved in the Republican Party. He remembers raising money to attend the Republican Lincoln Day dinner where Spiro Agnew was the speaker. "I sold bumper stickers that said, 'Missile defense makes sense,' and 'Work for peace. Nixon does every day,'" Crews laughed, acknowledging the absurdity of the phrases.

When he graduated, Crews chose to attend a Methodist university in Denver. He had been awarded a scholarship because he was smart and because his father was a Methodist minister, having moved his family to Iowa to take a job when Crews was two. His major, not surprisingly, was political science.

After his first year in college, Crews realized that spending his time in Colorado was not the way to launch a political career in Iowa; he moved back and attended the University of Iowa at Iowa City. It was 1971, the year that the 26th Amendment to the U.S. Constitution was ratified, giving eighteen-year-olds the right to vote. Crews registered to vote in his old hometown, thinking that it would be where he would eventually run for Congress. Even at that tender age, Crews had the wherewithal to call up the local newspaper and have a photographer take a picture of him as the first newly eligible young person in the county to vote in a 1971 school board election.

Another example of his instincts for what grabs the media's attention occurred when he attended the Republican Party's National Convention in Miami in 1972 as an alternate delegate. After Nixon's nomination for a second term, a reception was held that Crews wanted to attend. As he waited in the long line, Crews yelled out to Nixon's handlers, "Let some young people in; it'll look good on TV." The stunt worked, and then some. A photo essay in *Newsweek* about the convention included a picture of Nixon shaking Crews' hand.[10]

After graduating in 1974, Crews attended law school at his alma mater, the University of Iowa. Gradually, he become more comfortable with his sexuality. Strangely enough, Nixon and Watergate played a small part in his acceptance of himself. As Crews put it, "I realized that I can determine for myself what is right and wrong. It had something to do with Nixon and realizing that he and his aides were not infallible."

After passing the bar and being hired by a small law firm, Crews got a call to run Republican Governor Bob Ray's 1978 reelection campaign. At the time, Crews had been moving away from politics, but he felt managing the governor's campaign was too great an opportunity to pass up.

Crews and Kehoe met in 1975 through a fraternity brother of Kehoe's. They soon found they shared mutual interests, such as canoeing, bicycling, and camping. They also had a common ideology—Republican politics. "I wasn't initially attracted to Steve so I felt pretty comfortable being around him," recalls Crews. "He was fun to be with. Steve was in complete denial about being gay, even though he had these desires. One of the first things we did was go on a canoe trip together in Iowa. It was a great day; later we went on a three-day bike trip in Wisconsin."

At that point, Crews had not had much gay sex. Little happened in college or law school. Like Kehoe, he, too, was trying to deny his homosexuality. "They don't elect gay people to Congress," is how Crews summarized the conflict he faced between political reality and his sexual orientation. He had the fleeting idea of marrying a woman he liked from the University of Iowa but knew it would be a front. He rejected the idea.

After the election, they traveled to the Northern Rockies to go camping and cross-country skiing. After a year-end winter camping trip back in Iowa, they celebrated New Year's Eve together. That night, they stayed at a friend's house where they were put in the same bedroom. Said Crews, "By then, we had fallen in love, but we hadn't talked about being gay. He was having the same feeling but not realizing where I was coming from. We got undressed. I was in one bed and he was in the other, and I just went over and climbed on top of him. Afterward he asked if we could do it again."

It has always been Crews's dream and ambition to be a U.S. Representative. One of the initial obstacles to fulfilling this dream was Article I of the Constitution, which says that "No person shall be a Representative who shall not have attained to the age of twenty-five years." The year before Crews was eligible to run and still in law school, a Republican by the name of Jim Leach beat an incumbent Democrat. Twenty-one years later, he is still in office. In fact, Leach was one of the Congress members that Crews lobbied when he was in Washington for the march. The two have become friends.

In 1984 came the mayoral appointment. By 1992, Crews had lowered his sights from Congress and decided to run for state senate when the incumbent retired. It was then that Crews had to resolve the "gay issue."

Crews and Kehoe had never hidden their relationship since moving to Melbourne, but neither had they publicized it. This strategy worked more or less successfully until the race for state senate. Crews made a bargain with himself during the campaign: While he would not come out, neither would he lie and say he was not gay; if questioned further, he would respond that his private life was not relevant. As usually happens in politics and life, he couldn't have it both ways. All through the campaign, rumors spread about his sexual orientation. Crews believes that had he been more open about his sexual orientation, he might have won the fifty-six votes he lost the election by.

There was one incident related to the campaign that still bothers Crews and Kehoe. Two people with whom Kehoe works had good locations for yard signs. After the signs went up, both co-workers received calls telling them that Crews was gay. The co-workers then called to say the signs had to be removed because they could not be seen as promoting the gay lifestyle.

The defeat for state senate convinced Crews to be more forthright about his homosexuality. So, when the March on Washington approached, he saw it as an opportunity to increase people's awareness of who gay men and lesbians really are. There was a political consequence, however: an opponent in the November 1995 mayoral election.

Crews's homosexuality was never an overt issue in the campaign, but then there was no reason to publicize it since all 700 people in town knew. A more important issue was whether Crews was pushing his own agenda at the expense of the town. Wrote Crews's opponent in a questionnaire published in the newspaper: "It will be my job to listen to the needs and concerns of the citizens of Melbourne. I don't plan on leading Melbourne anywhere. I only want to represent the people that elect me. They will decide where we go. I believe the citizens of Melbourne to be intelligent, progressive-minded people!"[11]

Crews had to psych himself up for the race. Still disheartened by his loss in the senate race, he also was mindful of the defeat of three-term Des Moines school board member, Jonathan Wilson, in September. Wilson, who announced he was gay after much speculation, was targeted by the religious right. In a very contentious race, Wilson lost badly, coming in fourth. It was Kehoe who convinced Crews to run again, not just because of Wilson's defeat but because it would be the first time he would face the voters since coming out. If he won, Crews would be the first openly gay person in Iowa to be elected to office.

The campaign was probably the best thing for Crews. He was able to focus on his accomplishments as mayor over the previous eleven years, such as building the new fire station, improving the reliability and quality of the water supply system, lowering the property tax, and improving the financial condition of the city. His plans for the future included building a better library, creating new housing, improving the highway that runs by town, and further tax reductions. As he walked door to door, he was encouraged by the positive feedback he received.

When it came to running a campaign, Crews hadn't just arrived in town on a hay truck. Although there were only 425 registered voters, he ran the type of campaign befitting a population a hundred times that size. He mailed two campaign pieces. He walked door-to-door. He put up lawn signs. The day before the election he sent out a letter with fifty-one supporters on it. On election day, he had someone check the polling place to see who had voted and then started to call supporters who had not yet voted. After several calls, he realized he was overdoing it for a town as small as Melbourne. He put down the phone. He had done all he could do.

Which turned out to be enough. Out of a record-setting 289 votes cast, Crews received 167, or 58 percent of the vote.

Although Crews survived the political challenge, there have been repercussions for his professional career. After holding numerous government jobs, he set up his own consulting and legal business, specializing in public policy for local government. However, it has not been as successful as Crews had hoped. "Because of my visibility, the consulting practice doesn't do as well as it should. People won't say, 'I'm not giving you the business because you are a fag,' but when you don't get responses back, you have to wonder. I was talking to the city attorney for a small town called Guttenberg, and it was interesting because he didn't put two and two together until I told him my last name. I sensed that he recognized who I was. He never called back."

Living principally off one salary has meant that finances are tight. Although they both like to travel, vacations usually involve camping. And while they would prefer to leave the state sometime during the cold winters, they do not have the funds do to it.

*   *   *

There have been other repercussions from Crews's coming out. One involves his neighbors. Two weeks after the March on Washington, Penny Pfantz, the daughter-in-law of Crews and Kehoe's backyard neighbors, the Pfantzes, wrote a letter to the *Marshalltown Times-Republican*.[12] She stated that she was from Melbourne and knew them both. "I like them, and Crews has been a good mayor. But their lifestyle is wrong and I feel acceptance of it is being forced upon us."

Next she argued that people cannot take bits and pieces of the Bible just to fit his or her lifestyles. Then she stated that she saw film coverage of the march. "I was shocked by the public behavior which I was seeing and began to feel that I have been very naive as to what homosexual behavior means." After ambiguously saying that "those of us who have children still to raise cannot afford the luxury of a blasé attitude," she concluded that she still does not believe in desecrating a person's house just because one disagrees with his or her lifestyle. "If I had a good friend or a son who was gay, I would not stop loving them or ostracize them, but neither could I sit back and say that their lifestyle was OK."

After the letter appeared, Kehoe talked with his neighbors and asked if they knew about their daughter-in-law's letter. Mrs. Pfantz told him that it was a free country and she could write whatever she wanted to. Kehoe asked her if she felt the same way, and she said that she did not care what he and Crews did in their bedroom. "My response was, 'What does our bedroom have to do with this?' Then she made a comment about our lifestyle, and I said, 'You've seen all of our lifestyle there is to see. You live right behind us.'" Later Kehoe spoke with their son—Penny Pfantz's husband—and said that he wanted an apology. Not surprisingly, he was told not to expect one. "I said to him that what Penny did to us in the letter was no better than what the people did who spray-painted our house, except that what she did was legal."

A month later, Pfantz was in her in-laws' yard with her children, and Kehoe yelled to her, "When are you going to apologize for writing such a nasty letter?" Pfantz responded that there was nothing wrong with having her own opinion. "It definitely went downhill from there," said Kehoe. "I ended up saying things I wasn't proud of. I let people antagonize me and then say things I shouldn't."

The result of the exchange was that Kehoe no longer felt comfortable in his own backyard. He did not want his neighbors looking over at him like he was "some kind of queer." Kehoe decided he wanted to build a fence, an action that has much significance in the Midwest where few fences exist between homes. Because of the cost, they waited a year to construct it. The next spring saw the birth between their properties of a 60-foot-long, 9-foot-high fence that they built for $800.

If life in Kehoe's backyard has been rough, so has life at his workplace. Kehoe was closeted at work until the March on Washington. Coming out was not easy for him. He described it as like jumping into a cold lake. "You can stand there and look at it and look at it, and you know it's going to be a shock. Now, I wish I hadn't looked at it so long and had jumped sooner and gotten it over with."

Instead of being greeted with smiles in the hallways as he used to be, most of his co-workers began to divert their eyes and purse their lips when they passed him. Kehoe, who recently earned his BA degree in psychology, believes in the power of behavioral therapies for overcoming homophobia. According to Kehoe, one such therapy is flooding, which he describes as saturating a person with the thing that bothers him or her. An example of this would be to allow a kid who eats too much candy to have so much candy that he or she gets sick. He decided to put this theory into practice. One day while talking to an engineer who was recruiting prospective employees, Kehoe asked if he had interviewed any cute gay boys. "He was speechless," chuckled Kehoe, "as though someone had jumped out and said boo. He said 'no' and then mumbled something about not discriminating against gays." When he told Crews the story, Crews told him that what he did could be considered sexual harassment. Kehoe's first thought was "How many times could I use the word gay in my apology?"

One comfort to Kehoe is the close relationship that he and Crews have with Crews's mother. (Crews was in college when his father, whom he adored and still misses, died in an automobile accident.) Mrs. Crews always gets Kehoe a present at Christmas and sends him cards on his birthday and holidays. The rest of Crews's family includes them in their activities, while Kehoe's family has not been as accepting.

*   *   *

Then there is the matter with the local church. Crews's relationship with organized religion has, until recently, been an uneasy accommodation. His father did not fit the stereotype of a Midwest Methodist minister. Throughout his career, Rev. Crews ministered to migrant workers and to the poor. Later he left the church for two years to become a Vista Volunteer supervisor. From his father and his mother, a social worker, Crews and his two brothers were instilled with a sense of social justice and service to community. His battles with organized religion usually occur when Crews believes a church's teachings fall short in one or both of these areas.

The United Methodist Church is small—fewer than a hundred members with thirty regular worshipers. When he moved to Melbourne, Crews did not attend the church because he found the minister too conservative. However, Crews reevaluated his position in 1992 when he found, as have legions of politicians before him, an earthly reason to attend: candidacy for political office.

Just before the senate race, the church had a new minister appointed by the bishop that Crews liked, Rev. Beverly Bell, so he continued to go. He even was asked to be the lay member to the Methodist annual conference, a high honor.

But then the March on Washington and the vandalism happened. A week following the incident, Rev. Bell did a sermon denouncing the actions and calling for tolerance toward gays and lesbians. With Crews in attendance, two members got up and walked out. "And so," Crews stated with eyebrows rising, "the battle was on."

Church wars can be vicious and brutal. Such was the case in Melbourne. After an attempt to oust Crews as the lay member in the fall of 1993, his opponents were successful in 1994. The person who replaced him also wanted Rev. Bell removed. Recalls Crews about a meeting to discuss Rev. Bell's evaluation, "Her main opponent started by saying that he was not sure if the church would survive without her, but he was certain that it would not survive with her. He had already called the district superintendent and said she had to go."

And so she went, replaced by someone Crews did not like.

But the final blow came when the new minister and his wife signed Crews's mayoral opponent's nomination papers. Crews started attending a Methodist church in Marshalltown, but, he slyly interjected, "I didn't change my church membership until after the election."

Despite the church wars, Crews's faith in God remains strong. "When I was young, it never occurred to me for a second that God didn't love me because I was gay. I've never had a problem with being gay and being a Christian, nor do I think God has a problem with it either. I believe that God's love saves everyone and promises us all eternal life.

"The most amazing thing that has happened to me since coming out has been the strengthening of my faith," continued Crews. "I know that God loves me. I believe in one God and life everlasting, but don't believe that you have to be a Christian to enjoy life ever after. There are many paths to that. I try not to be judgmental. That has been a strength for me. So much of our opposition is done in the name of Jesus, and I know that isn't right. And if I can just work a little harder, I can help change these people and help them understand the wider breadth of God's love. That's where I think the battle is."

Along the way, Crews also became estranged from the Republican Party. Having fought long and hard for women's rights, environmental protection, reproductive choice, and gay and lesbian rights, he finally acknowledged that the party had grown too conservative. He is now registered as "no party."

*   *   *

The following are bumper stickers on Crews's 1983 Chrysler New Yorker: "Protect your family from the Christian Coalition"; "Equal Rights—Nothing more, nothing less"; "Clinton/Gore '96"; "The United Methodist Church—A Hate Free Zone" (with "should be" handwritten by Crews after the word "Church"); and a rainbow flag decal. Inside the house are more rainbow flags and stickers than adorn most San Francisco homes.

Crews and Kehoe are both proud of being gay. They clearly receive great emotional and personal fulfillment from fighting for gay rights and from being role models in a state where few exist. Nevertheless, the four years following the March on Washington have made them battle weary.

Crews is not sure when it will happen, but he is resigned to the fact that one day he and Kehoe will leave Iowa for better jobs. Portland, Oregon, interests them because of the beauty of the Pacific Northwest and the wide range of recreational activities. But Crews still has some goals he wants to accomplish as mayor, such as building a new library that families can use and where kids can study after school and connect to the Internet. With a new library and a fire station to his credit, Crews knows townspeople will not be able to minimize his contribution by saying he was just "the gay mayor."

"I have to be a good mayor because that is my claim to fame. But it goes back to wanting to be of service and wanting to help oppressed people. It's a very spiritual, Christ-based theology and philosophy. I've always been involved in causes, and now that I'm out I can be a source of hope and change for gay people."

Speaking with fondness and without bitterness, Crews—the man who became the face of gay America for Iowans that April Sunday in 1993—summed up his feelings for his home state like this: "There is something magical about Iowa. Year after year, on this six to eight inches of topsoil, you can plant seeds in the ground and have the whole place turn green. There is no place greener than Iowa on a summer day before the corn tassels because it's all corn and beans. And generally people tend to be open-minded, more so than the stereotypes would portray. But it's still tough. Of course, it's tough anywhere if you're of a different sexual orientation."

Chapter 4

Love Is All It Takes to Make a Family: Seattle City Councilwoman Tina Podlodowski

Three years before her election to the Seattle City Council, Tina Podlodowski began volunteering at Rise n' Shine, an organization that Podlodowski described as a Big Brothers/Big Sisters program for kids who are HIV positive or whose parents are HIV positive. This is where she met her partner, Chelle Mileur, who shares Podlodowski's love of children. "It turned out that we both wanted to have kids," she said, "and our volunteer work was an opportunity to spend time with children who really needed attention." Podlodowski (pronounced Pod-lo-dow-ski) was matched with Alisa, a child who had AIDS and who has since passed away. Mileur was matched with a little boy named Ryan, who was part of their wedding and whose father was HIV positive. "It was a good overall experience," Podlodowski remembers, "and a good preparental experience."

The knowledge they gained has been put to good use. In November 1995, the love of their lives was born to Mileur, a girl named Grace. With her, the two women became part of the lesbian baby boom that is sweeping the country. Even though there are no national statistics documenting the trend, most gays and lesbians have

---

Photo (left to right): Chelle Mileur, children Grace and Jackson, Tina Podlodowski.

stories to tell of lesbian couples they know who are having children. "At some point you get a critical mass, which is where I think we are," commented Podlodowski, age thirty-six. "There's one couple, then two couples, and then all of a sudden you realize just how many gay couples are having children." Added Mileur, age thirty-four, "Lesbians who are in their thirties and forties are just like other baby boomers. They've decided they want kids."

Both women believe that while people are beginning to accept gay relationships, a majority overwhelmingly disapprove of gay parenting. "Once you bring a child into a gay relationship, the whole issue changes," Podlodowski stated. "Some people don't think it's in the best interest of the child to be raised by two mothers or two dads. It has to be one mother and one dad. In their view, that's the ideal, that's perfection."

Podlodowski and Mileur disagree, of course. They feel their household is as nurturing an environment to raise a child as any other home. After spending time with Grace, it is difficult to refute the claim. Absolutely charming and engaging, Grace is a poster child, if you will, for the lesbian baby boom.

"I have a friend who says that being a gay or lesbian parent is the equivalent to *Star Trek:* the 'final frontier' of gay and lesbian activism because it's generally a place where we haven't publicly gone before," said Podlodowski. "We are able to dispel so many stereotypes that surround gays and lesbians and children by being loving, caring parents. It's hard for people to buy into a stereotype of what a gay or lesbian person is when they're in your baby group each week."

The two women will have an opportunity to educate members of another baby group because, when this interview was conducted, Mileur was eight months pregnant with their second child, a boy to be named Jackson.

*   *   *

In 1995, three years after volunteering at Rise n' Shine and meeting Mileur, Podlodowski ran for Seattle City Council. Podlodowski's lesbianism wasn't so much an issue as was her past employer and her economic status. The two words her opponents used to describe her were "Microsoft millionaire." Unlike most political name-calling, the epithet was true; indeed, she is a former Microsoft executive who, like many others from the company, became a millionaire from being given generous stock options when hired. However, with Microsoft being headquartered in nearby Redmond and Seattle's economy becoming more dependent on high technology, the label did not have the negative effect her opponents would have liked. The story of how Podlodowski came to be a Microsoft millionaire is one that mirrors that of other young engineers who, through hard work, intelligence, and a bit of luck, became successful beyond their wildest dreams.

Podlodowski is the daughter of Polish immigrants who met in the United States following their arrival in early 1950s after President Truman lifted the immigration quotas on Poland. Her father, who fought for the British Armed Forces during World War II, was a gardener when he met her mother, who was working as a maid. After their marriage, they moved to New Britain, Connecticut, to work for a defense contractor. "People who couldn't speak English but were good with their hands could always get jobs as machinists in these factories," she explained. Podlodowski is their only child. When she got older, the family moved to an adjoining town, which Podlodowski described as a slight step up in the blue-collar range. "As a first-generation immigration kid, I was taught by my parents that education is very important," Podlodowski recalled. "Everybody had a job, and my job was to make sure I got A pluses. Not As—A pluses."

Podlodowski considered herself fortunate that she was involved in sports all through high school because many of her teammates turned out to be lesbians. These friends were a support network for her when, at fifteen, she began to realize her sexual orientation. "I was part of a great girl gang—I can't think of any other way to describe it," she stated. "We were all national honor society members and three-sport athletes. We played soccer and basketball and then did a different third sport like softball or track. Mine was tennis." She remembered one prophetic conversation she had with her best friend: "I said to her that she had better stay friends with me because I was going to be a millionaire by the time I was thirty. We laughed hysterically because we were both blue-collar kids and having a million bucks was way beyond our comprehension."

Podlodowski wanted to be a radio disc jockey, so she attended college at the University of Hartford, which has a highly regarded public radio station. Ever the pragmatist, she chose an engineering major because DJs don't earn much money. She knew she would be more valuable to the radio station if she had her FCC license and could do her own engineering. "It was a simple matter of economics," she said about a decision that would lead her down a professional career path far, far from radio broadcasting. "I was looking at majoring in general engineering, but I was offered a scholarship in computer technology, so I majored in that. I was the first woman to go through their program."

Not only was Podlodowski the sole woman in her area of study, but in her three and a half years at Hartford, she was the only woman in her computer classes. "It taught me a lot about working in a male environment, that's for sure," she chuckled, "and it prepared me for subsequent successes in the computer industry because there still aren't many women there today." An overachiever, she was on the dean's list each quarter, served as a student member of the University Board of Regents, and started a gay and lesbian student group on campus. She did not readily let go of the dream of being a DJ, however. She still found time to produce and host several gay and lesbian-themed radio shows.

After graduating in 1981 at the age of twenty-one, the brown-haired, brown-eyed Podlodowski spent two years designing microprocessor-based hardware and software for AMF Incorporated. In 1983, she was hired as a project manager for the Hartford Insurance Group to run their microcomputer development center. Possessing a strong sense of fairness and justice that has followed her throughout her adult life, Podlodowski soon discovered the inequity of the company's compensation policies. "I was managing a group of programmers who were developing some pretty innovative software programs for insurance agents on this new computer which was just introduced, called the IBM PC," she said. "Not only was I doing my job, but I had the responsibilities of someone four grades above me. When it came time for my first performance review, I only got a 3 percent raise. That made me stop for a minute. I thought, wait a minute, I'm doing the job of someone four grades above me. How do I get recognized for this; how do I get compensated? I learned that employees had to spend time in their grade before they got promoted. It wasn't based on performance. But the way I had always gotten feedback with sports and academics was based on performance. You do the schoolwork; you get an A. You work hard at practice; you score the goal in a soccer game. So I decided that this was not the place I wanted to stay."

In 1984, Podlodowski took a job at MultiMate, a small software start-up that produced eight software products for the IBM PC. She was the company's product marketing director. In what would soon become commonplace in the nascent industry, the company quickly grew into a $100 million enterprise. In 1986, the founder sold the company to Ashton-Tate, a large software company. Suddenly unemployed, Podlodowski had two job offers, one with Ashton-Tate, the other with a computer start-up. She took the offer from Ashton-Tate and moved to Los Angeles, the company's headquarters. After a week, she decided she hated Ashton-Tate and hated LA. She then accepted her second choice job offer, the one with Microsoft. When she arrived in Seattle, Microsoft, whose stock had not yet gone public, employed about 800 people. She was to be the product manager of Microsoft's extraordinarily successful word-processing software program called Word.

"The primary reason I came to Microsoft was because of a female vice president named Ida Cole," Podlodowski recalled. "It was very unusual to see women in any positions of power and authority. The job gave me an opportunity to work with a role model and have someone to talk to about differences in managerial styles, such as the way that women look at the world versus the way that men do, at least in the software industry."

As product manager, Podlodowski spent a year overseeing the development, marketing, and sale of Microsoft Word 3.0. After the product was released, she was transferred to the East Coast to be Northeast sales manager for Microsoft products. "I was twenty-five years old, had never sold a thing in my life, and was sent to Manhattan to sell products to the big guys," she said with a lingering sense of awe. "In three years, the office went from almost nothing to employing 100 people and generating $30 million in sales."

Her next promotion was to international marketing manager and a chance to work again with Cole. Her job was to assist subsidiary general managers in Europe, South America, Asia, Mexico, and Canada. "There were five of us, and we had visas for every country on the planet. When something went wrong with one of the subsidiaries, one of us was dispatched to fix it." The position taught her a great deal about international business and viewing a company from a worldwide perspective.

This was followed by another employment opportunity in 1991. She was offered the job of director and general manager of Microsoft University, one of two businesses that had its own profit and loss statements separate from "Mother Microsoft." The university is where Microsoft employees and product users learned about Microsoft products. "The position gave me a chance to be a manager and to see if I could get people to work together. All the decisions were my decisions, and nobody interfered with me." In a year, Microsoft University went from having one location to having eight domestic locations and four international sites with 150 employees, $15 million in revenues, and a million dollars in profit.

Reflecting on her life in the computer industry, Podlodowski commented, "Microsoft was an incredible ride and an incredible experience. I was there when an entire industry was being created. For seven years I had no life outside the company. And for six and a half years that was okay. But it got to the point where I said, 'Hey, I've made a million dollars in stock options. I've proved to myself that I can do this kind of work and can run a business the way I want and be successful.' However, I realized that the component of giving back to the community wasn't there for me, a value my parents instilled in me in a very profound way. So in February 1992, I decided to leave Microsoft. I told myself I would take a year or two off to decide what I wanted to do, then do it. In the meantime, I wanted to use my business skills to help gay and lesbian nonprofits."

One of the first things Podlodowski did was become a board member of the Pride Foundation, an organization that works to strengthen the gay and lesbian community of the Pacific Northwest through grants and scholarships. When she was board president from 1993 to 1995, the Pride Foundation went from granting $25,000 a year to $250,000. She took their endowment from $200,000 to $15 million with $6 million in irrevocable trusts, making it the leading gay and lesbian foundation in the country. In 1993 she became interim house director of Lambert House, a drop-in center for gay and lesbian youth. She also became the first director of Hands Off Washington, a statewide gay and lesbian civil rights organization. And there was Rise 'n' Shine, where, in 1992, she met Mileur, who was working for a large computer firm as head of their consulting group.

By early 1995, Podlodowski and Mileur had decided to have a baby. Podlodowski had always wanted to have a child, but knew it would be difficult raising one as a single parent. "I didn't want to physically get pregnant, so I thought I would end up adopting a child," she recalled. Her idea of parenthood included being in the right relationship and sharing the parental tasks with someone. She found that person in Mileur, a tall, energetic woman whose fair skin and strawberry blond hair reveal her Irish ancestry. A good friend of theirs agreed to be the father.

Given that 60 percent of the pregnancies in the United States are unplanned, Podlodowski believes that gay and lesbian couples are the most prepared of all parents because their pregnancies are never an accident. "Gay and lesbian couples think through everything, from preschool to the kid's wedding," she said. "When it comes to children, I want to say to the radical religious right, 'Can you tell me that every member of your church has been as thoughtful about having children as gay parents are?'"

But then, as has happened so many times in her life, a new opportunity presented itself to Podlodowski. An incumbent Seattle City Council member decided not to seek reelection. After much thought, Podlodowski realized that the position could provide her with the means to combine her business skills with her desire to help the overall community. The couple discussed whether they should proceed with Mileur becoming pregnant that year. They decided they would.

* * *

Seattle, a city of 550,000, elects its council members citywide. Although initiatives have been on the ballot over the years to switch the system to district elections, voters continue to reject the change. Candidates run for specific seats on the nine-member council. Races are nonpartisan, with the top two voter-getters from the September primary competing against each other in the November runoff. Initially, ten candidates filed papers declaring their intent to run for Seat #7. However, when the official filing period closed, only four candidates remained.

Because candidates run citywide, communicating with Seattle's 360,000 voters is an expensive undertaking. In addition, Seattle's campaign reform law limits individuals, businesses, and PACs to donate only $400 per candidate every four years. This forces candidates to have a broad base of support in order to raise the $200,000 needed to win. A relative newcomer to politics, Podlodowski did not start out with the requisite level of support, even though she had proved herself to be a capable fund-raiser while president of the Pride Foundation. Podlodowski's strategy was to have friends hold small fund-raisers in their homes as a way to build her volunteer and donor base. Through much hard work, 100 house parties were held during the primary and general elections. She also received an estimated quarter of her funds from outside the Seattle area. In all, 2,500 people contributed a total of $210,000 to her campaign. Combined with the $40,000 that Podlodowski and Mileur contributed of their own money, the campaign budget reached $250,000. Few donations came from Microsoft or other high-tech employees, despite the fact that one of their own was running. But as candidates have found in cities with high-tech firms, getting money from computer engineers is an almost impossible task. Podlodowski observed with a shrug, "Many people who work for Microsoft think that politics is irrelevant to their world, so they can't imagine spending $400 on a politician when they can spend that on a piece of software."

On the campaign trail and in her literature, Podlodowski emphasized her business background and what she could do for Seattle. Recalled Podlodowski, "I wanted to make sure government was more aware of technology and how the changes could affect Seattle. The city needed to think about technology in terms of its schools, public policy, businesses, transportation, mass transit, and land use. High-tech businesses, be they biotech or software, will be a test of whether Seattle's economy survives or not, and I wanted to be sure that we as a city were going to be players in the twenty-first century."

When the ballots were counted on the night of the primary, Podlodowski came in second, winning 35 percent of the vote to Jesse Wineberry's 35.7 percent. Several days later, however, after the absentee ballots were counted, Podlodowski proved to be the top vote-getter by 800 votes, an impressive achievement for a first-time candidate. Wineberry, who is African American, was a former state legislator who, over the years, had become a perennial candidate, having run for U.S. Senate and for county councilor. He was also the self-declared "open, heterosexual, Christian, father candidate."

With only two months between the primary and the general election, the campaign became nasty very fast. It all began during a joint appearance on a Seattle radio show when a reporter asked if either candidate had a criminal record. "Criminal record?" Podlodowski thought to herself. "That's a weird question." Both she and Wineberry answered in the negative, although Wineberry added that once he had been arrested at a civil rights demonstration, a boast that turned out not to be true.

Then the campaign, in Podlodowski's words, "went nuts." The next day, Wineberry issued a press release stating that Podlodowski had lied about not having a criminal record. The accusation referred to an incident five years before when she and a friend were in a city park having a picnic. An officer approached them and said it was illegal for them to have an open container of beer. After pleading ignorance of the law and dumping the beer, they were given $50 tickets, which they promptly paid. Podlodowski had not given the incident another thought.

Next, Wineberry upped the stakes even more when he mailed a campaign piece that resembled an official police document. "Criminal Violation: Podlodowski, Tina M." read the large headline. After citing the case number and date, the violation was disclosed: "Intoxicating liquors prohibited in public parks." The next line said, "Judgment: GUILTY." The bottom of the flier read, "When asked by a journalist about past criminal violations, Podlodowski denied any knowledge of her criminal violation."

Mileur, who grew up in Chicago and was involved in Democratic Party politics, eagerly volunteered to do the opposition research. She soon earned the nickname "Terminator." "It was great to have such a focused rival to go after," she said with a devilish grin.

Mileur discovered that Wineberry had received a number of traffic violations, including driving without a valid license. He was caught driving with a license plate that bore a renewal sticker from a license plate reported stolen. He had been cited for failing to comply with state and federal campaign disclosures in past elections. In addition, court records showed that he was sued by Harvard University for $5,687 in unpaid miscellaneous charges he incurred while taking courses at the John F. Kennedy School of Government. What amazed Mileur was that someone with his past would be the first to fling mud. "Did he really think I wouldn't find out about those things?" she asked in a tone that would have made Richard Daley proud.

Podlodowski believed Wineberry's negative tactics misfired. "The mudslinging was something I wasn't used to, but I actually think it swung the election in my favor. We had front-page press all the time. People were talking about it on the radio. This is who she is, this is who he is. Why is he always mentioning her beer citation?" Both the *Seattle Times* and the *Seattle Post-Intelligencer* sided with Podlodowski. Wrote the *Post-Intelligencer* in their endorsement of her, "Wineberry's lapses are much more troubling than Podlodowski's picnic beer."[1] Furthermore, "Podlodowski has a set of strong goals, including working to attract more high-tech and other new industry, strengthening Seattle's position as an international city, keeping downtown as well as neighborhoods economically vibrant and streamlining city regulatory processes."

In terms of contacting voters, the campaign adapted to Seattle's climate and terrain. Precincts were telephoned, not walked. Podlodowski called this phone door-belling. "In August and September, no one is home in Seattle because it's the best time of year. It doesn't rain as much, and it's light until 11 p.m. By October, it's dark and rainy again. Because of our dollar limits and the geography of running citywide, we used phone door-belling and house parties in a way that no one had used before." She also took full advantage of her technology background. She had a Web site and utilized a sophisticated database to communicate with volunteers and supporters.

Running at the same time was Sherry Harris, Seattle's first openly lesbian council member, who was elected in 1991. Harris, who is

African American, was opposed by an African-American man. Having two lesbians running for office did not create a problem for Podlodowski. "Seattle is a very liberal city," she said. "Even though 80 percent of our population is white, we have an African-American mayor, and of nine council members, seven are women, two are Asian, and one is a lesbian. Of the two men, one is African American and one is Asian. There are no white guys. So did I think there was room in the diversity market for two lesbians running at the same time? Yeah."

There was not much gay-baiting in the council race. This is because Seattle has been accepting of its gay and lesbian residents, with gays and lesbians being well integrated into all aspects of political and social life. Seattle was one of the few cities whose voters did not repeal its ordinance banning discrimination on the basis of sexual orientation after Anita Bryant took her antigay campaign nationwide in the late 1970s. In fact, voters turned down the referendum by an astonishing 60 percent. In 1992, Cal Anderson, an openly gay man, was elected to the Washington House of Representatives. He was elected to the state senate in 1995. He died of complications from AIDS in 1996. Ed Murray, also a gay man, was appointed to Anderson's old house seat when the incumbent was elected to fill Anderson's vacant senate seat.

Given this history, it was not surprising that when Wineberry made his comment that he was "openly heterosexual," he was criticized for it, as he was when he attempted to make an issue of Podlodowski's lesbianism when he spoke before several black churches. To offset any negative impact, Podlodowski attended the First African Methodist Church. During the sermon, the minister said that he did not care if someone was black or white, gay or straight—it was the content of their character that mattered. After the service, the minister led Podlodowski to the entrance of the church and stood by her as they shook the exiting parishioners' hands.

As occurs in most gay candidates' campaigns, there was a debate over "how lesbian" Podlodowski should be. In her literature, Podlodowski looked very much like the corporate executive that she was, not the radical lesbian that some desired. Some community members wanted her to be more out in her campaign brochures, arguing for a photograph of her embracing Mileur. Podlodowski rejected the idea, believing that the campaign's main message was her plan to run city hall in a more businesslike fashion.

A year and a half after the election, Podlodowski tried to be philosophical about the differing points of view, but some resentment remained. "Gay candidates carry a lot of hopes and dreams and expectations for this thing we call the gay, lesbian, bisexual, transgender community, but you can't be all things to all people," she said, sighing. "I'm being who I am. I'm a lesbian, but I'm also a woman, a child of immigrants, and a high-tech person. Being a lesbian is one of the things that defines me, but not the only thing, so for me to focus only on being a lesbian would not be true to myself." As far as advice she would give to other gay candidates, she reflected, "I think candidates have to be prepared to have the gay community be their harshest critic because you're never out enough for some people, whatever their definition of out is. At some point you just turn off those critics, even though you know you're going to get grief from them."

Apparently, Podlodowski found the right combination in portraying herself to Seattle voters as a high-tech businesswoman, a child of immigrants, and a lesbian. She handily defeated Wineberry with 65 percent of the vote.

* * *

Because she stressed her high-tech background in her campaign and talked about making government more cost-efficient, one of the first projects that Podlodowski undertook as a councilwoman was having an audit conducted of the city's use of computers. "One question I asked was 'How much do we spend on technology?' Nobody could answer that question," she stated. "There wasn't someone like a chief technology officer running the shop. We hired a private consultant to come and tell us how much we were spending and to compare our business practices with the best business practices in the private and public sectors."

What the auditors found was fairly typical for a governmental operation, even though it would make a techie shudder. Besides observing problems with lack of training and inadequate wiring, the auditors discovered that each city department had its own technology fiefdom. Because standards differed in each department, computers that should talk with each other couldn't, such as those in the police department, municipal court, and the city attorney's office. This meant that if a warrant was issued for an arrest by the courts, it had to be hand-entered into the police department's computer, which could take days. Conversely, if the warrant was removed, it might not be deleted from the computer for three or four days.

Nor was there any management of the city's technology assets. "We had no idea how many computers we had because there was no list of them," said Podlodowski. "If one disappeared, there was no way to track it. There were no records of which computers needed maintenance or upgrades. Training was haphazard at best. Also, workers in the field had no access to computers at all. We needed wireless laptops for them."

Some of the recommendations made by the auditors included establishing a single point of contact for all users of technology, creating a database of all software and hardware assets, investing more in training since untrained users consume three to six times more support than trained users, and linking employee technology skills to job requirements. The auditors projected that the city could save between $16 and $32 million annually if their recommendations were implemented.

Podlodowski's colleagues on the council seemed relieved to have someone of her caliber to guide them in these matters. To the uninitiated, the world of computers remains foreign—and expensive—territory. "I bring to the council an expertise in technology, finance, and business that allows other council members to rely on me," she acknowledged. "They're glad they have a technology expert on council who can say, 'No, we're not going to spend $10 million on that because it isn't going to work.' Then, as they trusted me in that area, they came to trust me in other areas as well."

Podlodowski has worked hard to get city hall to shift its focus toward a private-sector mentality, one in which employees share a common vision. "On council, we're all very different people," she explained. "I try to corral everybody into thinking, hey, you know what, it really doesn't matter who gets the credit for this. We're all in this together, so why don't we think about what is best for the city?"

So far the shift is working. For example, while Podlodowski did not support district elections, she believed that the 45 percent of the voters who favored it needed to be heard. She was able to get consensus on matching each council member with a specific geographical area of the city. Now, when residents have a complaint, they can contact the council member assigned to their neighborhood. Podlodowski has also made strides with the unions. Before her election, the City of Seattle had thirty-five different labor unions and over fifty bargaining units with their own separate contracts. Due to her efforts, the city now negotiates with a coalition of unions instead of each one separately. The city has also stopped contracting out work to the private sector, a practice that is strongly opposed by the unions. Now, it is done only when there is union agreement, and this has created a more cooperative spirit between management and workers.

But political life is not without its hazards. Shortly after her election, Podlodowski was asked to be a chair of Washington State's Clinton/Gore Reelection Campaign, an invitation she gladly accepted. Then came along DOMA—the Defense of Marriage Act, a federal bill that denies federal recognition of same-gender marriages and permits states not to recognize same-gender marriages performed in other states. Introduced by conservative Republicans, it was meant to be an election-year wedge issue. To the disappointment of the gay and lesbian community, Clinton signed the bill. Out of principle, Podlodowski resigned from the president's reelection committee, an action that did not endear her to local Democratic Party leaders and which may hurt her politically in the future. She has no regrets. "Gay and lesbian people should have the same choice to get married as anyone else and have the same access to benefits. It's a simple matter of discrimination," she said with conviction. "Gay and lesbian people stay together for twenty, thirty, forty years in relationships, even though they could lose their housing as a result of that relationship, or their jobs, or even their kids. To me, that's what marriage and commitment is all about."

After she and Mileur established the Podlodowski/Mileur Fund for Gay and Lesbian Families with Children, Podlodowski found that she had unintentionally stepped into quite a fracas. In its first year, the fund distributed over $21,000 in grants. The grant that created the most controversy was awarded to the Seattle Public Schools to buy literature appropriate for elementary school students to promote visibility and inclusion for sexual-minority students and families. These included books such as *Heather Has Two Mommies, Daddy's Roommate,* and *Who's in a Family?* The Washington Family Council, a conservative Christian organization, demanded the district return the books. In addition, a state legislator introduced a bill to prohibit the teaching in public schools of homosexuality as "positive, normal, or acceptable." In response to the bill, Podlodowski commented in a newspaper article, "There is no reason for adults to organize a discriminatory movement to tell my child that her family is immoral."

In a powerful argument in support of keeping the books, Beth Reis, creator of a national Family Life and Sexual Health curriculum, wrote in the *Seattle Times* that "every child, gay and straight alike, is endangered by antigay prejudice, and only education can overcome prejudice. Every child is at risk of being ostracized with antigay slurs. If a boy is *too* quiet, *too* interested in the arts, *too* likely to walk away from a fight, or *too* academically successful, he may be branded a 'faggot.' If a girl is *too* athletically inclined, *too* assertive, *too* likely to walk away from a boy's come-on, *too* academically successful, she may be presumed to be a 'dyke.' Unfortunately, embodying any gay or lesbian stereotype qualifies a child for abuse. As does having two moms or two dads."[2]

Podlodowski believes that the big battleground for gay and lesbian civil rights in the future will be over children. "In the 1960s and 1970s, gays and lesbians were portrayed as people who molested children—more so gay men because lesbians were invisible in that context. Now, it's turning out that we are having children. We are presenting ourselves as positive role models as parents, and that provokes a lot of fear in organizations that make all their money trying to turn us into child molesters."

Like parents everywhere, Podlodowski has learned how difficult it can be to balance family life and work. She and Mileur are fortunate in that Mileur is able to stay home and raise Grace. In order to spend as much time as she can with her family, Podlodowski limits the number of events and night meetings that she attends. One of the great joys she receives is when Grace visits her at work.

All the political headaches fade away when she sees her daughter rushing toward her, shouting "Mommy, Mommy."

*   *   *

For the record, Grace calls Podlodowski "Mommy" and Mileur "Momma." Grace, who is being raised to view her biological father as a regular father, calls him "Dada." Her father's partner, who is seven inches shorter, is called "Short Dada."

Podlodowski had the honor of picking Grace's name because, as she said, grinning, "Chelle got to have her." She chose Grace, after Grace Kelly. Giving their daughter a last name was more problematic. Both women felt that giving her the hyphenated last name of Podlodowski-Mileur was "too much a burden for any child to bear." Instead, they gave her the last name of Gannon, which is Mileur's birth mother's maiden name. Their second child has the same father as his sister and will have the same last name. Both women hope to change their names to Gannon one day, but as they said, laughing, they do not think it wise for an elected official to change her name when in office.

Both women's names appear on the birth certificate under "parents." King County, where Seattle is located, has always been liberal in terms of adoptions for gays and lesbians. Podlodowski's adoption of Grace was treated as a stepparent adoption, which is less rigorous than two women adopting a baby. Said Mileur, "The county recognizes the fact that, as the biological mother, I get to have Grace live in this house whether any legislative body approves of it or not. I had the baby, so I get to keep the baby whether I'm gay or straight. What they do have the right to say is whether the other person living in the household is able to adopt." Mileur stated that it would have been difficult for the county to reject Podlodowski as a fit parent given that 150,000 voters thought she was worthy to be their representative.

Because Mileur is with Grace during the week, she is the one who has the most interactions with strangers about Grace. Grace, who is precocious and appears likely to accomplish great things in life, is always the focus of the conversation. "Usually what happens," explained Mileur, "is I am in the supermarket when an older woman comes up and asks if Grace looks like her dad. If I'm in a hurry, I'll say yes because she legitimately does. But normally, I answer that Grace does look like her father. I then explain that she has two dads and two moms, and that she's a lucky girl to have all those parents, even though she's not legally related to her dad, and that she lives with both her moms. As I say this, I can see their eyes getting bigger and bigger. People are just amazed by it. Fortunately, Grace is right there, attracting attention. She thrives on it. She interacts with them, she smiles, and totally wins them over so they can't pass judgment because they have this totally well behaved, adorable kid in front of them."

One question strangers often ask is, "What does Grace think about all of this?" Said Mileur, "I respond, 'Well, I haven't had that conversation with her yet, but she seems like a happy enough baby, doesn't she?' People will answer, 'Yes, it seems that way.' Then they might ask, 'What's it going to be like when she grows up?' I say, 'I'm hoping that people like you will accept her and help make her life easier.' You can see them processing this. They tell me, 'Oh, I guess I have a role to play in this.' I say, 'Absolutely.' Then if I'm not in a rush and the person wants to talk more, I try to put all the different kinds of families in context. I say that some kids have one mom, some kids have one dad, some kids have no parents, some kids live with their grandparents. This is just another variation."

Podlodowski and Mileur know they will have such conversations for many years. They also understand the need to be patient. "A lot of people ask questions because they genuinely have no experience with lesbian parents," Podlodowski said. "That's why we're the first line of defense for every gay and lesbian parent on the planet because the interaction people have with us will color how they feel about every gay or lesbian parent they ever meet."

* * *

In an article Podlodowski wrote that combined her politics with her child-rearing experience, she argued, "What better place to fight 'the gay agenda' than in the 'best interests' of the child? The radical right seems to believe that only male/female biology is what makes a family. But biology doesn't necessarily breed love and affection. Semen never read a story to a sleepy child. An egg never got up in the middle of the night to chase a nightmare away. Nothing means more in the life of a child than a loving, caring, active parent—gay or straight, biological or adopted. Nothing. And any legislation that keeps a child from his or her loving parent is just wrong.

"Gracie reminds me every day that a happy life is a simple life. It's based on how well you do these six things: sleep, eat, potty, play, learn, and love. Especially love. Watching Gracie laugh, I know that love is all it takes to make a family."

Chapter 5

Even Potholes Can Be Interesting:
San Diego City Councilwoman
Christine Kehoe

Observing San Diego City Councilwoman Christine Kehoe talking to two engineers about their plans to refurbish an abandoned movie theater reveals her success as San Diego's first openly gay elected official. The three become fast friends as they rapidly move from topic to topic, discussing the history of the neighborhood, historic movie palaces, common friends, and the headaches of starting a business. Throughout the meeting, Kehoe provides the civil engineers some names of people and companies who may be useful. At the end of the productive meeting, she tells the young entrepreneurs, "I really, really, really hope you can do it."

The three repetitions of "really" are an example of Kehoe's style—congenial, enthusiastic, encouraging. The fit between her personality and her politics is a good one, as she much prefers dealing one-on-one with people who are trying to improve the quality of life in San Diego rather than wasting her time with the myriad minor details that can consume policy matters. She enjoyed talking with the two men about their project for the same reason that she likes city government—it involved working with real people who have real problems. She must be doing something right because in 1996 she was reelected with 79 percent of the vote.

Part of the reason for her success is that she is very approachable. "People in the grocery store tell me stuff; people in the post office tell me stuff," she said. "I don't feel a loss of privacy 99 percent of the time. Once in a blue moon, someone will catch me off guard, and I won't feel like dealing with it. But I can count those incidences on one hand. I'm very much a people person. I'm always happy to talk with the next person."

This attitude explains why Kehoe is not considered a "movement" type. She seldom travels to Washington or Los Angeles to attend gay and lesbian events. Her philosophy—one shared by many lesbian and gay men who did not migrate to the meccas of New York, Los Angeles, Washington, DC, and San Francisco—is that equality cannot be legislated from above; rather, it is achieved by working closely with people from one's community.

Kehoe's style works well in San Diego. Andrew Collins, in his Fodor's *Gay Guide to the USA*, explains that even though San Diego is California's second largest city and has a sizable gay population, the presence of the military has a subduing influence. "The city's conservative demeanor mitigates the sort of flamboyant gay presence you often see in other large cities. The military has made San Diego very gay, but it's made San Diego gays and lesbians something far short of militant."[1]

*   *   *

Kehoe, who looks much younger than her forty-six years, has light brown hair that is slightly graying, and is a tall 5'10". Her arrival in San Diego in 1978 from her hometown of Troy, New York—"just like Greece but nothing like Greece," she laughed— was through a high school friend who was moving to San Diego from Phoenix. At the time Kehoe, who had married at twenty-two, realized she was not happy in her marriage. Having received her BA degree in English from the State University of New York at Albany and separated from her husband, she had nothing to keep her home. After helping her friend pack, the two drove to San Diego. "That was the first time I saw San Diego, and I loved it."

The change did her good. Although she considered herself a strong feminist, she had not yet realized she was a lesbian. Her first job in San Diego was working at the Women's Center, where a few lesbians were on staff. Gradually, she came out. "The women were really good to me and probably understood more about what was going on than I did. And I just went that way. I don't know how else to describe it. I never gave being a lesbian any thought when I was married. I attribute that to my Irish-Catholic upbringing. I was a deeply uninformed woman when it comes to sexual issues. Really, I was out to lunch."

Her job at the Women's Center led to editing the weekly gay paper with the not-so-subtle name of *The San Diego Gayzette*. It was her main introduction into the gay men's community. Where once she was unfamiliar with bathhouses and bars, she was now having discussions about how much pubic hair to show in the ads. "We aim to please" was her motto. It was a time when AIDS was beginning to take its toll, and gays and lesbians were demanding equal rights in California. A month after she became editor, Governor Deukmejian vetoed AB1, a bill that would have given gays and lesbians equal protection in housing and employment. So relatively new was she to politics that she admits not knowing many names of the area's state legislative delegation.

In 1984, Kehoe hired a new art director named Julie Warren. A year later, the two became lovers, eventually buying a home together. And despite Warren's initial warning that if Kehoe ever ran for office she would leave her, they are still together.

Next came Proposition 64, the 1986 California ballot initiative sponsored by Lyndon LaRouche, which called for people infected with AIDS to be quarantined. San Diego, like many areas in the state, wanted to conduct its own campaign away from the shadow of Los Angeles and San Francisco, which had historically dominated the political scene. The two cities still controlled most aspects of the statewide campaign, such as media and fund-raising. However, cities such as Sacramento, San Jose, Long Beach, Fresno, and San Diego all demanded that they run their own local campaigns. In retrospect, this served the gay community well because many people learned firsthand how to organize and run issue-based campaigns. Kehoe was such a person.

Although Kehoe loved editing *The Gayzette* because it broadened her worldview, the paper was losing money and would soon fold. A gay community leader asked her to recommend a person to run the "No on 64" campaign. She knew that if she did not take the job another person less qualified would be offered it. So she left the paper and coordinated the No on 64 campaign for the remaining two months.

The No on 64 campaign expanded Kehoe's horizons further by giving her a chance to work on an issue-based campaign as well as one that encompassed all of San Diego County. But working with the coordinators in Los Angeles was not easy. "I could barely get them to return my calls. They thought San Diego was the end of the line," Kehoe remembers. Working around the clock, she organized volunteers to get the message out about the dangers of Prop. 64. "We phoned thousands of people. It must have paid off because San Diego County rejected the measure at the same rate as San Francisco and Los Angeles. I think that's an indicator that we're not living in the Dark Ages down here."

In 1987, Neil Good, the first openly gay man to make a serious run for city council, asked her to be on his staff. This position presented her with new and valuable experience because she had never worked on a candidate campaign. In fact, in her own campaign six years later, she thought about his campaign every day when she was running, particularly about follow-through with precinct walking. The campaign also provided her with her first opportunity to visit city hall.

The campaign had undertones of gay-baiting. One of Good's opponents was always challenging him, saying all his money was gay money and that Good should release the names of his contributors. It seemed Good was always on the defensive, unable to turn the tables. He lost, coming in third in the primary. Eventually winning the race was Bob Filner, who later became the main supporter of the gay community's attempt to redraw city council districts that were favorable to gay candidates.

The next phase of Kehoe's career was two part-time jobs. One was with the Hillcrest Business Association, a neighborhood business group in the heart of San Diego's gay community. Although not a gay organization per se, its members were very sensitive to the gay community because so many of their customers were gay and lesbian. The second part-time job was as a volunteer coordinator with the AIDS Assistance Fund, a San Diego AIDS organization that provides services to people with AIDS and HIV.

The former director of the association, Joyce Beers, sat her down one day and advised her that working for the Business Association was more important to Kehoe's career than the AIDS Assistance Fund. "This blew me away," remembers Kehoe, "because it was the first time anyone ever talked to me like that. Joyce had run for city council years before, and I think she knew I needed to broaden my profile. Being the former executive director of the Hillcrest Business Association stood me in very good stead when I ran for council. Joyce did me a good turn." Kehoe left the AIDS Assistance Fund and devoted herself full-time to the Hillcrest Association. She worked there for two years before moving to her next job, which was inside city hall working for Councilman John Hartley.

After two and a half years with Hartley, she went to work for a local state assemblyman. A year later, she returned to City Hall as an employee in the city manager's office. It was while working there that a friend called and asked if she knew what Councilman Hartley was going to say at his press conference the next day. Kehoe had no idea what political announcement Hartley was about to make.

*　　*　　*

Before any gay community can elect an openly lesbian or gay man to high office, the groundwork must first be laid. Usually this occurs over many years as a result of dedicated individuals working behind the scenes. Sometimes their work bears no fruit; other times it pays off in the election of their candidate. In San Diego, the latter happened because of the efforts of a few far-sighted people who accomplished two things: winning district elections and drawing council boundaries that favored a gay candidate.

Prior to 1988, San Diego elected its eight council members under a system that was a hybrid between district and citywide elections. In the primary, candidates ran from specific districts. Then, the top two vote-getters ran in a citywide election in which all voters cast ballots. The consequence of such a system was that a minority candidate might win in the primary but lose in the general election, where more Anglo voters participate. The exception to this is the mayor, who runs citywide in both elections and who has one vote on the council.

Twice before, voters had rejected the idea of having the council members run by districts in both primary and general elections, but the third time was successful. San Diego's largest gay organization, the San Diego Democratic Club, was always a vocal supporter of district elections because it knew that without them if a candidate such as Neil Good had won in the primary, his chances of being elected citywide would be substantially lower. They feared that even if a gay candidate won his or her primary, ultimately it would be for naught. Many club members, including Doug Case, joined with other minority groups in the campaign to change the city charter.

The second and perhaps more significant event was the redrawing of council boundaries following the 1990 census. The San Diego City Council appointed an independent redistricting commission to draw new lines in response to a lawsuit brought by the Chicano Federation, which felt the current lines were in violation of the Voting Rights Act by depriving Latinos of representation.

Up until 1990, the gay community was split among three districts—District 2, District 3 (Hartley's seat), and District 8 (Filner's seat). Charles McKain, a lawyer, San Diego Democratic Club member, and San Diego native, understood that redistricting was a great opportunity to create a consolidated district where a qualified gay person could run and win. He looked at the zip codes and addresses of the club's 4,000 members to determine where to best draw the lines for a new District 3. Taking into consideration incumbent office holders and other minority communities when drawing all the other districts, McKain submitted his map. As it turned out, McKain's map became the alternative to the one that was drawn by the Chicano Federation, whose map was endorsed by the redistricting commission.

The coalitions that formed over the two maps demonstrate how vicious and bizarre politics can be when the stakes are high, as they were in this case. Republicans generally supported the Chicano Federation's map because they felt it created more districts with a Republican majority. The Log Cabin Club, San Diego's gay Republican group, also supported the map, believing—as did some other gays—that their community was better served when gay voters lived in multiple districts. That way, council members from those districts had to pay attention to their gay constituents, thus giving the gay community more clout. The San Diego Democratic Club could not have disagreed more, saying that "divide and conquer" meant being conquered. Thus, the Democratic Club found itself fighting alone, without a unified front or its natural allies from the minority community.

McKain and the San Diego Democratic Club had one thing that the other group did not have—five votes on the city council. That is the main reason why McKain was so undeterred by the criticism. At the time, the council was ruled by the so-called "Gang of Five"—three Democrats and two liberal-to-moderate Republicans. The leader of the group was Bob Filner. Filner knew that McKain's map was one that his majority of five could agree to, while at the same time not damaging Latino representation. When the issue came before the city council, Filner, at the last moment, presented his own map. His map heavily favored Democrats and environmentalists, but it replicated the lines of McKain's District 3. It was this map that was approved five to four.

The story does not end there. The Chicano Federation filed another lawsuit, saying the city acted improperly by voting on Filner's plan without proper notification. Meanwhile, one of the Democratic council members was recalled, replaced with a Republican. Also, new census data had become available. With the political landscape changed, an altogether new map was proposed. However, the lines for District 3 were not substantially altered. When the final map was approved, McKain's District 3 with its estimated 15 to 20 percent gay voters was left intact.

It was a hard battle for all those involved, and some scars still remain. McKain says that the two-year process taught him how hard-nosed and demanding politics can be. "Some people said that gays had more power than the Latino community," recalled McKain. "I don't believe we did."

Although McKain knew of Kehoe, he did not draw the lines specifically with her or any gay or lesbian candidate in mind. Nor were the lines drawn for a gay candidate's campaign to be waged in the 1993 election. It was assumed by everyone that Councilman

Hartley, who was elected in 1989, would run for reelection in 1993. The earliest the new boundaries would benefit a gay candidate was in 1996. Little did McKain or anyone else know that Hartley would suddenly announce at his press conference that he was not running for a second term. Thus the stage was set for Kehoe's run for city council.

*   *   *

There isn't much in Christine Kehoe's past to predict that her future would include holding public office. Although her parents were dyed-in-the-wool Democrats, they never attended political meetings. Her mother worked in the Albany State Capitol when the wheelchair ramps were built for Franklin Roosevelt. Her parents were FDR Democrats who believed in the labor movement, but they were never active in party politics. Nor was Kehoe ever involved in politics in high school or college.

Not that running for office hadn't crossed her mind as she became more involved in San Diego politics. In 1992 when she and her partner, Julie, were looking to buy a house, she instructed the realtor to show them houses only in District 3. Moreover, as she became more visible in the community, people said to her that they would volunteer if she ran for office. "There were just a lot of little things like that," said Kehoe. "Maybe I was preparing for it unconsciously."

When she heard that Hartley was not running for reelection, Kehoe knew she did not have much time to decide if she would run. Hartley's announcement came in February; the primary was in September. Foremost on her mind was her belief that it was now or never. "I felt I had enough experience at city hall to convince people that I could be organized and competent. Plus, I was still a fresh face. I examined my conscience. I talked with Julie. I felt very strongly that this was the time to do it. If I stepped aside now, I might not get the chance again."

One of Kehoe's council aides, Toni Atkins, said that, in retrospect, her boss couldn't have planned her ascent into politics better if she had tried. Kehoe had worked in the business community, in the gay and lesbian community, and in the political world as a legislative aide and campaign coordinator. She understood the issues, had a vision for the city, and was a quick study and a hard worker. In addition, San Diego, like all urban cities, had lost many prominent gay men to AIDS. Thus, of all the possible gay candidates, Kehoe had the best chance of winning. "Many gay men might have been in her position if it had not been for AIDS," said Atkins. "Circumstances just came together to make Chris the first elected gay official."

The first task was to raise enough money to establish Kehoe as a serious candidate and to scare off other opponents. She had the early support of several well-connected gay men who knew how important the election was for the community. "I remember a couple of the meetings at Don Belcher's house where these guys were," recounted Kehoe. "I know they were all thinking, 'Look at her hair!' They were so disappointed that I wasn't more glamorous. I didn't dress up enough for them. They knew me, maybe too well, from walking around Hillcrest in jeans and T-shirts on my days off. I don't think they thought I could make the transition to being a candidate." One person who was particularly helpful was San Diego businessman and longtime Kehoe supporter Dr. William Beck. "Bill just kept putting one foot in front of the other and got checks." At her first fund-raiser, Kehoe raised $32,000, almost a third of the $100,000 she collected in her primary. She recalled proudly, "The event blew everybody away." The Gay and Lesbian Victory Fund also raised money for her, collecting a total of $20,000 for the primary and general elections.

Like all gay candidates, Kehoe had to learn how to walk the tightrope of being gay without being marginalized as single-issue. In terms of telling voters she was a lesbian, Kehoe and her campaign staff felt the *San Diego Union Tribune* did a more than adequate job of making that information public. "Each candidate knows you're going to get about four column inches over the course of the whole campaign unless you set your hair on fire or jump off the Coronado Bridge," she explained in her usual light-hearted way. "This is because the paper has five local races to cover, plus all the others. In every single article that mentioned me, they included virtually every gay credit that I had, from editor of *The Gayzette*, to cochair of Lesbian/Gay Pride—there's a million of them—cochair of the Human Dignity Ordinance. They knew I had been active in the community for a long time. I tried to talk to them about including my business background, but they were like 'yeah, yeah, yeah.' So that message of my being gay was already out, and we didn't touch on that again."

Because of McKain's work, the district's demographics were receptive to a lesbian candidate. The population of District 3 was 142,000. It contains some of the oldest communities in San Diego, such as Balboa Park, Hillcrest, and North Park. Hillcrest is also the area where many gay bars and businesses are located. The ethnic makeup of the district is 56 percent white, 23 percent Hispanic, 11 percent African American, and 8 percent Asian/Pacific Islander. In addition to many gays and lesbians, there is a large senior population. Electorally, it is one of the few political districts in San Diego County where Democrats are a majority, even if barely: 50 percent Democrat, 35 percent Republican, and 15 percent Decline to State, Independent, and others. Although there is a wide variety of people with different income levels living in the district, overall it is fairly affluent.

The consulting firm of Evans/McDonough conducted a poll for Kehoe early in the campaign. It gave Kehoe and her consultants two important pieces of information. First, there was no leading candidate in the race. This meant that Evonne Schultz, the best known of all the candidates, was not a shoo-in. Although Schultz had the highest name identification—largely because she had run for council in another district three times and was currently an elected trustee on the community college board—her support was tenuous. Her support quickly eroded when respondents were told that she had only recently rented an apartment in the district and that she still owned a house in another district. Second, the poll found that a candidate who ran a competitive campaign and happened to be gay could be elected.

Evans/McDonough believed that a qualified gay candidate could win because about one-third of the respondents gave favorable answers to questions dealing with gay rights. For instance, 34 percent strongly supported domestic partner benefits; 30 percent strongly opposed the Boy Scouts because they discriminated against gays; and 39 percent were more likely to support a candidate because she is a lesbian.

That was the good news. As expected, some respondents felt the opposite. For instance, 31 percent opposed domestic partner benefits; 32 percent did not support full and equal civil rights for gays and lesbians; 34 percent were much more likely to support a candidate because they support the Boy Scouts; and 34 percent were less likely to support a candidate because she is a lesbian.

The balance of the respondents were indifferent, but they appeared to be willing to consider supporting a gay candidate. In several cases, gay issues won the support of a solid majority, even though the support was not strong. Thus, 54 percent supported domestic partner benefits; 68 percent supported full and equal civil rights for lesbians and gays; and 55 percent said the district was ready to elect a gay person to the city council.

Based on this information, Evans/McDonough concluded that one-third of the voters would likely support a lesbian candidate, one-third would not, and a third was indifferent. Because there were eleven candidates in the race, the even distribution made a gay candidate an almost sure bet to make the runoff. Also, they saw an opportunity to reach the one-third that was indifferent if there was the right connection between voter and candidate.

As is common in polling, respondents were read information about the candidates and then asked if they were more or less likely to support them based on that information. Respondents were most favorable to Kehoe promising to have open office hours, to making crime a priority, and to protecting and preserving the neighborhoods. This meant that in order for Kehoe to win, she would have to compliment her "liberal" positions on gay issues with a crime-fighting agenda and a message of openness and accessibility. And, in fact, this is what she did.

Not everyone in the gay community was happy about Kehoe's strategy to focus on nongay issues. As frequently happens, one of the gay papers was the loudest critic. Several gay reporters voiced their opinions at gay community forums that she was not running an "out enough" campaign. In addition, there were other people who wanted her to have a stronger gay profile or to run a more gay-centered campaign. But all in all, many of the activists bit their tongues and allowed her to put out the profile and message that she wanted. "They realized that the most successful way to run a campaign is to try to reach out to all San Diegans and to make everybody in the district understand that you know their issues," said Kehoe. "I don't think they all agreed, but in the end they were happy because we won. I think my campaign will be a good model for anyone who decides to run next. They might not choose to follow it, but I think they'll at least consider it."

Ruth Bernstein, Kehoe's campaign manager, remembers how hard it was to convince some supporters of the need to constantly stay "on message," which was that Chris Kehoe is an accessible candidate who knows the issues and who will be tough on crime. "It was so easy for people to get distracted by infighting or by the issue of the day. We just had to keep everybody focused."

This was particularly hard when, early in the campaign, Evonne Schultz sent out a brochure that was a comparison piece. As is typical in races where a gay or lesbian is running, one of the categories of comparison is "family." Schultz's family column showed two grown sons. Kehoe's family column was "0." The activists took off like a bullet, labeling Schultz's piece as gay-baiting and saying it discounted gay families. Some were ready to protest in front of Schultz's campaign office. Bernstein and Kehoe knew that if Kehoe countered with statements that her partner, Julie, and she were a "family," then the focus would be on her being gay. Kehoe thought it best not to draw more attention to the issue. She asked supporters not to protest, and they respected her wishes. Throughout, Kehoe resisted publicizing her own family. "We never mentioned Julie. She didn't want to be mentioned either. She's the last person to want a public life. So we ruled that out."

Although the hit piece had little effect on voters, it had a big effect on Kehoe's volunteer base. "It totally energized the campaign," said Bernstein. "It gave everyone a greater sense of purpose and helped our momentum. Straight families called us up wanting a lawn sign." This is not to imply that the campaign was ever sagging. People associated with the campaign still recall the large number of committed volunteers who dedicated themselves to getting Kehoe elected. Bernstein remembers that most of the early volunteers were men who did not know Kehoe well, but supported her because she was gay. "This slowly changed when people got to know her better, and then it became a Kehoe thing," Bernstein said. "I think her being a lesbian helped. It broadened her base to include many women. The district was walked twice, lawn signs were everywhere, and the campaign office was a constant flurry of activity." Thus, the Kehoe campaign became a gay crusade for the community.

Many of the elements needed for a winning campaign came together for Kehoe. Although Schultz was able to get most of the key endorsements, Kehoe was able to capture several that brought her the credibility she initially lacked. Councilman John Hartley supported her as did Councilman Ron Roberts, a moderate Republican. Because of their backing, Kehoe could not be considered just a "gay movement" candidate. Besides volunteers, she had the money to conduct a strong mail campaign. In total, she sent out five pieces of mail in the primary, as well as follow-up letters to each household that was walked. Several of the mail pieces were hit pieces on Schultz, focusing on trips she had taken as a college trustee and on the fact that she recently moved into the district.

"Chris was an amazing candidate," said Bernstein. "She wanted to run because she likes city government. She wanted to be an effective council member as much as she wanted to be the first gay person elected."

Out of the crowded field of eleven candidates, Kehoe came in first with 28 percent of the vote. Schultz came in second. In the November runoff, Kehoe beat Schultz 55 to 44 percent.

In 1996, Kehoe won reelection with 79 percent of the vote. This high percentage was achieved despite the finding in the 1993 Evans/McDonough poll that one-third of the voters said they would not vote for an openly gay or lesbian candidate. Kehoe is gratified by the progress. "Clearly we've moved some of these voters. Sometimes an older person will say, 'I didn't support you the first time, but you've done a really good job,' or 'You've made a difference.'" Thus, in politics as in life, people's attitudes toward gays and lesbians often change once they get to know a gay person and can see beyond the stereotypes.

* * *

When Kehoe was sworn into office, the San Diego City Council had already passed several pieces of important progay legislation. First was the Human Dignity Ordinance, which made discrimination based on sexual orientation illegal in housing and employment. Second, there was an AIDS/HIV antidiscrimination ordinance. Third, city employees were allowed to pay extra to have their partners included in the city's health plan. This was all done despite San Diego's overall reputation for being a conservative Republican town. With this, Kehoe was spared from fighting any large, potentially controversial battles on gay/lesbian/bisexual rights. Instead she has been able to focus her attention on more unglamorous, day-to-day activities that build a better city.

For instance, the federal government has an urban aid program called Community Development Block Grants, or CDBG. These funds are used by cities to provide programs and services. Each year, San Diego has approximately $18 million to allocate. This is divided among the city's eight council districts. With her portion of the funds, Kehoe has been able to support a variety of programs, some of which are aimed at the gay community. Never has the city council questioned or opposed Kehoe's recommendations. In addition, she is proud that the city has built a police substation, formed a redevelopment agency, and invested millions of dollars in economic revitalization in her district.

As with any elected official's office, a large part of Kehoe's staff duties revolve around constituent services. And while many elected officials dislike dealing with constituent problems, Kehoe does not. According to staff member Jeffrey Tom, many of the calls and letters deal with such issues as barking dogs, traffic, potholes, deteriorating sidewalks, and crime. "Part of what I love about the city council," Kehoe said, "is talking about safety, streets, and housing. If people don't feel safe in their homes, then it's my problem. I absolutely believe that. We bring the police officers out there, we tell people what phone numbers to call. We do the Neighborhood Watch—whatever it takes. I love that stuff. And people go, 'Oh my god, the minutiae. Potholes!' Well, potholes are interesting if you look at it the right way."

There are other issues that staff must contend with because of Kehoe being a representative of the gay community. As is customary in political offices, whenever anyone calls, staff first learns if the person is a district resident. If not, they are politely referred to the right office. Not so if the person is gay or lesbian because often they have issues they only feel comfortable about discussing with Kehoe's office.

The number of hate crimes were increasing in her district, so after her first election, Kehoe held a town hall meeting where people gathered to talk about what could be done. Prior to the meeting, the police chief marched with Kehoe and others from the substation to the center of the gay business area. As a result, a police storefront was leased in the Hillcrest business district. Better statistics on hate crimes are being kept, and business owners and residents are informed on how to minimize risk and increase safety.

Kehoe knows that just as there are tangible benefits of having a lesbian council member, there are intangibles as well. Having one of their own in office makes lesbians and gay men feel they have more clout. Plus, people from the community are appointed to boards and commissions. Volunteers gain campaign experience. Gay and lesbian staff members are hired. There is a sense of political empowerment, of pride. As Kehoe said, "It's synergy; it sort of snowballs. The election of a gay person raises the level of expectations and the level of access."

As far as the future is concerned, Kehoe is unsure what the year 2000 will bring when she is term-limited out of office. At the moment, she is contemplating a run for Congress against an incumbent Republican. But whatever happens, she wants to continue to work with people because that is where she receives the greatest satisfaction and feels most adept. It is where she can help residents such as the two engineers who are trying to make their dream of refurbishing a movie house come true. Moreover, there is work to be done on AIDS education and on overcoming sexism, racism, and homophobia. There are complaints to hear, solutions to be proposed.

"I feel fulfilled professionally in a way I never have before," concluded Kehoe. "This is very much the right spot for me. The constituents I represent are people that I believe in. And I love the challenges of my district. They're right there in front of my door. There's never a dull moment, which I really like. And as to the quality of life for me and for my partner, when you're happy, your relationship is usually happy," she added, smiling.

Chapter 6

Living, Fighting, and Governing with HIV: New York City Councilman Tom Duane

"In one sense, it's nobody's business that I've tested positive for the presence of HIV in my blood," read the August 1991 letter that New York City Council candidate Tom Duane mailed to 40,000 voters. "But I am a candidate for public office, and I believe in being candid. I've never denied who I am—or what I believe—and I can't imagine starting now."

Duane, who had been involved in New York politics for fourteen years, knew he was breaking political ground with his announcement. In a city where gays and lesbians are always on the cutting edge, Duane had done what only a handful of political leaders in the country have done: he disclosed his HIV status.

In the letter's next paragraph, Duane preemptively answered a question he assumed would be asked by readers: How was his health? "You should know that I'm not sick. I likely will be some day, but nearly everybody can say that. And I've undertaken a difficult task: To run for the City Council and to try to make a contribution if elected. You simply can't attempt such a task without a lot of stamina, and in that I'm lucky."

Duane personalized the issue when he addressed the need for the city to play a greater role in health care and education. "That's what I believe and have for a long time. Maybe I believe it a little more strongly because of my own circumstances. Because I know that no matter now healthy I am now, some day I'll need help too, the help that together we can bring to all New Yorkers." Duane ended the letter dramatically by saying, "I'll fight for human needs, including health care, on the city council. Like so many people in New York City, my life depends on it."

At the time of his announcement, the fear over AIDS transmission was much higher than today. Many people still believed that AIDS was easily transmitted by casual contact—a sneeze, a handshake, unsanitized utensils. Anyone working with the public—doctors, teachers, food workers—could lose their jobs if it became known they were HIV positive. Although the hysteria from Lyndon LaRouche's attempt to pass an AIDS quarantine initiative in California was beginning to subside, much ignorance remained. In 1991, Magic Johnson had to quit basketball after he announced his infection. That same year, several patients of a Florida dentist who died from AIDS were found to be HIV positive, reviving unsubstantiated transmission theories. Duane understood that the political fallout from his disclosure could be substantial. As John Magisano, president of the New York Gay and Lesbian Independent Democrats, observed at the time, "I don't know how it will play out with the voters. It's hard to say. This has never happened before."

The idea for the letter came from veteran Minneapolis City Councilman Brian Coyle. Coyle, who had AIDS at the time, wrote a letter to friends saying that he was HIV positive. He acknowledged that he was "taking a risk that people will write me off politically or actually fear working beside me. But being honest now is as important to me as being effective, which I have been during all these years of secretly living with the virus." Coyle never had the chance to see how voters would respond to his disclosure. He died in August 1991 of complication from AIDS several months after the letter was written.

Duane knew Coyle from meetings of the International Network of Gay and Lesbian Officials (INGLO), an organization formed to allow gay officeholders to meet annually and share experiences. When Duane decided to make his announcement, he called Coyle. "I asked him how he did it because I heard he did it in a powerful and empowering way. He told me the different things he did. He worked with a print journalist and a television reporter so he could have some control over the story. Shortly before the announcement, he decided he wanted to reach out to people in his district in a more personal way, so he sat down and wrote a letter. I thought that was great. If I was going to disclose my status, I wanted to do it in a way where the people who were going to decide if they would vote for me would get a letter from me explaining my decision to disclose my HIV status."

Of concern to Duane was the effect the announcement would have on people with AIDS or with HIV. "I wanted people to know that they could have HIV and still lead a full, active, stressful, busy life. I wanted people to know that HIV-positive people are their next-door neighbor, the person on their block." Because of the letter, people came up to him throughout the campaign and confided that they were HIV positive. "Other people," Duane stated, "wished me well in a nice, supportive way." A *Village Voice* article thought the disclosure might provide Duane some political capital. "Being openly HIV-positive could even help Duane in District 3, lending him an aura of courage and integrity. It might be harder to find babies to kiss on the campaign trail, but voters—at least in the Village—could be attracted to a candidate who would bring such a sense of urgency to the job."[1]

Duane was not in the race simply to educate New Yorkers about HIV disease, however. He was in the race to win. In order to learn as much as he could about people's reactions to his announcement in advance, Duane commissioned a poll. He was heartened by the results. Most respondents said a candidate's HIV status would not make a difference in how they would vote. Whether people would react differently once inside the voting booth was something that Duane could not know until election day.

Oddly enough, straight voters were more supportive than gay voters about Duane announcing his HIV status. "Gay men felt I shouldn't tell because of the discrimination I would face," he explained. Duane's mother had a similar response. "My parents are practicing Roman Catholics, and they were great, although my mother's first reaction when I told her I was HIV positive was that I shouldn't tell anyone. I had to tell her I was going to tell *everyone*," said Duane.

Unlike what might occur even today in cities where ignorance about AIDS is high, the announcement did not end Duane's political career or lead to calls for withdrawal. This is in no small part due to the fact that approximately 25 percent of District 3's voters are gay. However, this is not to say he wasn't criticized. He was, and severely: he was faulted for not disclosing his HIV status sooner.

Duane had been involved in New York gay politics and tenant rights issues most of his adult life. As a member of ACT UP, he participated in its HIV-positive caucus. This is how some members of the gay community knew of his HIV status. When asked by critics why he had not disclosed it during his previous campaigns for office, Duane said that he was not emotionally ready at the time. "I found out I was HIV positive in 1988, but I internalized it," he explained. "I didn't tell my family, and I didn't tell most people. It was only later that I got comfortable with the knowledge that I was infected."

In New York politics where concern over political repercussions has never stopped people from saying exactly what was on their minds, ACT UP founder and playwright Larry Kramer wrote in a letter that he was "disgusted" by Duane's dishonesty in keeping his secret for so long. AIDS activist Roger McFarlane was quoted in the *New York Post* as comparing Duane to Jews who kept silent during the Holocaust. To the accusation that he was being politically opportunistic, Duane responded, "It's an opportunity I'd rather not have."

Duane's main opponent, Liz Abzug, Bella Abzug's daughter, was also criticized by gay activists for not announcing she was a lesbian until her campaign kickoff. "It's a very bizarre campaign," a campaign consultant was quoted as saying. "She tells the world that she's a lesbian. Then he ups the bet by saying he's HIV positive. It's a game of 'Can you top this?'—the kind of thing that could only happen in New York."

Ultimately, it wasn't much of a contest. The main issues for voters were housing and health care, two areas in which Duane had a much longer history of involvement than newcomer Abzug or a second opponent in the race. Duane easily won the Democratic primary with 60 percent of the vote. He went on to win the general election with 75 percent of the vote, becoming the first openly gay, openly HIV-positive candidate elected to office in the United States. Also winning a council seat in the East Village was Antonio Pagan, another openly gay candidate. The two share joint honors of being the first openly gay people elected to the New York City Council.

Concerning his health, Duane said, "I don't have to be on any treatment because my health is stable. I haven't had any AIDS-related anything." Having made that statement, he quickly added, "I want to be as clear about this as I can. It would be fine if I were on a treatment. I feel I'm very lucky because my blood levels have held up, so I haven't had to make the difficult decisions about what kind of treatments to follow. A part of me wants to hold off until the next generation of drug therapies comes along, which will probably be better than the last one."

Duane remembers the earlier days of the AIDS crisis when every case of the flu or every fever was a cause for alarm. "I'd think, this is it, I'm going to die. Or if I got a twenty-four-hour virus, I thought, I'm dying. Part of this is because, in the 1980s, so many people would get sick and be dead in a few days. So when you got the flu, it was a nightmare. It was really a scary time. I'm glad that period is over, even though I remember it really well."

Medical advances have given Duane a different set of issues to worry about. "Now I have to start thinking about putting money into a retirement account and IRA accounts. It used to seem ridiculous, but now it doesn't seem ridiculous at all. I'm still very clear that my blood levels could drop precipitously tomorrow. You never know. And there's still no cure. I know I have at least a few years, so I don't think I have to pick out my retirement community yet," he said with a smile.

*　　*　　*

Tom Duane's experience with his New York City council district began forty-two years ago when he was born at the old French

Hospital on Thirtieth Street in Chelsea, which is within his district's boundaries. He was raised in Flushing, Queens, where he attended St. Andrew Grammar School and Holy Cross High School. He was the third in a family of four boys.

Because he lived in New York, Duane has been aware of gay culture since he was a teenager. This explains, in part, why he was comfortable in coming out at the age of seventeen. "I was lucky that I was raised in New York because somewhere in the back of my mind I knew that the Stonewall Rebellion took place. I was in ninth grade at the time and must have heard about it on the news," Duane said. "So early on I knew there were other people who were like what I thought I might be. And I knew how to make my way to the Village on the subway. I knew there were homosexuals, and I would go out to find them." Duane, who stands at 6′3″, and has wavy, light brown hair, would have been impossible to miss.

In the early 1970s, he attended his father's alma mater, Lehigh University, in Bethlehem, Pennsylvania. "The college is famous for engineering and wrestling, neither of which I participated in," Duane said with a grin on his still-boyish face. Duane remembers Lehigh being a conservative campus, with most students supporting Nixon's 1972 reelection. Not surprisingly, there were only a handful of out, gay students. Undaunted, he proceeded to start the school's first gay organization. Though there was little encouragement for his activities, he was fortunate that he could return to New York to attend Gay Activist Alliance meetings. Said Duane, "At these meetings, I would get pumped up to again try to generate some gay activism at Lehigh." He graduated with a double major in Urban Studies and American Studies.

Duane's Irish Catholic parents didn't take the news well when he told them that he was gay. "It was pretty traumatic for them," Duane said. Over time, they became more comfortable with this aspect of their son. His father, who was a stockbroker, died several years ago. His younger brother, who also happened to be gay, died of complications from a brain tumor that developed when he was a teenager. Duane's mother, whom he visits regularly, still lives in Queens.

After college, Duane moved back to New York to live in Chelsea. In 1977, he saw a flyer calling for gays and lesbians to meet their neighbors. This was the beginning of the Chelsea Gay Association, the first gay neighborhood organization in New York and, to Duane's knowledge, the country. Here he began his involvement in tenant matters, which, Duane stressed, "are big issues in New York."

Duane held numerous jobs during this time. He worked as an ESL teacher, and was employed by a public relations firm, city government, and the gay press. From 1982 to 1988, he worked with his father as a stockbroker, an experience that allowed him to get to know his father better. After leaving that job, he became a staff member for New York City Comptroller Elizabeth Holtzman.

In 1982, Democratic neighborhood activists asked Duane to run for Democratic District Leader against an incumbent they thought had grown too conservative. The position was a party post that only registered Democrats could vote for. Asked why he was approached by party activists, Duane explained matter-of-factly, "I had been involved in the neighborhood, was energetic, and willing to do the work." Duane campaigned hard for the office, handing out literature on the street and sending out several mailings. He beat the incumbent by a two-to-one margin. With his victory, he became the second openly gay Democratic District Leader in New York. The first was Ken Sherrill, who represented the Upper West Side.

Over the past ten years, several gay activists have tried to win election to the city council, none with success. In 1977, Jim Owles tried. David Rothenberg tried in 1985. In 1989, Rothenberg chose not to try again, providing Duane the opportunity to take a shot against a twenty-year incumbent. Duane proved to be a tough challenger, raising $175,000 and receiving the endorsement of *The New York Times*. But it was not enough. He fell short in the Democratic primary, winning only 46 percent of the vote.

Part of the reason why gay candidates had a difficult time winning was that the council districts were too large to allow for minority representation. In 1991, however, New York City voters approved a new charter that created fifty-one smaller council districts intended to be more representative of the city's population. Though no gay person served on the fifteen-member Districting Commission, the gay community worked with other groups to ensure that the large concentration of gay and lesbian voters in Chelsea and the West Village was not divided among several districts. The new district was considered a viable one for a gay or lesbian candidate to win. "Even though the district was not majority gay," said Duane, "the belief was that voters who were accustomed to taking out their garbage with gay people and going to tenant meetings with gay people would vote for a gay person." With the lines redrawn, the gay press speculated that the incumbent would have a difficult time defeating a gay candidate. As it turned out, the incumbent decided not to run, leaving the seat open for Duane.

And what a council district it is. It includes the West Village, Chelsea, Clinton/Hell's Kitchen, and parts of Soho and Murray Hill. It incorporates all of Midtown, the theater district, the garment district, the flower district, the printing district, Rockefeller Center, Radio City, Madison Square Garden, Times Square, and the Empire State Building. "In short," said Duane proudly, "all the places that people want to visit when they come to New York."

As a way to stagger the terms of the new council, half of the fifty-one members were up for reelection in 1993, including Duane. He had no Democratic opponent in the primary, and won the general election with 75 percent of the vote.

A year later, in 1994, Duane ran for Congress. His opponent was Jerry Nadler, a politician whom Democratic Party leaders had chosen in 1992 to replace Congressman Ted Weiss, who died during the congressional campaign. Nadler, who easily won the general election, was up for reelection to Congress in 1994. Some Democratic Party activists asked Duane to run, saying that rank-and-file Democrats did not have a voice in their party's candidate in 1992. The congressional district covered all of Manhattan and the South Brooklyn communities of Brighton Beach, Coney Island, Borough Park, and Bensonhurst.

Duane lost, obtaining 30 percent of the vote, but he found the campaign challenging and exciting. "It was worth it to go to neighborhoods where an openly gay person running for office was an unlikely situation," stated Duane. "I really liked that part of it. In retrospect, I should have learned from my 1989 council race that it's almost impossible to beat an incumbent. The higher the level of office, the more difficult it is. It's really hard to beat an incumbent member of Congress, given that districts are 575,000 people. How do you meet them all?" he asked rhetorically.

In 1997, Duane was up for reelection to city council. He was unopposed in the primary and won the general election with a whopping 94 percent of the vote, with his Independent opponent receiving 6 percent.

Duane will be term-limited out of office in 2001. As new medical breakthroughs occur, his attitude about term limits has changed. "When the whole issue came up, I wasn't very compelled by it. It seemed so far into the future. I wasn't sure I'd be kicking around to have to start worrying about what my next career will be. But believe me, these kinds of problems are a luxury to have."

*   *   *

Duane acknowledged that trying to describe how AIDS has affected New York isn't easy. "It's been devastating," Duane finally said. "The health care costs and the emotional toll have been huge. In addition to having incredibly high rates of HIV infection in my district, I have the theater district and the garment center, and these industries have been enormously impacted by the AIDS crisis as well."

Statistics back up Duane's analysis of the catastrophic impact of AIDS on metropolitan New York. As of June 1997, the Centers for Disease Control reported 95,275 adult AIDS cases and 1,828 cases in children under thirteen, for a total of 97,103 cases. This is almost one-sixth of all reported cases in the United States. No other city comes close to these staggering numbers. Los Angeles is second with 36,000 cases; San Francisco is third with 24,800.

Duane's personal life has been devastated, too. "I'd say that 75 percent of my friends have died of AIDS. Last fall, one of the people I loved most in the world died. He was thirty-two and had known he had AIDS since he was twenty-five, so he spent most of his adult life living with AIDS. Just recently, a good friend committed suicide because the quality of his life was deteriorating. And these are just the recent deaths."

AIDS has consumed much of Duane's political life. One of the first AIDS issues in which he was involved in the 1980s was related to his activism in tenant matters. "When people started dying, their life partners started getting evicted from apartments because their names weren't on the lease," explained Duane. "We had cases where someone would die of AIDS and the next day the landlord would be there nailing the eviction notice on the door. So a group of us fought for succession rights of nontraditional family members. We put together a broad coalition of people and had several street rallies. This led to the Braschi decision, which was the State Supreme Court's decision that nontraditional family members and lesbian and gay life partners were entitled to rent-regulated apartments in New York City. This was incredibly significant because it was the first time that gay life partners were recognized by state law. It led to a circuit court judge approving same-gender, nonbiological parent adoptions based on Braschi, even though New York State still doesn't have a nondiscrimination law protecting gay people."

An important accomplishment that Duane has made since serving on the council is saving the Division of AIDS Services. When he was first elected, the city was allocating more money for services for AIDS patients, but when Mayor Guiliani was elected in 1993, he tried to cut the budget and made threats to eliminate the Division. Duane was successful in 1997 in passing a bill that permanently established the Division of AIDS Services, making it impossible for any mayor to abolish it.

Just as Duane has worked hard to fund housing and social service programs for AIDS patients, he has spent time preventing bad policy from being enacted. "You think you get elected to change the world and make it a better place and to move things forward," Duane said, reflecting on the nature of politics. "But what happens is you also spend a lot of your time stopping terrible things from happening." Duane recalled the battles he fought over proposed cuts in services, maintaining confidentiality of HIV testing, and preventing contact tracing. "All in all, I have spent enormous amounts of energy on AIDS-related issues," he said.

Another issue that Duane fought for was domestic partner benefits for city employees. According to Duane, when David Dinkins was running for mayor in 1989, he promised the gay community that he would provide the benefits. Because of the New York City mayor's enormous powers, he could do this without legislation passed by the council. However, after his election, Dinkins was only willing to establish a registry for gay and lesbian couples. This was unacceptable to Duane and other gay leaders. "We were relent-less," remembers Duane. "People constantly followed him around with signs that read, 'David Dinkins. Keep your promise. Full bene-fits.' Right before the 1993 mayoral election, he finally granted us domestic partner benefits." Whenever he can, Duane tries to get private companies and public agencies like the Metropolitan Trans-portation Authority to offer domestic partner benefits. More often than not he is successful. He is also thinking of introducing a bill similar to San Francisco's in which all companies doing business with New York City must provide domestic partner benefits to their employees.

Constituent calls to his office run the gamut, from complaints about barking dogs, loud neighbors, and fumes from dry cleaners to people receiving secret messages from fillings in their teeth. Be-cause housing is a major issue in New York, Duane's staff spends a great deal of time on housing and tenant issues. Staff member George Pender explained that many tenants in rent-controlled apart-ments are afraid of taking their landlords to court for fear of evic-tion. This is when Duane's office advocates on their behalf. Other housing issues deal with illegal evictions, discrimination, and envi-ronmental health concerns, such as asbestos in the building.

Crime is an issue in the district, especially assaults against gays and lesbians in Chelsea. Said staff member Andrew Beman, "There has been a great deal in the press about how Chelsea is the new gay mecca. When gay bashers hear that an area is a prominent gay location, that's where they go."

Duane himself has been the victim of gay bashing three times. The first was on Long Island in 1983. He was in the parking lot of a gay bar when two guys "just started pummeling me. They knocked me down and started kicking me," Duane recounted. "I started screaming, but the thing that saved me was when I finally started yelling 'help' and people from the bar came out and scared them off." The two assailants were apprehended and later pleaded guilty to misdemeanor charges. "I was furious," stated Duane, "because prosecutors never asked me what I thought the charge should be." The second assault occurred on Seventh Avenue in 1991 when he received a punch in the face that broke his glasses. Later that year, someone threw a beer bottle at him. "Violence toward gays is still a big problem," he commented. "Many of these crimes continue to go unreported and unprosecuted."

An issue that receives big coverage every year is the exclusion of the Irish Lesbian and Gay Organization (ILGO) from marching in the St. Patrick's Day Parade. The courts have ruled that the Ancient Order of Hibernians, which holds the permit, can exclude ILGO, declaring it a free-speech issue. This results in ILGO requesting a permit for their own parade to begin several hours before the official parade. "We're always denied it," said Duane, "but we try to march anyway." This means that every March 17 or thereabouts, Duane and other activists are arrested. "It is totally wrong that we are excluded. There are Irish-American lesbians and gay people, and they should be allowed to march under their own banner in the parade."

Duane is always getting himself arrested. In addition to the illegal marches of ILGO, he has been arrested supporting a wide variety of issues: abortion rights, disabled rights, human rights, and gay and lesbian civil rights. He often participates in ACT UP demonstrations as he did recently on Wall Street to protest price gouging by drug companies. He feels that his involvement in the protests lends extra support to the issues. He also believes that there is a smaller chance of a dangerous situation occurring when he is part of the group being arrested.

One reason why Duane becomes involved in street protests is because he is—in his own words—"willing to go to the mat" on issues he believes in. "A lot of the time I see elected officials who'll say that they're either for something or against something, but I want to actually make something happen or stop something from happening, as opposed to just being on the record. If that means getting arrested while exercising my First Amendment rights, then I'll do that. I'll fight until I can accomplish as much of my goal as possible." It is this attitude that led one of Duane's staff members to describe him as "a ball-busting activist type, yet someone who is still a big kid with a heart and good sense of humor."

*   *   *

For the thirty-nine fifth graders assembled at the back of the auditorium of Midtown West School on Forty-eighth Street, it was their big day. Their hair was combed, their shoes polished, their clothes crisp. They were of all races and nationalities, reflecting the beautiful diversity that is New York.

Duane was there to give the commencement speech at the school's "completion" ceremony. Later that day when Duane told people that he had given a speech at a completion ceremony, he took great delight in adding, "They don't have graduations in my district. They have completions."

When the students finished their processional and were seated in their chairs on stage, the program began. The speaker who introduced Duane commended him for his commitment to public education and his support of the school. She mentioned that Duane had been at the school earlier in the year to participate in the principal-for-a-day program.

Perhaps because Duane is still "a big kid with a heart and good sense of humor," Duane was in his element around the children. In his typical deadpan manner, he began by asking them, "Do you remember me? I was the nice principal. Is the mean principal here today? He's not? Then we're all safe." After a slight pause, he continued, "I'm kidding, of course. He was nice, too."

Like a smart politician, Duane came bearing gifts. "I do have good news to report. In this year's city budget, I was able to secure enough money to establish a computer lab at the school." This received thunderous applause. He then turned to the fifth graders on stage and added, "Of course, this doesn't help you out too much. But I know some of you have younger brothers or sisters, and if you're really, really nice to them, I bet they'll let you use the computers." Looking at the kids in the front section of the auditorium, he asked, "Am I right?" A few heads nodded.

Then he turned his attention to the parents. "Because of your commitment to public education, you really are what makes this city great. Public education is one of the finest things we have. Small miracles happen every day in our schools, and because you've decided to share your children with us, you're part of that miracle, too. So thank you for that." This received a big applause.

Next, Duane looked directly at the children and said, "We are very, very proud of all of you today. You are the future of New York City. We are very nervous about the world that you are going into," he admitted. "We know that you are not nervous, that you can take care of yourselves, and that you think the world is there with open arms to welcome you. But we are nervous for you. When we show that concern, try to be patient and tolerant of us. Just a little bit."

In his good-natured style, he warned them that "as the speaker, it is part of my job to give you advice, and I know you're thrilled about that. My first piece of advice is: Read, read, and read some more." This got much applause from parents and teachers. "I'm not saying you can't watch TV, but the most important thing is to keep reading. Read everything in sight. It's the one thing that will change your life the most.

"Second piece of advice: Be kind to others. When you have a chance, reach out your hand to someone who is having a little harder time than you are having. If you're going to err on the side of something, err on the side of being just a little bit kinder.

"Third piece of advice: Pursue your dreams. Think about things you would like to see in the future and go for it. But let me assure you. Joy is not in achieving the dream; the joy is in striving to achieve that dream. Along that trip, I guarantee you that a lot of wonderful things will happen."

Duane ended his talk by concluding, "That's really all I have to say. Read, be kind, pursue your dreams. I know your future will be wonderful."

After the applause died down, music selections followed. One of the songs, "If I Could Fly," from the movie *Space Jam,* recorded in a gospel style by Art Kelly, was quite inspirational. Three children stood in front of microphones on stage and took turns singing the verses, while the rest of children sang the chorus.

> I believe I can fly, I believe I can fly
> If I just spread my wings, I can fly.

When the song ended, the councilman slipped out the back door and onto the streets of New York, then walked to the corner of Forty-second Street and Broadway to catch the subway for city hall. Because he had stayed to listen to the children sing, he was now very late for his next meeting. But he didn't seem to care. It had been a great New York morning.

Chapter 7

Politics in a War Zone:
Dallas School Trustee José Plata

With 155,000 students, the Dallas Independent School District (DISD) is the tenth largest in the nation. The school population would be much larger if most of Dallas's white residents did not send their children to private and parochial schools. That is why the DISD student population does not match the demographics of Dallas. Whereas the overall population is 44 percent white, 31 percent black, 24 percent Hispanic, and 1 percent Asian, DISD students are 47 percent Hispanic, 41 percent African American, 10 percent white, and 2 percent Asian.

Racial issues consume Dallas school politics. In 1972 when the federal government began overseeing the district's desegregation efforts, the largest minority was African American. Today, racial problems still exist, but they are different. Now, Hispanics are the largest minority, with the gap steadily growing. By the next decade, it is estimated that Hispanics will outnumber black students two to one. The shift is tearing the district apart. Hispanics feel they have not received their share of the education dollars, and the African Americans are concerned that their hard-earned victories are in jeopardy.

What follows is a sampling of what has occurred over the past several years. Most of these incidents received extensive press coverage:

- The local president of the NAACP, Lee Alcorn, stated at a school board meeting, "I don't give a damn about Hispanic children. At some point you have to be selfish about those things that are of interest to us. I never hear Hispanics talking about African-American concerns. They are not going to take care of us. I see them as vultures. We go out and make a kill and then here come the Hispanics and feast on the results of our efforts. I'm sick of that."[1]

- Countered an Hispanic activist, "African Americans have only one agenda and one color, and that's black. If they were people of good faith, they would readily admit to the inequities of Hispanics in the DISD. But nobody wants to hear the concerns of the Hispanics, least of all the blacks."[2]

- A former teacher sued the district because students at several predominantly Hispanic secondary schools were not being issued textbooks. The teacher also reported numerous other problems, including widespread use of a bogus class that gave students credit for a course that did not exist. School officials replied that some teachers are reluctant to issue books to Hispanic students because many families move and instructors fear the books will be lost.

- For several weeks, African Americans shut down or disrupted school board meetings, calling for more black representation in decision-making roles. At one particularly contentious meeting, the school board president called in the police. Several members of the New Black Panther Party, a small but vocal black organization, were arrested.

- An NAACP officer asked school officials to provide a count of Hispanic children who were not legal residents or American citizens. "That's attacking the children," said the president of the League of United Latin American Citizens. "That's hitting below the belt. We're tired of the racial bashing, and we can only take it for so long."[3]

- In a controversial move, the school board hired a Latina, Yvonne Gonzalez, as superintendent. The vote was strictly down racial lines. After a month on the job, she was quoted as saying, "There was a concerted effort to humiliate me. Blacks started identifying me as a 'white Hispanic.' I couldn't go a single meeting without being heckled and taunted. They surrounded my car. They screamed in my face. They told me to go back to Mexico."[4]
- A white school board member, Dan Peavy, had his cell phone conversations recorded by a neighbor. On the tapes, which the neighbor made public, were racial slurs and antigay remarks made by Peavy. Peavy resigned from the board soon thereafter.

Such is the environment in which trustees must govern. While no one ever said that being a public official was easy, there should be limits on how horrendous it is, especially when Texas law prohibits the payment of any stipend. The situation is particularly stressful for José Plata, a forty-two-year-old openly gay trustee. Not only is he the first gay trustee on the nine-member board; he's the only Hispanic. This creates pressures on him from both communities to be a spokesperson for their issues. Plata tries to remain above the fray in order to advocate for the group most often forgotten in the bickering: the students.

* * *

Plata, who is 5'10" with brown eyes and graying black hair and beard, is the tenth of eleven children. His parents, who came to the United States as teenagers to escape political turmoil in Mexico, met in northeast Texas while working in the fields. They settled in nearby Lamar County where they became tenant farmers and ranchers. Plata's parents, who are both deceased, always stressed the importance of education, even though they had only the equivalent of a sixth-grade education. "The language we spoke at home was Spanish. We all succeeded despite it," he said with sarcasm, referring to the misconception that Spanish-speaking children cannot achieve in school. Five of his brothers and sisters have earned higher education degrees.

It wasn't until he was a teenager that Plata began to attend the local Catholic church. The priests were good role models for him, and several suggested he think of choosing the priesthood. This became a more serious option when he enrolled in the University of Dallas, a Catholic-run institution. "I eventually decided it was something I would not be happy with," he said. "Looking back, it was the right decision. I knew I would always be in service to mankind, just not as a priest. I've always been a civic-minded individual."

After completing high school, Plata attended Paris Junior College in Lamar County, graduating with an Associate of Arts degree in Liberal Arts. He received an academic scholarship from the College Entrance Examination Board, the organization that conducts the Scholastic Aptitude Test (SAT). This allowed him to attend the college or university of his choice. He chose the University of Dallas in Irving, Texas, and graduated in 1978 with a BA from Constantin College of Liberal Arts. His concentration was in elementary education, Spanish, and theater arts. While there, he was active in the Student National Education Association (SNEA), an offshoot of the National Education Association, the country's largest teachers' union.

Before he began teaching, Plata returned to Paris, Texas, to work for the Retired Senior Volunteer Program of Red River Valley and took additional classes at Paris Junior College. His enrollment allowed him to continue his participation in the SNEA. He was elected national vice president of the organization and moved to Washington, DC, to perform his duties. After his term expired, he returned to Dallas and began teaching at Rosemont Elementary School.

Plata may well have remained a teacher had it not been for Ross Perot and the Texas legislature. In 1984, Perot pushed through the state house a controversial proficiency exam for teachers. All teachers had to take and pass it if they wanted to continue being employed. Many resented being forced to take the test, believing that it was demeaning and insulting. Plata was one such teacher. "I earned my degree," he said, making reference to the University of Dallas and its reputation for high academic standards. "It was scary to me that more teachers didn't protest, but I would not sacrifice my personal integrity for expediency." Rather than take the test, Plata, who had taught for six years, quit. He was quickly hired by the

Baldwin Family Music Center to do the firm's administrative work. He got the job because he had taught the owners' children and had become friends with the family. He continues to work there.

Plata no longer attends a Catholic church, although he considers himself a Catholic. He has problems with religious dogma and the church's view of homosexuality. "I resented their denouncement of gays in the Vatican Letter," he said. "Everything the church says about gay people is a lie. This Pope has done more than his share of injustice in this world." Plata now attends the Dallas Cathedral of Hope, a Christian ministry that primarily serves the gay community and is associated with the Metropolitan Community Church. "It's a great congregation," he said. "I'm still very much a Christian; religion is something that has meaning in my life."

Prior to his coming out, Plata had been in love with two women. "The first one turned out to be a nun. Is that a sign or what?" he chuckled. It was while attending the University of Dallas that he became attracted to a man with whom he had an affair. "I'll never forget it," he laughed. "I went through the whole process of learning who I was at twenty-three. The relationship was working, and it was freaking me out." Gradually, Plata became comfortable with his sexual orientation, but, as with many gay people, it took him longer to be totally out in his public and political life. His campaign for school board accelerated the process.

*   *   *

Dallas school board trustees are elected by districts, meaning candidates run for specific geographic seats. Of the nine districts, the seventh contains some of the most impoverished areas in Dallas County. Although it includes the Oak Cliff section of Dallas, which has a growing gay presence, most of it is in the predominantly Hispanic area of West Dallas. District 7 has the highest percentage of Hispanic residents—65 percent.

In July 1994, the Hispanic trustee from the area resigned to work for the U.S. Department of Education. The board set January 21, 1995, as the date for the special election to fill the seat. Friends from the community and the school district encouraged Plata to run. "My bosses understood what it would cost in terms of my time away from the office," recalled Plata, "but they knew my work ethic—I'll go to the grave working. They were very supportive. It was marvelous how everything fell into place so quickly," he said, sounding still in awe of the speed at which everything happened. Four other candidates entered the race.

As to why he decided to run for office, Plata said it was because of the role that education had played in his life. "Even though my parents didn't have much schooling, learning was the centerpiece of my growing up," he explained. "Education helped frame who I am and made me into a more productive citizen. Now, it was my turn to give back all that others had given to me."

Plata, who had been involved in several other candidates' campaigns, benefited from attending a Gay and Lesbian Victory Fund candidate workshop. Led by political consultant Dave Fleischer, the workshop covered all aspects of campaigns, from management, to issues, to media. One valuable component was fund-raising. Fleischer recommended that candidates compile their Christmas card lists and ask those people first for money. Since Plata's campaign was during the Christmas season, the strategy was easily put into action. "I sent out the first letter, and you know what? I got a response," he said with a burst of laughter. "I thought, now I can mail out a slate card. I was later criticized for taking money outside my district, but I have a very wide network of friends and supporters."

Next, a logo needed to be designed. It was a daunting task because Plata wanted the logo to reflect both education and the Spanish culture. For this job, Plata turned to a good friend who was a graphic artist. In what Plata considered a stroke of genius, she chose green, white, and red—the colors of the Mexican flag—for the logo. The top green stripe read, "For Dallas School Board, For District 7"; in the middle white stripe was the word "Plata" scrawled in a child's handwriting; in the bottom red stripe was "For our youth, for our tomorrow." "It captured everything I was about," he said proudly.

During the campaign, Plata's sexual orientation came up only once publicly. At a candidates' forum, a Spanish-speaking woman referred to Plata's "homosexual tendencies," and asked him what kind of role model he would be as an elected homosexual. Responding to her in Spanish, he replied that improving education had nothing to do with the other candidates' heterosexuality, just as it had nothing to do with his homosexuality. "It's what you do to help people that matters," he said, adding that he had done more for education than any of his opponents.

Support of a major newspaper is crucial in low-profile special elections where most voters know nothing about the candidates. Thus, it was of enormous importance that Plata received the endorsement of the *Dallas Morning News*. In their editorial, the paper stressed Plata's experience as a public school teacher and his long involvement in local business and arts organizations. "Mr. Plata is energetic, articulate, and passionate about education," the paper added. "He out-attended other candidates at election forums, community meetings, and neighborhood gatherings. He is the best candidate for the job."[5]

Plata spent $25,000 in the primary, much more than any of his opponents. It was almost enough to allow him to forego a runoff. He missed by eighteen votes. Out of a meager 7 percent voter turnout, he received 49.1 percent of the vote. "I had enough gay people come up to me and apologize for not having voted in that first election," he said, shaking his head in disappointment. Jim Salinas, a retired data systems executive, came in a distant second with 25.6 percent of the vote.

A dilemma facing gay and lesbian candidates is how out to be. For candidates who have been active in their community for years, this is less problematic because the press and political insiders already know them as gay people. For candidates without a history of involvement, disclosure can be tricky. They are more apt to downplay their sexual orientation for a variety of personal and political reasons. Such was the case with Plata. Although some people knew he was gay, Plata chose not to mention it in his literature or speeches. This tightrope walk was successful in the primary, but not in the runoff. As Plata soon realized—as have other gay candidates—discussion of one's sexual orientation is not something one can control.

The first time a newspaper reported that Plata was gay occurred even before Plata was an official candidate. In an interview with a part-time reporter for a small weekly Spanish newspaper, *El Heraldo News*, Plata was asked if he were gay. Saying that he would not answer any questions about his personal life, Plata continued to confine his answers to school matters. When the interview ended, the reporter once again asked him if he were gay. Plata replied, "No comment." The writer, who was not a professional journalist, took the liberty to editorialize in his story that Plata would make a good trustee "even though he is gay." The remark was all but forgotten until two days after the primary when the host of a Spanish-speaking radio talk show said that voters had a right to know about Plata's homosexuality and referred to the six-month-old story. This might have been as far as the outing went had not the *Dallas Morning News* written an article about the matter and put it on the front page of its Metropolitan section. "Plata's sex orientation at issue in trustee race," read the subheadline.[6]

Plata remembers the interview with the *Morning News* reporter who wrote the story. "All he wanted to do was to out me," he said. "My advisors counseled me to not let the media focus on my sexual orientation; rather, I should talk about my campaign for better schools. So, during the interview I kept talking about the issues. The reporter got so frustrated with me because I wouldn't give him what he wanted that he finally ended it."

What started out as a sleepy campaign soon became a hot news story. Although the mainstream media never flatly declared that Plata was gay, stories always mentioned that he would not comment on his sexual orientation. Plata dodged the questions by responding with such statements as, "People asked me to run because they know I have served the community in making things better for our kids. It [my sexual orientation] has never been an issue in our campaign for better schools." In another interview, he repeated that his orientation was irrelevant to his qualifications for office. "It's never been an issue in my campaign. We're more concerned about school safety, overcrowding, site-based management, the dropout rate, and getting graduation rates up."

Plata later acknowledged that he had been unsure of how to deal with the issue, not an unusual reaction for some gay and lesbian candidates. For Plata, it was difficult getting to the point where he could state in public that he was gay. "It takes someone who is very self-confident and who knows that he will not be attacked," he said. "When they wrote those stories about me in the paper, they included my picture, and I felt like I had become a target. I called the general manager of the *Morning News* and said, 'You have to understand that this is about me and my life, not about me and my orientation.

You've made me a target now, and I'm the candidate your paper has endorsed.'" Reflecting back, he remarked, "All through the campaign I tried to hold my own, but sometimes I questioned how well I was doing."

The turn of events was not lost on Plata's opponent, Salinas, who had no hesitancy about discussing Plata's personal life. In a direct attack, Salinas, who was a Democrat, mailed out a letter from the chair of the Texas Republican Party. The letter read: "Jim Salinas's opponent is running a stealth campaign. Jim's opponent is receiving substantial political and financial support from those in our midst who are planning an aggressive homosexual rights agenda. We have seen in recent months that agenda being promoted by certain individuals on the Dallas City Council, and we do not need to see the Dallas School Board do likewise. My concern is that if Jim's opponent is elected he will promote a social agenda inconsistent with values of most of our city. Jim Salinas doesn't have any 'hidden agenda.' He just wants to do a good job representing you and the children."

Newspapers often do stories on whether a candidate's contributors live inside or outside of the district. Because gay candidates often have friends and contacts throughout the state and the nation, their financial statements show many donors who are not district residents. This was true in Plata's case. One-half of Plata's funds were from outside the district, although no direct mention was made of it being gay money. The article was part of the reason why Plata chose not to take advantage of the Victory Fund's national network of contributors in his May 1995 reelection race. "I went to some of my advisors in Oak Cliff," he said. "They told me not to do it. 'You don't need it. It will cause you more grief than it's worth.' They were right."

It is hard to know what effect Salinas's hit piece and the articles focusing on Plata's sexual orientation had on the outcome. Perhaps as damaging were tactical errors he made in his own campaign. Plata admits that he made a mistake by not getting his supporters to vote absentee, thus assuring their participation. Early voting, or absentee voting, is crucial in special elections because so few voters are aware that they are being held. "It was stupid," he said in retrospect. "I had no one in charge of it." Salinas, on the other hand, was able to get many of his supporters to mail in their ballots. This made the runoff, which was held three weeks after the primary, shockingly close. Plata, who received 49 percent of the vote in the primary, squeezed out a victory with just 51 percent.

*   *   *

The problems facing the Dallas public schools are monumental. For starters, students' SAT scores are dismal—they are consistently in the bottom 10 percent nationally. Moreover, the dropout rate, while high for all racial groups, is a scandalous 28 percent for Hispanics. Plata reported that it is typical for high school freshmen classes to start with 1,000 students but to graduate fewer than 200. A contributing factor to these problems is that a staggering 75 percent of the students live below the poverty line.

School officials failed to predict—or chose to ignore—the rapid growth of the Latino student population. Today, 47 percent of the students are Hispanic, but enrollment is expected to jump to 57 percent in three years. By the year 2010, it is estimated that 70 percent of the students will be Hispanic, with fewer than half being fluent in English. "There was a huge demographic change, but the district had no long-term plans to deal with any of it," said Plata. "They still don't. I kept telling them, 'Get ready for the onslaught of our population,' but administrators would not listen. Nothing was done in those areas with large Hispanic populations. Schools weren't built, and now they're all overcrowded. Infrastructure is crumbling, and schools aren't wired for current technology. It's a mess."

Another problem relates to how the DISD workforce is unrepresentative of the population it serves. With 47 percent of its students Hispanic, 41 percent African American, and 10 percent white, its employees are 44 percent black, 41 percent white, and 15 percent Hispanic. The same lack of representation applies to its elected officials. Although the school population is only 10 percent white, the nine-member board consists of five white trustees, three blacks, and one Hispanic.

Of all the demographic inequities, the most startling is that only 9 percent of the district's teachers are Hispanic. Few of the non-Hispanic teachers speak Spanish, compounding the educational problems of nearly half its students. Recruitment efforts to hire more bilingual teachers is underway, but the demand is too great and the supply too limited.

Low test scores. High dropout rates. Overcrowded schools. Low academic standards. What does it all add up to? Plata, who speaks candidly, said, "The district has forgotten that it is supposed to prepare children for the future, not just provide remedial education. We must raise our standards to help our students become critical thinkers so that colleges and universities with high academic standards will more readily accept our graduates."

Although there are certainly many teachers and administrators who care deeply about the education of all students, racial politics has taken center stage and shows no sign of exiting anytime soon. As a reporter for *The New York Times* observed, "Unlike confrontations in recent years between ethnic and racial groups in Los Angeles and New York, the issue in Dallas seems less a difference in culture and more a simple fight for power."[7] Echoed *Morning News* columnist Henry Tatum, "The real issue is one of power. As the changing face of the Dallas school population continues to evolve, which racial group will be in control?"[8]

The fight for power at the dais often spills over into the audience. At one particularly raucous meeting, an Hispanic parent became fed up with African-American activists who were protesting yet another board hearing. The Hispanic man yelled that the protesters were no better than the Ku Klux Klan. That led an African-American man to utter obscenities to the Hispanic man. Then all hell broke loose. With the board president futilely pounding his gavel, the men fought in the aisles. The police were called in. People were arrested.

Such skirmishes are becoming commonplace. Said one trustee, justifying the frequent cancellation of board meetings, "When people are telling you that there is a group of sixty people coming in to intentionally use violence to shut down the meeting, as leaders you have to be able to ensure the safety of the public. We couldn't guarantee that."

The animosity has led community members to resort to name-calling at the meetings and in the press. African Americans call Hispanics "vultures" and "scavengers," while Hispanics say that African Americans have become "oppressors" and "racists." Having only three of the nine votes, African-American trustees, angry at being on

the losing end of many issues, nicknamed the board's white majority—and Plata—"the slam-dunk gang" for blindly supporting the
administration. "I got called a white person and a slam-dunk member," he acknowledged. Showing his frustration, he added, "That is
not the way to go about building good board relationships." Once
during budget hearings, Plata was accused by several board members
of being a fiscal conservative. This amused him. "I looked at them
and jokingly said, 'You know what? I've never been called conservative anything, but I'm starting to feel proud of the title.'"

The name-calling took on a whole new dimension when tapes of
phone conversations of Dan Peavy, a white board member, were
released to the press by a neighbor who had secretly recorded them.
The tapes contained racist, sexist, and homophobic remarks. Not
surprisingly, the content of the tapes was big news. In the minds of
many, Peavy's statements were proof of what whites truly felt about
minorities. "It brought this school district to its knees on the issue of
institutional racism," said Plata.

Ironically, the tapes were beneficial in one regard—they served
as a catalyst for change. Six months after the tapes were released,
the board approved a policy that established procedures for reporting and investigating all allegations of harassment, be it "verbal,
written, physical, psychological (both climate and contact) and any
other demonstrative actions with regard to race, ethnic origin,
religious preference, gender, or sexual orientation." It was a major
victory that the policy included gay and lesbian students because it
is rare for school districts to protect gay students from harassment
by other students or teachers. Dave Gleason, a spokesperson for the
Dallas chapter of Parents and Friends of Lesbians and Gays
(PFLAG), was quoted in the paper as saying, "Many gay and lesbian students report that the worst harassment they receive comes
from teachers. They can handle their peers. When it's coming from
adults, it gets to be too much."[9]

When administrators first drafted the antiharassment policy,
sexual orientation was left out. This occurred despite the fact that
when Peavy's remarks first surfaced, the board included sexual
orientation in a resolution condemning his actions. When the omis-
sion came to the attention of Plata and other board members, they
voiced support for its inclusion. "The whole Peavy affair was a

blessing from God," noted Plata. "We were able to get sexual orientation added to all our policies. Do you know what a fight that often is? And it was all because of Peavy."

Other than the Peavy tapes, the only time that Plata's sexual orientation has came up since taking office was during the redrawing of school boundary lines. Such changes are often the most controversial facing any school board. "It is a time when parents become very territorial," explained Plata. "They lash out at you personally. Some parents who were unhappy over where the lines were drawn said that the reason for me not caring was because I was a gay man. They complained that I was the wrong person to be on the school board because I didn't have kids."

Over the two years he has been a trustee, Plata has grown more relaxed with being gay and supporting gay issues. For example, in his official school district photograph, he is wearing a red AIDS ribbon. "The photo blew people away," he said, "because it was my way of saying that I'm not the typical board member who conducts business as usual." In addition, he is now more apt to open up to fellow board members about gay concerns. "I feel so comfortable around them that when the discussion touches on sensitive matters, I am capable of saying—on the advice of my friend William Waybourn—'as a gay man.' I do this just to drive home my point. Sometimes, I also have to remind them that I am the only Hispanic person on the board, and that they need to listen to me because I bring a distinctive viewpoint to the board."

The trustees whom Plata enjoys working with the most are the four white women on the board. This is because, in his words, "They don't engage in male-ego bullshit." Once when the women were being intimidated by other board members, he told them, "Girls, there are four of you and one of me. If we girls stick together, we can pass whatever we want." From then on, Plata reported, the women learned how to count their votes.

In most school districts, the only person the trustees directly hire is the superintendent. It is the superintendent, not the elected board members, who has the power to implement policy. This is why school trustees strive to hire someone who reflects their overall philosophy. As with all matters before the Dallas school board, the decision to hire Yvonne Gonzalez, a Latina, as superintendent was controversial. The vote was six to three, with Plata joining the five white trustees. The three African-American trustees were angry because they felt Gonzalez would begin funding programs for Hispanic students at the expense of African-American students. They had reason to be concerned. With the backing of the majority of the board, this began to happen.

Shortly after Gonzalez was hired, Plata invited her to a meeting of the Stonewall Business and Professional Association, a gay chamber of commerce. She was the first superintendent to attend a meeting of a gay organization, and Plata was pleased she accepted. Plata, who has a very good relationship with the superintendent, summed her up by saying that "She is tenacious, ferocious, pretty, and mean." Laughing, he added, "Her other car is a broom." Once, after observing Gonzalez battle some harsh critics at a contentious board hearing, he leaned over to her and said admiringly, "You have more balls than most of the men I know."

At the gay business meeting, Gonzalez shared with the membership what it is like to be superintendent of the Dallas public schools. "I feel like I go into battle each morning like a big plump grape," she said. "But all day long people come in with little baby syringes, and they'll draw out a little of the juice here and a little there. By the end of the day, I'm like a dried-up raisin." She informed them that reading was the number one priority for children and encouraged them to get involved with programs to help children read. During the question and answer period, a lesbian teacher pointed out how good Gonzalez was on gay issues. She said that with Gonzalez in charge she felt "as safe and secure in my livelihood as any gay or lesbian employee in the state."

Plata believes that the biggest challenges confronting him as a trustee aren't related to his gayness but to his ethnicity. "Because I am the lone Hispanic on the board, I have the sole responsibility of being the representative of the Hispanic population. This has been tough, especially with Hispanic students growing to be the largest minority group in the district." He continued by saying that his efforts to improve education for Latinos helps all students because he will not lower the standards for anyone. "I'm not here to be good or nice," he said sternly. "I'm here to succeed and to be accountable."

Plata is aware of the expectations people have of him. He wants to be a good role model and to continue making a difference. He said that there are times when he is lonely and would appreciate someone to come home and rub his back, but for now a relationship is not in the immediate future. "It's too much work," he said with typical good humor. "Besides, who has the time? I have to attend board meetings, community functions, and meetings with parents and business groups. I want people to know that at least one board member cares about what they're doing. At the moment, this is the most important way for me to spend my time."

Few elected officials have to endure what Plata—and his colleagues—must face on a daily, if not hourly, basis. Every comment is a slight; every action a threat; every vote a battle. It is fair to say that most officeholders—especially those who serve on a part-time basis with little or no monetary compensation—would not put up with the grief. Life is too short. Even though racial politics continues to divert attention from the real education issues at hand, Plata shows no sign of giving in or giving up. He said that he is able to deal with all the insanity by "telling myself that this too shall pass. That, and I know I have more friends than I do enemies." As to how he is able to maintain his optimism, he paused and then said, "I keep going because there is so much to do, and there isn't enough time to get it all done."

*   *   *

Just when it seems that the problems facing the Dallas Independent School District can't get any worse, they do. The following are a few of the jaw-dropping events that were reported shortly after the interview with Plata:

- In August 1997, a federal investigation requested by Gonzalez led to the indictment of thirteen school district employees for overtime fraud. In total, eighteen employees were suspended or fired, nearly all of them African American.
- In September, the district's associate superintendent for management, Matthew Harden, an African American, filed a lawsuit accusing Gonzalez of sexually harassing him and sought $10 million in damages.

- Gonzalez denied the allegations and announced that she had submitted her letter of resignation to the board. The board placed her on paid leave for thirty days.
- The events surrounding Gonzalez served to escalate racial tension between African Americans and Hispanics, with Hispanics defending Gonzalez and African Americans demanding her ouster. Both groups held protest marches in front of the district office.
- Texas Governor George W. Bush weighed in on the matter, saying, "This business has to stop. Racial politics has got to end. This is inappropriate for a school district that is charged with educating children. It is essential that these school districts, this school district in particular, not go through racial war."
- A private investigator said that Gonzalez had hired him to conduct surveillance on Harden because Gonzalez feared that Harden would leak confidential information to the media.
- Federal authorities executed a search warrant at Gonzalez's apartment and removed items that included bedroom furniture possibly purchased with district funds.
- Federal prosecutors informed Gonzalez that they intended to file criminal charges against her, citing embezzlement, witness tampering, and obstruction of justice.
- With Gonzalez still on paid leave, the board appointed a new acting superintendent, a white man. An African-American Dallas County commissioner accused the board of resurrecting "a white boy from somewhere."
- On October 7, Gonzalez pleaded guilty to one felony count of spending more than $16,000 in school district funds to purchase furniture for her home and office. School board trustees voted unanimously to accept her resignation.
- In November, Plata, along with another trustee and a former administrator, were sued for $10 million by Harden, who alleged that they conspired with Gonzalez to force him out of office.
- The Texas Education Commissioner informed the board that he was concerned about the district's stability and financial management. He warned them that the Texas Education

Agency was following internal and federal investigations. A state investigation of a neighboring school district led to the state taking over its operations.

In a brief conversation with Plata to get his reaction to all that was happening, he said, "It's crazy." He then added, "It's getting to be too much, but I'm doing okay. I still have the challenge of improving the education of these kids in front of me. Come hell or high water, I won't stray from that course."

Chapter 8

Climbing the Political Ladder: California Assemblywoman Carole Migden

There are two aspects of California Assemblywoman Carole Migden's character that leave an indelible impression: first, she is bright and talented beyond measure; second, she is calculating to the point of being Machiavellian. By possessing these traits, Migden has accomplished more in her two short years in the California Assembly than most of her colleagues could dream of in their lifetimes.

In terms of being bright and talented, the well-respected *California Journal*, a monthly magazine that focuses on California politics and governance, chose Migden as its Rookie of the Year, a high honor. The accolades did not end there, however. When competing with all eighty members of the assembly, she also was named most hardworking. She was a runner-up in four other categories: intelligence, integrity, influence, and ambition. With the exception of her lesbian colleague, Assemblywoman Sheila Kuehl, no other legislator came close to racking up such recognition.

In regard to being calculating, a case in point is Migden's strategy on deciding whom to support for governor of California. By February 1998, Migden still had not decided which Democratic candidate to support—Al Checchi, Jane Harmon, or Gray Davis. When asked whom she would be endorsing, she replied, "I would have been with Dianne Feinstein had she run." Before continuing, she paused. "First and foremost," she proceeded, "I want to win." She repeated the words in a deadly serious tone: "I want to win." She then explained, "I have told Ms. Harman, Mr. Checchi, and Mr. Davis that I'm going to assess in the month of April whom I think has the best chance of beating Dan Lungren in the general election, and I will make my decision accordingly. This isn't about personalities. I don't care that one is delightful, that one has vigor, or that one is self-made. I don't care about those things. I'm going to make my decision on who can win the general election."

Picking winners is something that Migden does extremely well. When she was still a San Francisco County supervisor, she endorsed Willie Brown for mayor over former Supervisor Roberta Achtenberg. When Brown won, he resigned the assembly seat that he had held for thirty-one years. Endorsed by him, Migden ran unopposed in a special election to fill the remaining months of his two-year term. She was seen as so formidable that no other candidate ran against her in the regularly scheduled election. When the new legislative session convened in December 1996, many names were floated for Speaker of the Assembly, including Kuehl's. Migden backed the winner, Cruz Bustamante. Bustamante then chose Migden to chair the powerful Appropriations Committee—a move that created grumblings from veteran lawmakers who felt they had been passed over in favor of newcomer Migden.

* * *

Migden's outward appearance reflects her abundant physical energy, down to the tightly wound curls at the end of her blond-assisted hair. At 5'3" and 106 pounds, the forty-nine-year-old Migden is trim and muscular. To keep her body toned, she works out five to ten hours a week. "I don't lift great volumes of weight, but it's persistent," she said. "I'm almost fifty. If I was twenty and doing this, then I'd be something. I joked with a friend the other day that if someone was in better shape than me it was either because they were a movie star or a professional athlete." Besides keeping her in shape, weight lifting provides Migden some precious time for reflection. "There's a solitude, a clarity of mind that I get when working out. It gives me time to do a lot of thinking." Migden receives the same satisfaction doing yoga and Zen meditation.

Having extra time for anything has been noticeably absent from Migden's frenetic life. Her legislative career began in 1990 when she was elected to the San Francisco Board of Supervisors in what was tagged the "lavender sweep" because of the high number of gays and lesbians who were elected. They were Migden and Roberta Achtenberg to the Board of Supervisors, Tom Ammiano to the San Francisco Board of Education, and Donna Hitchens to municipal court. They joined two other long-term gay officials, Community College Trustee Tim Wolfred and Supervisor Harry Britt, who took Harvey Milk's seat in 1979 after he was assassinated. In 1993, Achtenberg was appointed by President Clinton as HUD undersecretary and Britt did not run for reelection in 1992. Where once there were three gays on the board, Migden kidded at the time, "Then there was one." The number rose to two in June 1993 when Susan Leal was appointed by Mayor Frank Jordan to replace Achtenberg. Today, the three gay elected officials serving on the board are Ammiano, Leslie Katz, and Mark Leno, with Leal now city treasurer.

Born in New York City in 1948, Migden was raised in suburban Yonkers. Her father was a GI when he met her mother, a French citizen, during World War II. Growing up, Migden saw her family as different from the norm. Her mother had a French accent and instilled in the family a European perspective on world events. They were Jewish in a suburb that was religiously mixed. Her father, a CPA, was a jokester and garrulous. Her mother, a homemaker, was introspective and academic. A middle child, Migden has a brother who is a CPA and a sister who is a public utility lawyer.

Migden says of herself as a child, "I had a sense of independence, and I thought that whatever I made of this life would be based upon my own efforts and initiatives. I was always strikingly mature. I had very few starry-eyed childhood illusions about life. I don't know why. It might be a sense of difference—a little girl with all the trappings who felt different from others. It might have been because I found the normal way of relating didn't apply to me, or that I had a willfulness that was different and was not traditional."

Both of Migden's parents are still alive and, although in frail health, were able to fly out to witness their daughter being sworn in as a member of the assembly. "They were touched and more than just a little surprised who their little girl grew up to be," she said with a twinkle in her eye. "They could tell it was a fancy event, so it had to mean something important. I'm glad I was able to make them proud of me."

Migden attended Adelphi University, earning a degree in English. She came to California in 1970 with her future husband and lived in Berkeley. Her marriage lasted two and a half years. She came out as a lesbian when she was twenty-six. "I learned how to fit in straight society, but it was an accommodation that didn't feel authentic," said Migden.

After her divorce, Migden, whose professional background is in mental health, earned a master's degree in clinical psychology from Sonoma State. She then was named director of the Pacific Center in Berkeley, a gay and lesbian mental health agency. She moved to San Francisco and became involved in the lesbian-feminist movement.

It was as an agency director that she first met Supervisor Harvey Milk. Their relationship had a profound influence on her and sealed her desire to become involved in politics. "I called up Harvey Milk to get my agency funded by the United Way," she recalled. "I said that my name is Carole Migden, and I represent gay people here in Berkeley, and we've been trying to get in the United Way for ten years. I said that gays give nationally to the United Way, but there is no funding for any gay program in the United States of America. He said that he would call the United Way trustees and say, 'I'm a supervisor. You must deal with me.'

"'Harvey,' I said, 'we get bubkes,' which is the Yiddish word for nothing. Harvey, who was a Jew from Woodside, New York, loved that. Bubkes is a word that he hadn't heard in years. 'Yes, you're right, we get bubkes,' he said. He said that he'd help and he did.

Together we fought, and that year the Pacific Center was the first gay and lesbian organization funded by a United Way."

Migden credits Milk with sparking her interest in electoral politics. "Harvey pushed the system. I became enchanted with that. Through political leadership, one really did have access and opportunity to make change. And often in life, one can't always realize tangible results of one's efforts and derive satisfaction from them because some are extremely subtle or long in coming. I liked Harvey, and he liked me." After Mayor Dianne Feinstein appointed Harry Britt to fill the remainder of Milk's term when Milk was assassinated in 1978, Migden flirted with the idea of running against Britt in the regular election. She campaigned for a couple of weeks, then dropped out of the race and supported Britt.

In 1981, Migden took the job of director of Operation Concern, an outpatient psychiatric clinic in San Francisco for gays and lesbians. "I built that agency from a $150,000 program into a $1 million program," she said proudly.

In 1982, Migden ran for community college board. She lost, coming in fourth in a field of nine for three seats, a respectable showing. The race taught her many lessons, primarily that she needed to have a broader political base. One of her first actions was to become president of the Harvey Milk Gay and Lesbian Democratic Club. Migden knew, however, that to be elected citywide she needed support from outside the gay community.

All aspiring politicians need a base, and Migden carved hers out of the gay community and the Democratic Party. That such a base exists says a great deal about San Francisco politics, not only because of the gay factor, but because of the influence that party politics plays in the city's politics. San Francisco is overwhelmingly Democratic and voters have elected Democrats to most political positions.

Migden methodically set out to become part of the city's Democratic machine. She did this by getting involved in the local party organization called the central committee. These committees exist for both parties in all counties in California and throughout the country. And although they have limited power, die-hard party activists take these posts seriously. There are several ways to become a member of the central committee, but the principle way is being elected to it by the voters of each party. Even though central committee candidates are listed on the ballot, few voters take much notice. There are usually a large number of people running, and the top vote-getters win. In 1984, Migden ran for one of these slots and won. It was a small step, but it got her connected to San Francisco's Democratic machine which, six years later, helped elect her to the Board of Supervisors.

Migden spent most of the 1980s serving on numerous Democratic Party committees and, in her own words, "methodically penetrating the party, for myself and community." As with any volunteer or service organization, this meant "just showing up." Migden sat on committees, went to conventions, attended fund-raisers, worked the room. Because she considered the work of the party as important, the stalwarts rewarded her. Over time, she became a member of the state Democratic Party, served as chair of its lesbian and gay caucus, and was appointed chair of the state platform committee. She became a member of the Democratic National Committee and a member of its platform committee. In these capacities, Migden strove to make sure that gay and lesbian concerns were addressed, even though the results of her actions were often limited to positions written in documents that few people read.

Migden was able to use her contacts to help promote her own political career. Even though she believes that party officials are suspicious of gays because they see gays as wanting to empower themselves rather than to help the party, Migden feels that her involvement opened doors for her. These early contacts gave her exposure to people and gave her legitimacy.

Migden's new legislative responsibilities have forced her to curtail her Democratic Party activities, although she continues to serve on the Democratic National Committee. Although she is pleased that the delegate selection process for the 2000 presidential campaign will include rules that will help guarantee that gays and lesbians are better represented at the convention, she notes that the party is not yet ready to reinstate a gay caucus.

One big change since the gay community helped elect Bill Clinton is that chief gay and lesbian fund-raisers now are demanding policy changes, not just having mimosa breakfasts with party luminaries. "In yesteryears, we would go for high tea, then they would pulverize us with such policies as 'Don't ask, don't tell,'" she explained. "Well, who cares if you have an opportunity to dine with the president if he puts a bayonet through your head? It's important that we are insistent upon results for our dollars."

Migden used the nomination of San Franciscan James Hormel as ambassador to Luxembourg as an example of how the gay community cannot settle for less than what they deserve. "I thought it was good that the president nominated Jim, but I think Clinton abandoned him. If the president wanted Trent Lott to have a hearing about a potential nominee, then it would occur. One can always say, well, I nominated you and then walk away. So Jim Hormel gets nominated. Well, we don't care about the nomination. We care about the hearing and the vote counting. And I think he should prevail upon Al Gore now, and all gay people should be pursuing Al Gore to insist that Jim Hormel get a hearing. Let us be cautious before we are too drippingly appreciative," said Migden sternly.

It could be argued that the Democratic Party remains cautious (at best) or exploitative (at worst) of the gay community. Migden understands these criticisms, although she still believes it is necessary to work within the party in order for it to reflect her values. "Let us not believe that we are tolerated or liberated," she said. "No one relinquishes power. We have to take it. As Phil Angelides [the former chair of the California Democratic Party] said, 'If you need a friend, get a dog.' Your friends are predicated on your ability to deliver votes and money. That's a very stark, perhaps cynical, but unshakable truth. And I'm Ms. Democratic Party. No one has my credentials that substantiates their entitlement to speak as a Democrat who has paid her dues. So I do party politics, and I enjoy it. I feel I've made a contribution, and I've benefitted by it. But I'm not disillusional about that system promoting gay and lesbian candidates. They may tolerate them, and they may acquiesce, but no one, no one besides lesbians and gays are working to give us a seat at the table. And maybe if we gained it, they'll move their seats over and allow us to sit at it. And that's what I've come to see and believe time and time again."

Having a seat at the table means getting elected to office, the prize that ambitious politicians strive for. The uninitiated probably have little, if any, concept of what it takes to run for office—the years of meeting people, of attending fund-raisers, of building coalitions, and of paying one's dues. In the rough-and-tumble world of politics, few campaigns are won on a lark. It takes years of mapping out a plan.

*   *   *

When Migden ran for supervisor in 1990, everything was in place politically. Because of her work in the gay community and in Democratic politics, she had access to money and to volunteers. As important, however, she had assembled a quality campaign staff, headed by Dick Pabich.

Pabich is a well-respected but unassuming political mastermind who advised some of the most prominent office holders in San Francisco, including Senator Barbara Boxer, the late Congressman Phil Burton, and former Supervisor Nancy Walker. The Wisconsin native moved to San Francisco in 1975 and a year later volunteered in Harvey Milk's campaign for state assembly. When Milk ran for the board of supervisors, Pabich helped design and write his campaign materials. When Milk was elected in 1977, Pabich was hired along with Anne Kronenberg for his city hall staff. After Milk's death, he served in the same capacity for Harry Britt. When Britt ran for election, Pabich left the staff and helped manage the campaign. He ran Britt's later reelection campaigns, as well as his unsuccessful campaign for Congress in 1987.

Pabich first met Migden in 1979 during her brief run for supervisor against Britt. They became friends, and Pabich helped with Migden's unsuccessful campaign for college board in 1982. In 1989 when she knew she wanted to run for supervisor, she met with Pabich and they began planning their strategy.

Of the five seats that were up for election in 1990, two were held by incumbents. Given San Francisco politics, it was assumed they would win reelection. This meant the remaining three seats were up for grabs. The presumption was that a lesbian or gay man could get elected, especially a lesbian, because historically women candidates receive more votes because of their gender. What wasn't clear was whether the public would elect two lesbians since Achtenberg also had decided to run.

The Migden and Achtenberg campaigns decided early on not to have the two candidates run as a team. Except for the gay community, they had different bases of support. For example, Achtenberg had close ties with then-mayor Art Agnos and had the backing of his extensive operation. Migden, on the other hand, had the support of the Democratic political machine. Nor did the candidates get the same endorsements. Migden, for instance, got the endorsement of the Democratic Central Committee, but Achtenberg did not. Recalling her campaign and how the strategy was devised, Migden said, "I built up a credible, professional record that said to the people of this city that I can serve you. Yes, I'm a lesbian, and, yes, I want to represent my community, but I'm a health professional, and I know about real people and real problems. I know how to raise money and balance a budget and meet a payroll and be a manager as well as a visionary. I'm a tough, practical administrator, who is also a compassionate, informed person."

Migden raised close to $250,000 for her election, as did Achtenberg. There is a $500 campaign contribution limit for city offices, so candidates must raise their funds from many people in small amounts. Migden, who took time off from her job to run, spent most of her time raising funds. Pabich estimates that less than half of her funds came from the gay community.

Migden was the third highest vote-getter, finishing behind the two incumbents but preceding Achtenberg. She said of the campaign, "I won in virtually every neighborhood in the city. I worked very, very hard. I've been called more than once a tireless campaigner. And I was committed that if I was going to lose by 100 votes, it wasn't because I didn't go to that extra party or try. My conviction was that I make sure that I did everything I could do that was in my control."

In terms of fund-raising, Migden said that she has never been skittish about asking for money. "I don't mind asking if I believe in what I'm advocating. I urge and encourage people to examine their own hesitancy, because I think it has to do with bad social messages we receive when we're young that it is not high-minded or serving of the public good. We have to reformulate our thinking about fund-raising and giving money for the agenda for social change. It's not repugnant, nor should it be. I think women are more reluctant than men in asking for money. I think that lesbians and gays are more inhibited than others because they sometimes are socially awkward or uncomfortable. It takes a certain degree of stick-to-it-iveness and confidence."

Those are ingredients that Migden has in spades, and they explain, in part, her success in Sacramento. Even though she was unopposed for her assembly seat, Migden raised over $400,000—an impressive sum even for politicians who have a tough race on their hands. She spent little on herself, choosing instead to strategically dole it out to other Democratic assembly candidates running throughout the state. Her prowess has made her one of the chief fund-raisers for the Democratic caucus. There is one condition she places on those who receive part of her largess, however. "I'm very clear to make the point that this is gay money. You can't take our money then vote against us."

* * *

As a county supervisor, Migden developed a reputation for being too scheming, too overtly political. "She's too abrupt," "she's too aggressive," "she's too ambitious" were frequent complaints spoken and written about her from people who like their politics genteel. To most observers, she came across as the type of person who, while talking with you at a party, was focused more on who was in the room rather than on whom she was with at the moment.

Such negative descriptions by someone's peers are not uncommon in local politics, where city hall air is filtered through frail egos, short tempers, and long memories. It is little wonder, then, that many local officials across the country yearn for the day they can move up to state or national politics where, in theory, issues take precedence over personalities. In that sense, San Francisco is no different from the Midwestern towns that thousands of gays and lesbians fled in order to escape small-town attitudes about what is and is not respectable behavior.

Asked how she likes state politics, Migden answered quickly, "I adore it. I feel pleasantly divorced from what I think are parochial, petty problems of municipal government." She added that there is an absence of personal discords, which enhance the civility of the climate. On a personal level, she stated, "I believe that I'm well liked, that no one is out to get me because of a feud, or because I'm a rival of somebody's, or because someone is in another camp.

These all happen when you have incestuous, sometimes petty and unpleasant rifts. I like the fact that I'm pulled back from the district, although I'm there when I need to work on constituent issues."

With her new role have come some trappings of power. As befits an influential committee chair, her office is enormous. At her disposal is, in her words, "a million dollars worth of staff." Then, with a sweep of her arm, she exclaimed, "Just look at the place," referring to the spaciousness of her second-floor capitol office. "It's the greatest. But it doesn't really ring my chimes. I would be happy with a more practical workspace."

On her desk sit a cup of coffee and a large glass filled with greenish-looking sludge. "I drink a health food concoction every day, which is sort of off-putting to some people," she explained. "It's full of algae and nutrients. I work at my desk. I'm not part of the hamburger set."

Nor is Migden part of the set that goes out for meals to conduct business—standard fare for most politicians. "When someone says they want to arrange a meeting with me, I usually say, 'What do you need? Got a problem? Well, tell me about it. Give me a one-page faxed summary, and I'll get someone on it.'"

Along with the green algae on her desk are an array of Post-Its and scraps of paper. This is her way of keeping track of constituent case work, something she monitors closely. "I have these here so I know to bug my staff if the constituent's problem isn't solved. 'Is it over?' I keep asking. The greatest pleasure I get out of life is crinkling up a piece of paper and throwing it away." Migden surveys her desk, takes a scrap of paper and crumbles it up. "Done. Next. Just tell me, done, done, done. I always tell my staff, 'Don't tell me you left a message. Tell me it's done. Leaving a message isn't getting the job done. If you have eight hours, what do you mean you called them at ten? Call them at twelve. Call them at two. Call until they're haunted by you so you get a response.' I do derive great satisfaction from helping people, and often it's just a matter of being persistent in calling to get results. Aggressiveness doesn't mean harshness or callousness. It means persistence. And that's what it often takes to get bureaucracies to bend to get results for real people."

For the meek and mild, Migden's way of dispensing office marching orders can be hard to take. It explains, in part, the reputation she has for being difficult to work for. Criticized harshly in the press for having a high staff turnover, she is making a concerted effort to be a kinder, gentler boss.

Alan Lafaso, who worked for another legislator until Migden spirited him away, said, "She's a tough boss; she does a great job at striking fear in all of us, but I can see the humanity in her every day beneath the tough facade. I can see she cares about gay and lesbian rights, civil rights, and health care. She is trying to do better with staff. She's much calmer than she was before."

One thing that has not changed is the accelerated pace at which she leads her life. "I do everything quicker than the rest of the world," she acknowledged. "It's what is; it's organic to me." She is well known in Sacramento for doing instant spots at cocktail parties and fund-raisers—dropping in just long enough to be noticed. "I'll be there for five minutes, but not for two hours. I don't drink or eat terribly fatty foods, but I say to people—because I never want to be disrespectful—that I'm popping in and out so they will not see me as being rude. Generally I'm very attentive to people when I'm there. My office is well regarded for our work, not because I'm eating too many pigs in a blanket on a platter, but because we are attentive and professional."

Migden's years of putting in her time to inch up the political ladder paid off when she was appointed chair of the Appropriations Committee, one of the most prestigious and sought-after posts in Sacramento. It is a job that is worthy of her many skills. "I think I handled my political career the right way," she reflected. "For twenty years, I worked assiduously as a grassroots activist, party person, elected official, assemblyperson. And that's the way it should be. It is inspiring, I believe, for others to take note that with hard work and a certain degree of talent that good things are possible."

To prepare herself for being chair, she spent weeks watching tapes of all the Appropriation Committee hearings held since 1974, a task that reveals her capacity for tedium that must be regarded with nothing less than awe. "I studied my craft," she said. "I learned techniques about presiding over meetings and came to understand the subject matter of issues by watching countless, numberless tapes of old hearings." The video watching must have paid off because journalists and political insiders give her high marks for the way she handles the enormous volume of legislation that passes through her committee. In fact, most observers are shocked that a rookie is doing what they thought only a seasoned veteran could handle.

Although Migden's legislative role is new, her experience at running budget hearings is not. When she chaired the board of supervisors' budget committee, Migden spent hundreds of hours reworking Mayor Jordan's figures to find ways to cut $200 million out of a $2.7 billion budget. It was Migden, not Jordan, who worked on the compromises and found ways to save services while cutting costs. As chair, Migden worked to stabilize funding so important services could continue to be provided. She believed that the more money that was available, the less friction there would be among groups competing for it. "Rather than launch competing measures for meager resources, I tried to figure out how to stabilize government," she said. "It's the hard stuff, the boring stuff, it's the not-easy-answers stuff, yet I believe we must face these problems squarely."

As a supervisor and now as an assemblywoman, Migden has a reputation for being a hard worker and a pragmatic politician. She enjoys the inner workings of government, of doing the political arithmetic. In a setting where it is nearly impossible to get a consensus on important pieces of legislation, it can be exhilarating to successfully negotiate deals with friends and foes to get necessary votes. She knows that to make an imprint, a person must be willing to do her homework, be aware of what is politically feasible, and be able to work with colleagues on both sides of the aisle.

One aspect of Sacramento that surprised her the most was the lack of animosity between legislators. According to Migden, lawmakers in Sacramento tend to be congenial, even hard-line Republicans. "Some Republicans who are the most hateful in their attitudes are the most genial and easy to get along with. Sort of like with Ronald Reagan, who many people found irresistible. Despite any lob you wanted to launch at Reagan, you wanted to warm up to a joke he told. You wanted to be in his company. I laugh sometimes. I think my guys are stale and humorless, and Republicans are often delightful and fun to be around. That's a little mind-blowing," she said, laughing at the paradox.

Another truth Migden discovered about Sacramento was that one's honor rests with being fair. "People expect you to be partisan and to hold different views, but it is important to be fair and not to lie." Then she gave a lesson in Political Science 101. "All things being equal, if you can cut someone's decision a certain way and it doesn't mean all that much, you give it to them. And it comes back in good stead. It's not to disburse favors without accountability, but just try to be fair and to help people out if you can."

It is this give-and-take attitude that Migden uses to coax legislators who are dead set against supporting the numerous bills that she introduced. "I understand that certain people are not going to vote for gay rights," she said, "but if you take people in their context and understand them, then maybe you can get them to budge around the edges. It's all about incremental gain. Or, all things being equal and something matters to me and doesn't hurt you, are you inclined to say aye or nay? It's not about assaulting or assailing someone in their core beliefs, but gaining ground in the gray area."

Although neither she nor Kuehl were overly successful in getting their legislation signed into law, Migden firmly believes that headway was made in discussing gay and lesbian issues in an honest and open way that has never before happened. "Issues were highlighted, discussions were held, minds were changed," she said. "If it wasn't an election year, I believe we would have gained ground this year."

The high ratings that both Migden and Kuehl received from the *California Journal* reflect the prevalent opinion that both are doing a good job. "I think we are well liked and well respected, and that we are seen as powerful members," noted Migden. "It's an irony that gay issues are difficult or anathema for some of our colleagues, yet it is the gay members who are the most praised."

Staff aide Lafaso agreed. "A lot of politicians are committed to being antigay, but the great thing about having Carole and Sheila here is that people have to deal with lesbian political activists on a daily basis. It helps to have them see gay people as individuals. It slowly chips away at the bigotry."

Getting her legislative colleagues to support her bills is just one part of the equation, however. "You learn that the object is getting a bill signed by the governor, not just having it pass the legislature," stated Migden. "If we can elect a Democratic governor, I think we can make great strides."

Migden knows how hard it will be to bring about fundamental change, but she is philosophical about the speed of progress. "Law-making isn't for the easily frustrated. What I say to my staff when something doesn't work out is 'Who said it would happen in a month, a year?' It may take ten years, it may take twenty. I don't expect it to come easily. I don't expect to be exhausted by these issues. We'll continue to struggle."

From the time Migden was a supervisor, she understood the importance of looking at the long term. She believes it is even more so now. "Not to use baseball terms—which is when I hate the patriarchy because the images fail us—but I play the long ball, if you will. Immediate gratification or a little spike in the press is fun, but I focus on which course of action will help in the long run to actualize some profound change. The movement made some prog-ress, but not to the degree we expect or we seek, but we're going to keep moving forward."

An important element in Migden's world view is her outlook on oppression, which, she believes, comes from being Jewish as well as a woman. "Sometimes—and I mean no disservice to my gay brothers—if you emerge from a privileged, middle-class, white background, albeit you are gay, you may be startled by the resist-ance you encounter in the world. But if you are a person of color or a woman or a Jew—someone who is used to being an outsider in the world—you aren't surprised by the hostility."

* * *

Part of the reason why Migden is able to keep fighting the daily battles is her partner of twelve years, Cris Arguedas. Arguedas is a renowned criminal defense lawyer who received her fifteen minutes of fame when she helped the O. J. Simpson defense team with preparing Simpson for possible cross-examination by the prosecu-tion. As it turned out, Simpson did not testify on his own behalf, reportedly because of the merciless grilling he received from Arguedas.

"Cris is very calm, centered, and smart. She's been called a compact Buddha. She keeps me on an even keel. She has been very supportive and accepting of my political life. We have a strong relationship. I'm lucky to have her. She offers me unconditional love."

Conducting a relationship is not easy for any couple that lives and works in different cities. Coordinating schedules is particularly hard, but when they don't spend the night with each other, they talk on the phone. "I have nothing but black shoes in the trunk of the car when I'm going to different locations," said Migden. "Cris has a house in the Oakland Hills and practices law in Emeryville, I have my apartment in San Francisco, and I have a place here in Sacramento. Because I've got to have clothes everywhere, I buy everything in triplicate."

For relaxation, Migden is happy to be with Cris on a Saturday night, wearing sweats. "There is nothing I covet more than a night off. I'm trying to do fewer nonmandatory outings. As I've gotten more established and am where I want to be, I can be more selective. I don't have to be everywhere. I'm trying to restore some balance in my life, and there is nothing better than going to the movies with Cris and getting a malted afterwards."

Migden does not know what she would do if she were not in politics. Nothing else feels so important to her. "I didn't choose in this world to go make money, so I suppose I chose to have influence. I used to say that if I lost an election that I would be a weight trainer. But I enjoy the political process and the opportunity to impact decisions that are fundamental to people's lives."

Chapter 9

The Outing of a Gay Republican Mayor: Mayor Neil Giuliano, Tempe, Arizona

As a show of support for nonprofit groups holding events in Tempe, the city often reduces the amount of fees they charge. In 1996, Arizona Central Pride applied to have their fees lowered. A citizen advisory committee recommended that $1500 of their $8100 fees be waived for their annual gay pride festival in Tempe. The committee then forwarded their recommendations to the city council.

Listed in a newspaper article about the committee's action were all the groups recommended to receive a fee reduction. Along with the Boy Scouts Jamboree, the Ms. Arizona parade, and so on was Arizona Central Pride. When members of Tempe's religious right read the May 1996 article, they immediately took up arms to overturn the committee's recommendations. Shortly afterward, the city council began receiving calls and letters demanding that Central Pride's waiver be denied. A Baptist minister wrote, "You have hastened the day when the sign leading into Tempe says, 'Welcome to Sodom and Gomorrah.'"

Little did Neil Giuliano, the forty-one-year-old Republican mayor of Tempe, suspect that this series of events would eventually force him to publicly disclose his sexual orientation.

On the day of the city council's vote to accept the advisory committee's recommendation, many fundamentalists came to city hall to speak against the waiver. They were greeted with the news from Giuliano that it was the council's established policy to only take testimony on items designated as a public hearing. All other agenda matters, such as the fee waivers, were considered routine and were voted on by the council with no public discussion. Members of the audience could speak on the waivers or any other issue at the end of the meeting. "When I told them that we were going to consider that item and that they couldn't speak on it until afterwards," recalled Giuliano, "you would have thought I declared that the Second Coming wasn't coming." The waivers for all the groups were approved unanimously without council discussion.

From that day on, a handful of fundamentalists began to regularly attend council meetings, waiting until the public comment portion to denounce the council for endorsing the homosexual lifestyle. At a July meeting, one speaker said he wanted them to know that he was still upset over the city's sponsorship of the gay pride festival. He then said the words that Giuliano knew he would one day hear. In rather dramatic fashion, the speaker said he happened to know that one of them was leading the gay lifestyle. Giuliano's first thought was, "This is it, they're going to out me."

Giuliano, who had never publicly discussed his sexual orientation and who, in fact, had only completely come to terms with being gay several years earlier, assumed that the other council members would know that the speaker was referring to him. An incident during his 1994 mayoral race provided the first public hint that Giuliano might be gay. In a poll assumed to have been commissioned by one of Giuliano's two opponents in the race, a question was asked of respondents if it would make any difference if they knew Giuliano was single and didn't have a family. The very next question asked if they would support a proposed statewide initiative giving special rights to homosexuals. Enough respondents were incensed by the implication of the two questions that they called both mayoral candidates and demanded that the second question be deleted. The backlash was great enough that whoever paid for the poll changed it. Even though no one ever directly asked him if he were gay, Giuliano knew that the seeds had been sown.

The day after the speaker's allegations, Giuliano flew to Atlanta to attend the Olympics. He brooded all weekend, wondering what to do. When he returned to Tempe, he began to receive anonymous phone calls and letters telling him that he and his "homosexual agenda" were going to be exposed. Several weeks later he went to San Diego to attend the Republican National Convention. Ironically, it was while he was there that he listened to his voice mail and heard a caller say, "I want you to know that this Thursday we're coming to the public meeting, and we're going to ask you, the council members, and the city manager why the city supports this homosexual event in Tempe. We're going to ask everyone point blank if they're homosexual."

Giuliano remembers his first reaction as being, "What am I going to do with this?" It was on the plane home from San Diego that he decided that life was too short to let these people control it. "I'm just going to be honest with people; whatever happens, happens," he told himself. Fortunately for Giuliano, the caller did not realize that the next council meeting had been canceled months before. The message gave Giuliano ten days of lead time to put everything in order. He called his chief strategists and other supporters to explain the situation. He didn't sleep much; he lost weight. It was a very difficult and emotional time for a public figure who had spent his entire adult life in service to others.

*   *   *

Giuliano was born in 1956, the second of four children. He grew up in a modest middle-class Italian-Catholic family in the New Jersey town of Bloomfield, population 60,000. His parents, like most residents, were registered Republicans. When Giuliano was in junior high school, his father, a banker, was elected to the city council. From junior high to high school, Giuliano was known as the councilman's kid. Because his parents believed in doing as many things as possible as a family, Giuliano became accustomed to going to community events and being in the public eye. "Even before family values was the politically correct thing to do," he reflected, "our family practiced it. They didn't bring us kids along for political reasons; my mom and dad were just that way."

In school, Giuliano was involved in sports that suited his lanky, athletic build: soccer, basketball, and track. As befitted the councilman's son, he also became interested in politics. "I lost everything I ran for in high school," he said with a laugh. He ran for and lost junior class vice president, senior class vice president, student body vice president, and president of his Key Club chapter, a high school service organization sponsored by Kiwanis. When he lost the Key Club presidency, he decided to run for state treasurer of the organization. Giuliano, along with a slate of outsiders, miraculously got elected. "Here I was, just elected as treasurer, and I didn't even know how to endorse a check," he said with typical self-deprecating humor. "In fact, I didn't even have my own checking account. I had no idea what I was doing."

When Giuliano was completing his junior year in high school, his father suffered a heart attack. An avid reader of Zane Grey novels who had always dreamt of living in the West, the senior Giuliano decided to make a life change. He resigned his city council seat and moved his family to Arizona. His son pleaded with his parents not to take him "to the middle of God-knows-where" so he could complete his senior year in Bloomfield. They let him stay with his grandmother and two aunts. After graduating from high school, Giuliano planned on attending New Jersey's Rutgers University. However, before the fall term began, he spent the summer with his family in Phoenix. One day he visited Arizona State University, which is located in nearby Tempe. He liked it so much that he decided to stay. Sadly, his father never saw him graduate. He had a fatal heart attack after only four years of living in the West.

Giuliano's first major at ASU was political science, then business. He finally settled on communication. He was involved in intramural sports and in Circle K, the college-level version of Kiwanis. It was as founder and president of the ASU chapter of Circle K that he finally started to win elections. First, he became a district governor, then president of Circle K International, the world's largest collegiate organization for service and leadership development. Giuliano believes that what got him elected was his personal relationships, not his social skills. "In many respects, I was a late bloomer," remembered Giuliano. "In high school and college, I was more introverted, shy, and insecure than I am now. I was a gangly kid with long black hair, standing just under six feet tall. I might have weighed 130 pounds soaking wet."

When Giuliano graduated in 1979, he thought about going to law school. He even took the LSAT. But then he realized that he would only be going into law because everyone told him that he should because of his interest in politics. "It wasn't because I wanted to be a lawyer," he said. "I didn't like to study; I wasn't even a good student. I didn't kill myself to get good grades."

Giuliano, who has always been religious and who still attends Catholic church weekly, took a job as a lay youth minister at an ecumenical church in Colorado. He heard about the job from the pastor, who had been a Kiwanis International trustee. His main responsibility was to take groups of high school and college students to work in rural, impoverished areas of the state. It was hard, demanding work. After five months, any thoughts he had about joining the Peace Corps quickly vanished.

After his return to Tempe, Giuliano read an ad in the paper that would haphazardly start him on his career path. The position was for a male counselor and a community education specialist for the Center Against Sexual Assault. Despite having no counseling background, he was hired. His way of helping the husbands and boyfriends of rape victims was mainly to listen. His other responsibility was to give speeches at high schools about rape prevention and sexual assault. He burned out on the job quickly. Next, he applied for a position at ASU as a counselor for disabled students. He was hired to work with blind students and deaf students. After eighteen months, he decided to attend graduate school. He knew that he liked the college environment, and that he wanted to be in a helping profession. Giuliano spoke with the vice president of student affairs. He was told he could get a degree in university administration and work full-time with college students. Giuliano decided it was the type of career he wanted. In the fall of 1981, he entered the master's program in higher education administration.

During his time in graduate school, Giuliano became involved in what he calls real politics. He was the campaign manager for several candidates, one of whom was his roommate, who was elected student body vice president. The following year, Giuliano ran for president and won. Although he was older than most of the students, he always looked younger than he was. Even today, he is so lean and youthful that he could be mistaken for a college student.

In 1983 he finished his master's degree and was ready to take a job at another university when the ASU president and vice president asked if he would consider working with student leaders and teach a leadership class. He applied for the job and was hired. Over the fourteen years that Giuliano has been associated with ASU, he has held seven different positions, all of which he was asked to apply for. After serving as director of the alumni association and associate executive director of university relations, he is now director of federal and community relations. He still teaches the leadership class.

In 1989 while doing community outreach for the alumni association, Giuliano was asked by several friends to think about running for city council. "They told me that everybody knew me from being student body president and president of the Tempe Kiwanis Club," said Giuliano. "My first reaction was to say no. I then remembered that I teach my students that you don't get anywhere in life if you don't take risks, and here I was afraid to take a risk. Besides, my friends said that we'd have lots of fun, but not to worry because I wouldn't get elected."

Giuliano's supporters knew a good candidate when they saw one. He was well known by people in business, nonprofits, and government. In addition to working on the ASU campus and with the alumni association and being past president of Kiwanis, he had been president of a civic program called Tempe Leadership and served on numerous nonprofit boards. He knew the old-timers as well as the recent college graduates. Moreover, he had a positive message that appealed to voters. "I wasn't running mad, I wasn't running angry," he stated. "I was running because I loved Tempe." The theme of his campaign was "positive leadership for the future."

There was one nagging problem: Sooner or later he had to come to terms with his sexuality. "This was another area where I was a late bloomer," he explained. "I think that people acknowledge to themselves that they're gay at different points in their lives. That was the way it was with me. There's the first inclination, but you dismiss it. There's the second inclination, which you dismiss a little bit less. After a while, you realize you can't dismiss the inclinations anymore, that it's sort of the way it is."

The first time Giuliano had a fleeting thought he might be gay was as an undergraduate. He ignored it because he was too socially immature and lacking in self-confidence to do anything about it. By his late twenties and early thirties, he began to understand what was going on. When the opportunity to run for city council arose, he rationalized that if he got elected, then he would have even less time to deal with his sexuality.

In Tempe, city council candidates run citywide, not by districts. Any candidate who wins a majority in the primary is automatically elected. When Giuliano ran in 1990, ten candidates, including three incumbents, competed for four seats. Two of the incumbents received more than 50 percent of the vote to avoid a runoff. To the surprise of city hall observers, Giuliano came in third, ahead of the remaining incumbent. In the general election, Giuliano and the incumbent captured the last two seats.

Because elections in Tempe are not held in conjunction with presidential or gubernatorial races, they are relatively low-key and inexpensive affairs. Out of Tempe's 160,000 residents, there are 85,000 voters, of which only 10 to 15 percent vote in the city's nonpartisan elections. The average cost of a council campaign is approximately $12,000, which is what Giuliano raised and spent. Tempe is overwhelmingly white, with 80 percent of the residents being Caucasian and 11 percent Hispanic. Like Arizona as a whole, registration is predominantly Republican, 55 percent, and 43 percent Democrat. Neither the mayor nor the city council posts are considered full-time jobs with full-time pay, although similar to their counterparts in cities across the nation, the officeholders often put in a full day's work.

One of the first constituents' meetings that Giuliano held after his election was with members of Arizona's gay and lesbian political organization, the Human Rights Fund. They were also the first gay activists Giuliano had ever met. As is standard practice among these groups, they called Giuliano to request a time when they could get acquainted. After their call, Giuliano remembered thinking to himself, "What could their issues be? I'm just a city councilman. I'm not in Washington, DC." Then he got nervous. "Are they calling me because they know? Are they calling me because they can tell? What's going on with all of this?"

As it turned out, there was no hidden agenda. The meeting, which took place at the Coffee Plantation coffee shop, was cordial and relaxed. A variety of issues were discussed, including the possibility of the City of Tempe having a nondiscrimination ordinance. But most important for the gay leaders and Giuliano, the meeting was an opportunity to get to know each other.

When Giuliano got back to city hall, he asked the city manager if the city discriminated against gays and lesbians in hiring and promotions. He was assured they did not, even though no written policy existed. To make certain that all employees were aware of the policy, the city manager agreed to send a memo reaffirming the city's position. Afterwards, Giuliano was surprised by the reaction that gay leaders and other council members had to his involvement. "They saw it as a really big deal and gave me a lot of credit, even though I didn't see it as much of anything," he recalled.

Now in his mid-thirties, Giuliano no longer dismissed the clues that he was gay. As he put it, "I finally knew what the story was. In one sense, I was dealing with it, but in another sense, I wasn't. Privately, I now had some gay friends, some of whom were friends from college and who probably knew I was gay but never put any pressure on me." Dating, however, was problematic, not only because there was AIDS to worry about, but because Giuliano had no experience with relationships. "I knew I wasn't in the Ozzie and Harriet mold," he said, smiling, "but I wasn't sure what my other options were."

Being in the public eye, Giuliano realized that people would eventually learn he was gay. As he became more comfortable with himself and with being around gay friends, he assumed that people would either figure it out or he would disclose it. But, as with many gay people, Giuliano did not think his sexual orientation was a big issue; moreover, he did not want to make it one. Regardless of what happened, he ruled out ever calling a press conference to talk about his private life. He was not the type of person to discuss personal issues in a public forum.

As Giuliano began to think about a second council term, the current mayor, who had served for sixteen years, decided to step down. Giuliano's core support group encouraged him to seek the more powerful post. "I figured it had been fun serving on the council, but if I was going to do this, I might as well really do it," he said. "If I win, fine; if I don't, that's fine, too. If I don't win, then maybe I could get a life and do things outside of public service."

For his 1994 mayoral campaign, Giuliano produced a twenty-page pamphlet outlining his positions on issues facing the city. Even though some people told him no one would read it, he went ahead with it because he felt people needed to know his stances. The piece was called "Bridging to the Future." "I wanted people to think in terms of the next generation of leadership in Tempe," he stated. "I felt that of all the candidates I was the one who could help build that bridge to the future."

Besides Giuliano, two former council members ran for mayor. In the March primary, Giuliano came in second, 110 votes behind the leader. The two candidates met head-on in the May runoff.

Given all the segments of the community that Giuliano's life intersected, it was not surprising that he enlisted scores of volunteers to run a strong grassroots campaign. As important, he was able to learn from his mistakes in the primary. One part of town in which he did not do particularly well was a retirement community called Friendship Village. His mother, a seasoned veteran from her husband's campaigns, called these voters herself. "We used Mom because it was a more personal approach," Giuliano said. It was a successful strategy. Whereas he lost the precinct in the primary with 289 votes, he won it with 462 in the runoff.

The *Phoenix Gazette*, which had endorsed Giuliano in the primary, once again supported him. They wrote, "Neil Giuliano offers Tempe a balance of youth and experience, of solid accomplishment and well-directed ambition. His candidacy promises a 'bridge to the future,' bringing in new elements to municipal politics: An even closer relationship with Arizona State University, which dominates the city, the younger generation of adults who remember him as an ASU student in the 1970s, and the larger political arena he entered as a community representative of the university. [His opponent] would be a fine mayor. But Mr. Giuliano might be an outstanding one."[1]

In a race that was expected to be close, Giuliano won handily—6,919 to 5,819 votes. He spent $51,000; his opponent, $58,000.

In politics, where some closeted gay people may take antigay positions to remain above suspicion, it is to Giuliano's credit that as a council member and as mayor he never shied away from issues dealing with the gay community. As mayor, he has taken the lead on a variety of policies: creating a controversial human relations commission, designating a hate crimes liaison officer in the police department, and approving a resolution supporting diversity awareness. In addition to favoring the fee waiver for the gay pride festival, he issued one of the few proclamations throughout the state for gay pride week. (The mayor of Phoenix issued one, too, but called it "Tolerance, Anti-Discrimination, and Non-Hate Week.") Giuliano acknowledged that his life might have been different had he never taken a stance on these issues, but added, "That's irrelevant. Other people could think whatever they wanted about me. If I was in the closet, that was my business. But all along the way, I still had to live with myself."

*   *   *

When Giuliano returned home from San Diego with the fundamentalists' threat occupying his mind, one of the first people he called was six-term Republican Congressman Jim Kolbe of Tucson. Earlier in 1996, the fifty-six-year-old Kolbe had incurred the wrath of the gay left by voting for the Defense of Marriage Act, a federal bill that allowed states not to recognize same-gender marriages in other states. When Kolbe learned that he was about to be outed by the national gay magazine, the *Advocate*, he decided "to beat them to the punch." Kolbe's announcement drew substantial media attention, which probably muted some of the coverage that Giuliano might have received. With the departure of Wisconsin's Steve Gunderson, who did not run for reelection, Congress was without a gay Republican until Kolbe unexpectedly joined the ranks.

Kolbe, who is a friend of Giuliano's, offered him good advice. "He told me to be very honest and direct with my supporters, family, and friends. This way they wouldn't be surprised." A month earlier, Kolbe had done the same thing. Just as Giuliano had a ten-day lead time to put his house in order, so Kolbe was given a five-day notice from an *Advocate* reporter. He spent his time phoning people and preparing press statements. Right before the *Advo-*

cate story broke, Kolbe issued his press releases in Washington, then flew home to Tucson to meet with constituents and the local press. Kolbe stated that 97 percent of the calls and letters he received were supportive of him.

Giuliano called his close circle of friends and family to tell them the news. Support was unequivocal. On the Tuesday before the Thursday council meeting, he informed the council members. To a person, they backed Giuliano, saying they would join him at a press conference if he held one. On Wednesday, he spoke to reporters from the *Tribune* and *Gazette*. The other media received faxes. Giuliano was adamant about not giving any television interviews, even though TV crews followed him around for several days. "This is not a big issue to me," he told them, "so I'm not going to treat it like one by letting you do stories about it on TV. Someday, someone saying they are gay will not be a news story at all, so for me there is no interview."

Giuliano's press release is remarkable for how understated the issue at hand is. His being gay is referred to almost as an afterthought. In keeping with his philosophy, Giuliano's focus is on what he had done for the city and what he hoped to do in the future. His statement is as follows:

> Recently, a number of citizens shared their strong opposition to the unanimous recommendation of the City Sponsorship Review Committee and the unanimous City Council acceptance of their recommendation to waive a partial amount of the city fees associated with the 1997 Arizona Gay Pride Festival to be held, as it has been since 1991, at Tempe Diablo Stadium soccer fields. Like other events, this group of citizens met the criteria as a non-profit organization whose event is open to the public, without operational problems and whose proceeds go to other charities. For the rare occurrence when the sexual orientation of event organizers or attendees is known, the City of Tempe does not discriminate based upon this information.
>
> It is unfortunate that some citizens uncomfortable with these decisions have sought to make the issue personal with comments and innuendo and speculation about the personal lives of myself, other council members, and city employees.

Let me state clearly that my private life, although I happen to be gay, or that of any other council member or city employee, is not and will not be a topic for discussion at a city council meeting. Meetings of the council are to conduct the business of the city, not to discuss the personal and private lives of individuals serving either as elected officials or employees.

While I regret that some people have an interest in my private life, I accept that such is a part of elected service. Having lived in Tempe for twenty-two years, since I was eighteen years old, and through my commitment and work as a student leader, volunteer, councilman, vice-mayor, and mayor, I believe the community knows well the quality and content of my public service and leadership for Tempe.

With the end of summer comes a great deal of city activity: advancing the Rio Salado project, neighborhood enhancement programs, our community policing efforts, downtown redevelopment, and transportation issues are just a few of the current topics under discussion. I remain focused on these important issues and will continue to build bridges to a brighter future for all Tempeans.

Despite Giuliano not wanting his sexuality to be big local news, it was. His coming out was the lead front-page story of the *Tribune*. "Giuliano says he's gay; feared 'inquisition'" rang out the headline.[2] In his talk with reporters, it is clear that Giuliano wanted them to know the disclosure was not his choosing. "Some of these people feel the need to expose my private life," Giuliano is quoted as saying. "They're not going to do that because people already know. Partially, they have won, but it's on my terms."

On the night of the council meeting, security was tight. Extra security precautions had been taken in case of trouble. As the start of the meeting approached, large numbers of people began to arrive. By the time Giuliano called the meeting to order, the council chamber was full. Fortunately, it was packed with Giuliano supporters. Although fundamentalists were in attendance and ready to ask each council member and staff member if he or she was gay, for whatever reasons, they decided not step up to the microphone.

*   *   *

With Kolbe's and then Giuliano's announcements, some conservatives began to wonder what was in the water that Arizona Republicans were drinking.

Besides being white and Republican, Kolbe and Giuliano share many things in common, particularly their belief that being gay is not a central part of their character or their political lives. In a 1997 speech before the San Francisco Log Cabin Club—a gay Republican political organization—Kolbe spoke about how being gay is not his defining persona; that he is someone who just happens to be gay. The quandary for Kolbe was how to be a gay Republican congressman without becoming ineffectual on other more important issues. "If I talk mostly about gay issues, do I reduce myself to irrelevance with the Republican brethren and have Republicans everywhere tune out my message on trade, taxes, and a balanced budget?" he asked in his speech. "Conversely, if I speak only about the macro and micro political issues, do I fail to make myself heard as a voice of reason on issues of civil liberties and individual rights for homosexuals and others in our society?" To answer that question, Kolbe discussed Jackie Robinson and how he broke down the color barrier in sports. "Can anyone doubt how Jackie Robinson paved the way for the African-American community? It wasn't because he held frequent press conferences or made speeches, or participated in boycotts, important as those might be at critical moments. It was because he played baseball and played it well. He paved the way for countless other minorities in professional sports, not because he trumpeted his color, but because he played baseball so well." That, then, was how Kolbe saw his new role. Do not focus on gay issues; rather, lead by example.

Giuliano takes a similar tack. He, too, believes that he can increase understanding of gay people by simply doing his job and doing it well. Like Kolbe, he refuses to classify himself by his sexual orientation, or to classify others by theirs. "I don't feel a need to wear the gay/lesbian/bisexual elected official ribbon when I go to conventions," he explained. "Why does someone have to know my sexual orientation to know what I'm all about? If it's a public policy issue that's involved, then fine. But my sexual orientation isn't the first thing that people need to know about me. I certainly don't deny it, nor would I walk away from discussing it, but it doesn't have to be a banner that I wear."

Barbara Jones, the former director of the Lesbian Resource Project, acknowledged that the local gay community does not see Giuliano as having a gay agenda. "He's not that kind of mayor," she said. Although she believes that he has been an effective leader for Tempe, she is disappointed that he has not taken more of a leadership position on gay issues. "I wish he would do more on domestic partner benefits for city employees. He hasn't pushed it as much as I would hope."

For Giuliano, a political moderate, being gay and Republican isn't always an easy fit. He knows, as do many gay and lesbian Republicans, that rather than writing off their party, they can make a bigger difference from inside the walls than outside. "There is no denying that the right wing of the Republican Party is rather anti-gay," he said. "A lot of my Democratic friends say that I should be a Democrat, but that'd be too easy. If I chose not to interact with those people anymore, what influence would I have in changing their perceptions of us?" he asked. "None. In my position, I have the opportunity to influence them. Jim Kolbe and I have done that because we're there; they know us."

For some Republicans, a person's gayness is too blinding to see beyond. The Republican state senator from Tempe is quoted as saying in a newspaper article about Giuliano's sexual orientation, "I just don't think it's something I can get past."[3] Most others have been less rigid. In Michael Lewis's book on the 1996 presidential election, *Trail Fever*, he tells the story of how a staff member ran up to Arizona Republican Senator John McCain with a cell phone and said that the mayor of Tempe had just declared he was a homosexual. "The revelation, in Arizona, could kill a politician," wrote Lewis. "Indeed, it might tarnish a politician too closely associated with the victim. All of the reporters were calling to see what McCain thinks, and McCain doesn't hesitate to tell them. He takes the cell phone and says, 'The mayor of Tempe is a friend of mine. He is a fine man. Who the hell cares if he is gay?' "[4]

Giuliano believes that except for fundamentalists whose views are based on their religious beliefs, McCain's attitude is shared by most of the Republicans he has spoken with. Giuliano knows that while privately many conservative Republicans are comfortable with gay people, it does not always translate into support for public policy. "How do we move from the personal to the political?" he wondered out loud. "That's the dilemma."

The same dilemma exists when it comes to voters who know gay people but are opposed to gay and lesbian candidates. Paradoxically, voters are likely to vote to reelect an incumbent after he or she has come out. This may explain why coming out seldom is a death knell. Examples abound, but the best-known cases are the four U.S. congressmen who disclosed their sexual orientation while in office and continued to be reelected: Gerry Studds, Barney Frank, Steve Gunderson, and Jim Kolbe. Giuliano believes that the reason for society's reluctance to support gay candidates is because homosexuality is so foreign to them. "My own view is that many gays and lesbians thought they might be heterosexual at least once in their lives or tried that lifestyle, so heterosexuality isn't foreign to them. But it's not true the other way around. I think the majority of the population has this overwhelming fear of the unknown. So if people know you by your sexual orientation first, it's going to be hard for them to build a relationship of trust. And people only vote for candidates that they trust."

There may also be a difference in the eyes of voters between candidates who are gay and those who are seen as gay activists. Unless a politician's constituency is overwhelmingly gay, most voters will not support a gay candidate—or any candidate that they view as single issue. Giuliano is quick to stay at arm's length from the activist label. "When I talked to reporters about my coming out, I told them that I am not an activist, I don't consider myself an activist, and I don't think I will become an activist," he said, shutting off all possibilities that he is likely to have a change of heart. His position draws no arguments from local gay leaders. As Bill McDonald of the Arizona Human Rights Fund told Giuliano after his announcement, "We don't need you to be an activist. There's enough of us already. We just need you to do your job as mayor."

*   *   *

Business at city hall has gone on pretty much as usual since all the commotion. Giuliano remains focused on development of the city's recreational lake, resolving downtown parking issues, and creating stronger neighborhoods. "My detractors and opponents say that I have this new special-interest agenda, but that is clearly not the case," he said.

His mother, who had asked him two years ago if he were gay, continues to be very supportive. "I told her about all the threats I've been getting," he said. "We have extremist groups in Arizona that feel there shouldn't be a mayor who's gay. She's more concerned about my safety."

Giuliano, whose church is solidly behind him, has had his religious beliefs strengthened because of the ordeal. "For me, a real walk in my faith occurs when there is a challenge," he said. "There have been other people of the same faith who no longer accept me or feel I can no longer make a contribution because of my sexual orientation. That's just reality and I have to deal with it, but I think it's too bad."

It has not been all trial and tribulation, though. Some fun has been had along the way. When the 1997 U.S. Conference of Mayors convention was held in San Francisco, Mayor Willie Brown asked Giuliano if he would present the city proclamation for the annual San Francisco Lesbian and Gay Film Festival. Giuliano, who had never been to the Castro Theater before, was blown away by the huge crowd in attendance and the reception he received. He remembers that when he was introduced as the openly gay mayor of Tempe, the place went crazy. When the star of the movie, Alexis Arquette, spoke, he commented on how he had never followed politics before but he might start if he could just get a date with the mayor. Several days later Willie Brown joked about what a big splash Giuliano had made in the city.

Aside from come-ons from gay Hollywood actors, however, Giuliano's life has changed very little. His social life still revolves around being an elected official. "When I don't have activities involving my being mayor, I have some close friends that I do things with," he stated. "But I'm not sure anyone could really date me. I'm always going to events or giving speeches rather than spending time with just one person. Who would put up with that? I'm not totally opposed to dating, but I just don't know how it would really fit. Besides," Giuliano added, "no one ever perceived me as anything but being single. It wasn't men, it wasn't women. It was just Neil. Which is probably what it still is," he said, laughing.

Whether dating or not, there are psychological benefits to coming out. Bill McDonald, who has known Giuliano for several years, feels that Giuliano's actions have had a positive impact not only on Tempe but on Giuliano himself. "I think he's more at ease with himself, that's he's a happier guy," he said. "He can lead a more normal life now."

Although his work at Arizona State University coordinating governmental affairs does not involve counseling, Giuliano hears a knock on his door about once a week from a student who wants to talk. He is also asked to speak at the gay student group on campus. His message is one of letting the students know that while the community needs people who will be frontline activists, it is also all right for them to simply voice their own opinions and live their lives within their own comfort level. "Over time," he tells them, "they may evolve one way or the other—they may be officers of this group today and consider themselves big activists, but in five years they may have settled down in a career and relationship and may not have that role. They'll make the biggest difference when they're comfortable in the role they're in. My advice is, 'Don't try to be something you're not.'"

Giuliano also cautions young gay people to refrain from sexual activity until they're really sure of their emotions and sure of themselves as people, just as straight kids should. He knows how difficult that is, but thinks it is better in the long term for health reasons and for their own emotional well-being. How mature they are about this depends on their family environment and how supportive their parents are. "I was lucky," he said. "I grew up with really supportive parents."

One rewarding aspect of Giuliano's coming out has been the number of people who come up to him to tell their own stories. "As an openly gay official, I never thought that I would be in a situation to have an impact on families," he stated. "I can control their water rates; I can control their property tax; I can control when their garbage will be picked up. But to be able to have a positive influence on a family makes me feel very good."

He recounted one story of a woman who wrote him and said that her son, who was born and raised in Tempe, was gay. After graduating from high school, he did not think he could go to college there. And after he graduated from college, he could not move back because he would not be comfortable living there as a gay man. "At the end of her letter," Giuliano commented, "she said that she wanted me to know that she called her son and told him he could come home to Tempe because now we have a mayor who's gay."

Chapter 10

Working for a Fair and Equitable Society: U.S. Shadow Representative Sabrina Sojourner

In elections in which few voters know much about the candidates on their ballots, having a name that resonates can be a great asset. Sabrina Sojourner, the shadow representative from the District of Columbia, believes that she has such a name. "Isn't it wonderful?" she asked, a wide grin passing over her face. "People told me after my last election that they voted for me because they liked my last name."

The stock of Sojourner's name rose exponentially when the Pathfinder spacecraft landed on Mars this summer, and its land rover, Sojourner, captured the imagination of the country as it crawled over rocks on the planet's surface. According to *The New York Times*, the rover received its name from a fifteen-year-old Connecticut high school student who submitted it for an essay contest. The student was writing a report on Sojourner Truth, a former slave who took to the road to preach emancipation and women's rights, when her teacher gave her a contest entry form. She chose the name for the land rover because of the harsh conditions that Sojourner Truth experienced during her years as a slave and when touring the country speaking for emancipation.

Sojourner Truth and Sabrina Sojourner share many things in common besides a name. Just as Sojourner Truth spoke out against slavery, Sabrina Sojourner travels the country talking about civil rights, racism, homophobia, and multiculturalism. Just as Sojourner Truth lectured on granting women and African Americans full rights as citizens, Sabrina Sojourner works for federal voting rights for Washington, DC, residents.

Sojourner, who is 5′5″ with stunning black eyes and distinctive white streaks in her black hair, is often referred to in the gay press as the only openly African-American lesbian elected to the U.S. Congress. That she is included along with Barney Frank, Gerry Studds, Steve Gunderson, and Jim Kolbe comes as a surprise to some gay historians who have never heard of her. Although it is true that Sojourner is a U.S. Representative from Washington, DC, she is an unseated or shadow representative, meaning she is not recognized by Congress as an official member.

DC has no congressional representation because the Founders wanted federal—not state—control over the seat of the new national government. Since it is not a state, the district does not have the representatives to which it would otherwise be entitled, even though it has more people than Alaska, Wyoming, or Vermont, and has about the same population as Delaware, or North or South Dakota.

Suffrage for DC residents has been slow in coming. It was not until 1961, with the ratification of the Twenty-third Amendment, that they could even vote for president. Ten years later, Washingtonians were granted permission to elect a nonvoting delegate to the House of Representatives; in 1973, they were given the right to vote for the mayor and city council. The creation of the three shadow representatives was approved by voters and was modeled after a plan designed by Tennessee in 1796 to achieve statehood.

Sojourner was elected to her position in 1994, winning 82 percent of the vote. Her main—and actually only—official responsibility is to lobby for the district to become the nation's fifty-first state, to be called New Columbia. To build support for her cause, she regularly speaks before groups in DC and around the country detailing how undemocratic the laws are that govern the area. "Colonialism is alive and well in the district," she said. "Even though we don't elect any of the 535 members of the House and Senate, they dictate everything that we can and cannot do. Congress can change any law that the DC government passes; it can change any budget item. This violates every aspect of self-determination." She has found that when people understand the issues, they are more apt to favor statehood.

Sojourner believes that lesbians, gays, and other progressives would support DC's position more actively if they understood what was at stake. For instance, statehood would result in the election of a liberal to the house and two liberals to the senate. These members of Congress would have voted in favor of a 1996 federal bill to prohibit workplace discrimination based on sexual orientation and would have voted against DOMA, the Defense of Marriage Act.

"We were the first city in the country to become a majority black city," explained Sojourner, referring to a finding from the 1960 census. "Today, we are 85 percent people of color and 85 percent Democratic. This is precisely the reason why the District of Columbia is discriminated against." Political observers agree that the real objection to statehood by Republicans and conservative Democrats are the three liberal Democrats who would surely be elected. This argument is hard to refute since one of their new colleagues would most likely be Sojourner herself.

*   *   *

Sojourner was born in Texas in 1952, but her family moved to San Jose, California, when she was two. Growing up in the Bay Area, she was exposed to the political unrest of the 1960s. There were protests at her high school against the Vietnam War, and many students carpooled to nearby Stanford and U.C. Berkeley to participate in campus demonstrations. Several students she knew were beaten when protesters took over People's Park in Berkeley.

Amid all the political activity, Sojourner excelled in academics. As a student, she fell in love with words and the arts, especially theater. She read all the great playwrights and was introduced to black writers. She became active in competitive speech and debate.

After graduating from high school, she attended Stanislaus State University in California's Central Valley. This allowed her to be away from the Bay Area without totally severing ties with her family. While at Stanislaus, she ran for a student body office but lost. This led her to being appointed to several student/faculty committees. Her life took a dramatic turn the end of her freshman year when, at age eighteen, she got married. "The relationship stabilized things in my life," she stated, then added, "until he started beating me." Her son, Chris, was born a year later when she was nineteen. The marriage lasted two and a half years.

It was a particularly rough time for her. "There was a lot of emotional struggle for me during that period," she reflected. "I was raising a child, trying to get an education, trying to figure out my marriage, trying to deal with what happened to me as a kid. At one point I just said, 'to hell with it,' and literally in the dead of night left my husband, left Chris with him, and moved to Santa Barbara." In the fall of 1974 she enrolled in U.C. Santa Barbara. Her son joined her a year later.

Her time at U.C. Santa Barbara was filled with joy and new experiences. She met many people of color with whom she shared similar interests. Her small group of friends worked to bring talented black artists and musicians to campus. "It really jelled my understanding and my belief of how politics and art can work hand in hand to make changes in people's lives," she said.

Two important events happened for her in 1976: She graduated from college, and she came out as a lesbian. "For several years, I thought I was bisexual," she acknowledged, "but I decided I really wanted to be with women." She moved back to the Bay Area and settled in the East Bay. She became involved with women's groups and was active in founding the San Francisco Women's Building, organizing the first violence against women's conference, and planning several black lesbian conferences. She worked with such people as Margaret Sloan, Pat Parker, Gwen Craig, Brandy Moore, Holly Near, Meg Christian, and Margie Adams. "Many of us were neighbors," she said. "It was a very exciting time for all of us."

Another person with whom she worked closely was Harvey Milk. "Before I moved back to the Bay Area, I got to know him through the films he had done with the American Film Institute," she remembered. "My favorite is still *Rhinoceros*. He was a very good actor. Harvey and I had a connection because we both came from the theater and saw the importance of the arts. He made a point in coming to my theatrical performances."

This was the first time that Sojourner thought about running for office. "The leftist, progressive movement had finally come of age in 1977," she stated. "Harvey ran for supervisor and won. George Moscone ran for mayor and won. Ron Dellums was elected to Congress. It was all unbelievable. Then there were all the devastating events in 1978: the Jonestown Massacre and the assassinations of Milk and Moscone. This all occurred within ten days of each other. It took the whole city several years to recover."

The last conversation Sojourner had with Milk was the summer before he was killed. They talked about her running for office in the East Bay or moving to San Francisco and running there. "He was the person who planted the bug in me," she said. "I wasn't at a point where I was ready, though. I thought that if I went to law school, then I would be better prepared for politics. I got accepted at University of Missouri Law School in Kansas City. Shortly after I moved there, I decided I didn't want to think the way that lawyers think, so I left."

After living in Kansas City for several years, she moved to Atlanta. During her six years there, she worked with the African-American political community. She also used part of the time as a hiatus to do some much-needed writing and thinking. "I knew that before I could be public about who I was, I had to resolve some issues from my childhood," she said.

Sojourner believes it was fate that brought her to DC in 1990. A recession had hit Atlanta, and when she was offered a job in DC to work with the National Organization of Women as director of its diversity program, she accepted. Later, she was the legislative aide to Congresswoman Maxine Waters, an African American from Los Angeles. Since then, her main source of income is as a self-employed management consultant. She works with private and public organizations to develop appropriate means of addressing social and organizational issues that impact employees, such as diversity and multiculturalism.

The nation's capital is where Sojourner finally succumbed to the call to hold public office. From 1992 to June 1996, she served as an ex officio member of the DC Democratic State Committee, and in May 1996, she was elected by voters as an at-large member to the committee. Then, several friends in the Democratic Party asked if she would run for shadow representative. Initially, two other Democratic candidates filed for the seat, but they eventually dropped out. She spent $25,000 in the runoff against a Republican opponent.

Sojourner admits to loving DC and working in politics. "If you're a political junkie, you can get your fill in Washington," she said, smiling. "Local politics, national politics, international politics, politics of the economy, politics of health care, social justice. You name it. Whatever politics you like, it's here." Stating the obvious, she added, "I'm definitely in the right place."

*   *   *

It has taken many years for Sojourner to come to terms with what happened to her as a young girl. She was nine when her father began to sexually abuse her; the abuse ended when she turned fourteen. In an emotionally powerful narrative poem entitled, "I Think I Was Nine When It Started," from her book, *Psychic Scars and Other Mad Thoughts*, Sojourner traces the beginning of the abuse by her father: "It was a weekend day. I think a Saturday. Late summer? Early fall? I don't know. You see, I've never tried hard to remember. I've always worked hard to forget that time."[1]

Understandably, Sojourner did not know how to stop the abuse. Ordered by her father to remain silent, she was afraid of telling her mother because it would break her heart to know the truth; moreover, her sisters might turn against her if their father went to jail. "I didn't want to be responsible for that. I didn't want to be the one to turn my whole family upside down. He must have drilled that into me."

For most of her early adult life, Sojourner did not reveal that she was a survivor of sexual abuse. "I was always afraid people wouldn't like me if they knew the truth about me—about me and my father," she wrote. "Sometimes, I still feel that way. I know that sounds silly. But it's true. He always referred to it as *our secret*."[2] Only in the last ten years has Sojourner understood the price she paid by being silent. "I knew keeping it a secret was not helping me," she explained. "I now understand how secrecy can kill us. Whatever the secret is—be it HIV disease, sexual orientation, cancer, madness in our families, depression—it will kill us if we permit it." Eventually she did tell her mother, who claimed she suspected nothing. Then, her mother went into denial. "She just totally would not hear me," Sojourner said.

Years later, Sojourner was able to confront her father about the abuse, but as far as she can tell, he has not been repentant. Although she can't forgive him, she realized that to maintain her anger would only continue to make her his prisoner. "I have forgiven him in that I have made peace with whatever hold he had on me," she said.

As a survivor of child abuse, Sojourner experienced several of the common pathologies that accompany child abuse, including a suicide attempt. Without parental support, she felt cast adrift. Each problem she faced seemed insurmountable because she had no one to turn to. In her narrative, "Black People Do Not Commit Suicide," she poignantly wrote, "Being black in the racist United States and not having a family is like a ship with no home port. There is no place from which to take off and no place to land."[3]

Sojourner knows that suicide is a taboo subject for her to raise because of the belief in the African-American community that it is a problem for whites. In her narrative, she discusses the prevalence of the problem in her community, mentioning that drug and alcohol abuse are a type of suicide as well. As to the reason for the high rates: "It's hard living the life we live. White people commit suicide all the time over emotional stress, financial stress, job stress, and stress stress. We have to deal with all that plus the stress of racism. And many of us are dealing with the stress of homophobia, sexism, religious intolerance and more in addition to all that other stuff— it's a wonder more of us do not commit suicide."

Another manifestation of the child abuse was the development of an eating disorder. In "Loving Us Both," a narrative addressed to her mother, Sojourner states how the issues she has with food stem from being emotionally rejected. "I binge in a desperate attempt to recreate some sense of being cared for by you, to ease the aching knot inside, to let my little girl know that she is loved. I purge because I don't see myself as worthy of the caring."[4] As Sojourner's self-esteem increased, her self-destructive behavior stopped. "I want to be visibly proud of who I am and whom I love," she continued. "I want to be more: more caring towards myself and other people; a better mother to my wonderful son. I want to have successful and caring friendships, including a loving/friendship/partnership with another woman. I want to be a successful teacher, writer, and filmmaker. I want to live a rich and full life."

Because of her childhood, Sojourner enjoys helping young people who, like herself, had a tough start. "I think it's really important for adults to talk about the problems they had as kids," she said. "Often, those of us who have survived hardships are reluctant to share our experiences. In so doing, we're doing a disservice to kids. They don't gain from our knowledge in how to take care of themselves when they've been discriminated against or abused in some way."

Recently, Sojourner was asked to speak to a group of high-risk teenagers who were completing a specialized program. She consented on the condition that she could present a nontraditional keynote. Rather than give the standard "Yeah, I know it's rough to be a kid" speech, she wanted them to know she could empathize with them because of her own situation. "I told them that I knew about sexual abuse, that I had to deal with it when I was young," she recalled. "I shared this because I wanted them to know you could put terrible experiences behind you. I ended by saying that the secret to being a happy and healthy adult is knowing that the things that hurt you as a child can never hurt you again; that what brought you joy as a child can be built upon and improved as you grow older."

Many of Sojourner's personal issues are past her now, enabling her to focus on her consulting business, her writing, and her politics. Moreover, their resolution has allowed her to run for public office without fear of being exposed. "There's nothing for anyone to dig up about me because I talk about the worst things that anyone could know," she said with a trace of defiance. "That's why being an out lesbian and a survivor of child abuse who is dealing with Congress and defending the District of Columbia is the right place for me now."

* * *

As an African American, lesbian, feminist, single mom, and political activist, Sojourner knows what it's like to be considered different by society's standards. Although other people have wanted to compartmentalize her, she has resisted, refusing to fit into predetermined molds. "It took me awhile to realize that the best thing I could do is to recognize that my identity is not made up of separate entities," she said. "I'm actually a weave of different things. That's why in my writings I hyphenate terms because they all have equal weight. However, there's really only one hierarchy for me in terms of my identity, which is I'm first and foremost a person of faith. My faith is woven throughout my identities and is the framework that holds who I am together."

Just as she has learned to appreciate and celebrate her own uniqueness, she knows people learn to be afraid of what distinguishes them from others. She believes that society teaches us to exchange our differences for conformity and assimilation. She finds it particularly disturbing when middle-class lesbians and gays put down other people in their community merely because they present another dimension of gay life. "I remember when people thought if the drag queens and the dykes on bikes went away, then everything would be fine. They forget that the reason we even have a movement is because of butch lesbians and drag queens. When they were arrested one night in a bar during a routine raid in New York City, they fought back. It was not the people at a nice, middle class, quasi-closeted club who led that fight."

An ongoing debate in the lesbian and gay community is deciding what the goal of the moment should be. Is it complete assimilation in which a person's sexual orientation is all but irrelevant, or is it to keep a gay sensibility intact while ridding society of homophobia? Sojourner hopes it is the latter. "Many gay people say that they want our differences to be invisible," Sojourner noted, "but there is no way that can happen. We're going after the wrong dream if we try to develop a society where all of our little quirks and talents can't exist."

Too often, Sojourner has seen people in oppressed communities pass judgment on others. She calls this lateral oppression. It occurs, she said, when people oppress others out of jealousy or fear of loss. She defines this phenomenon as "biased attitudes, actions, or inactions toward those with whom we should have some affinity, or with whom we ought to be building alliances." Sojourner offered numerous examples: Female managers and supervisors exhibit lateral oppression when they exploit others in the workforce; middle-to upper-class white gay men and lesbians do likewise when they mistakenly see themselves as the only people in society who are singularly oppressed because of their sexuality; people of color demonstrate it when they participate in the dominant culture's misconceptions and attitudes toward their own and other cultures.

"I was just in Florida where I told white, Latino, and black middle-class Republican gay men that if they were only interested in obtaining gay and lesbian civil rights, then their sights were too low," Sojourner said. "I'm not interested in that. I look at our national organizations, and though we often say our movement is a civil rights movement, there is not a full understanding of what that really means. Often what gets acted out in terms of behavior and planning is going after extensions of privilege as opposed to civil rights for all people."

Sojourner is often critical of gay national organizations when it comes to their lack of involvement in diversity issues. "At the national level, our organizations have demanded the support of other civil rights organizations; however, they fail on a large scale to reciprocate," she stated. "Look at California's Proposition 209, which banned affirmative action in education and in public contracts. I know there were people in the gay community who signed the petitions and voted for it. This stems from racism and hate. If the proposition had been something like Colorado's Amendment 2, they would have been writing letters and protesting. This is not to say that there weren't lesbians and gays fighting against 209, but our gay organizations were not involved in the fight."

Keith Boykin, the executive director of the National Black Gay and Lesbian Leadership Forum works with Sojourner on a variety of issues and has nothing but praise for her commitment to an agenda that encompasses multiculturalism. "It's important to have an articulate, vocal African-American woman who is willing to challenge the gay and lesbian community on issues of race, class, and gender," he said. "She's no shrinking violet. She won't ever back away from taking on a battle, no matter how difficult it is."

Sojourner said that she is working toward the goal of people overcoming their discomforts with those from other groups who are striving for their own rights. Until that occurs, she believes oppressed people will be their own oppressors. "If you're a white, middle-class gay man who is racist, anti-immigrant, and xenophobic, then you're working to keep the door to your own oppression open. The same thing is true about not working on class issues, education issues, or helping at-risk kids. We don't know which of those kids are lesbian and gay. We need to concern ourselves with all of these things because having a future in which we as gay, lesbian, bisexual, transgender, questioning people can live happy, healthy and safe lives is dependent upon transforming the entire society to one where everybody is safe. I'm clear about the type of America I want," she added. "I want a society that is truly fair and equitable for everyone."

Chapter 11

Taking Destiny into Their Own Hands: A Portrait of West Hollywood

The June 15, 1998, West Hollywood City Council meeting was not much different from those in thousands of city halls across America. There was discussion of garbage fees, a report on the new library, an update on the new fire station, and a review of the 1998-1999 budget. The participants looked much like their electoral counterparts elsewhere. The four council members (a fifth was absent) were well dressed and presented themselves professionally. They listened politely when members of the public and administrators spoke.

But the items under "Announcements" were anything but typical. The mayor mentioned that the next city-sponsored same-gender commitment ceremony would be June 27, the Saturday of Gay Pride weekend. He reported on the upcoming "Walk Against Hate" and encouraged people to read the city's pamphlet "Know Before You Go" about protection against hate crimes. Then members of the audience spoke on such matters as the thirtieth anniversary of the Metropolitan Community Church, the dedication of new AIDS panels, and the commendable work of the local Cannabis Club in providing medicinal marijuana to cancer and AIDS patients.

Nor was the budget they adopted characteristic of other cities. Out of an operating budget of $45 million, $3 million will be spent on social service programs, a figure that city officials claim is the highest percentage per capita of any city in the United States. This includes funds to support a wide array of programs, such as day care and in-house services for seniors and AIDS patients, a preschool, job placement, legal aid, mental health, and homeless services. This is in addition to the city's extensive recreational and affordable housing programs. Near the end of the almost five-hour meeting, the council adopted a noncontroversial ordinance that added "gender identity" to its already landmark nondiscrimination policy.

Budgets, garbage, same-gender ceremonies. West Hollywood, once dubbed the "gay city" and "gay Camelot," has matured into a well functioning, socially responsible city that strives to meet the needs of its 37,000 inhabitants. And while the council recently has placed more emphasis on infrastructure and routine services, it is still a place where rainbow flags fly freely down Santa Monica Boulevard, where 300,000 people come to enjoy the Gay Pride Parade and Festival, and where a majority of the council is gay, the only such city on the planet. For any activist who dreams of a time and place where gays and lesbians wield political power on an equal basis with other segments of the population, attending a council meeting can instill a sense of pride for all that the gay movement has accomplished and for all the hopes and dreams still to be fulfilled. If gays and lesbians can govern effectively here, then they can anywhere. That is the promise and challenge of the West Hollywood experiment.

*   *   *

For anyone unfamiliar with the story, West Hollywood did not become a city until 1984, when voters approved a ballot measure establishing cityhood. Until then, West Hollywood was an unincorporated "pocket" of Los Angeles County. This meant that along with seventy-seven other pockets that were not part of any city, services such as police, fire, zoning, and traffic were operated by the county. If citizens had complaints, they had to go to the five-member board of supervisors, who had jurisdiction over all unincorporated areas.

Because West Hollywood was not a city, it could not adopt its own policies and procedures. If residents wanted certain laws passed—antidiscrimination policies or rent control ordinances, for instance—the county supervisors had to vote on it. If West Hollywood residents favored a particular policy but people living in other pockets did not, the legislation would not be approved because it would be effective in all unincorporated areas.

Because 90 percent of West Hollywood's residents rent—a majority of them seniors—there was overwhelming support for strong controls to safeguard against rapidly increasing costs. But supervisors, who were probusiness and prolandlord, were opposed to passing a tough countywide ordinance. Although a rent control policy was on the books, it was full of loopholes. Moreover, it was scheduled to expire in 1985, which meant economic disaster for many.

Ironically, its unincorporated status was the reason why West Hollywood was where thousands of gays and lesbians chose to live. Because West Hollywood was not a part of any city, it did not have its own police force. The area was patrolled by the Sheriff's department, which had a tradition of being more lenient in policing bars and cracking down on alternative lifestyles than the more conservative and uptight Los Angeles Police Department. In the 1920s and 1930s, the area was known for its gambling, prostitution, and speakeasies; later, the stretch of Sunset Boulevard in West Hollywood became known as the Sunset Strip. In the 1960s, the hippies arrived. In the 1970s, as gays and lesbians began moving into the many high-rise apartment buildings located throughout the 1.9-square-mile area, gay bars and gay-owned businesses flourished. Although there were still raids on gay bars, gays and lesbians were less harassed there than elsewhere.

By the late 1970s and early 1980s, the gay and lesbian political movement was growing, and gay people were demanding more rights from their government. This included the freedom to mix socially with other gay people in bars and other establishments without fear of harassment. But because West Hollywood residents were such a small percentage of the county population, they had minimal representation and no political clout.

As fate would have it, in 1983, gays, lesbians, renters, and seniors found the right cause at the right time to achieve each of their goals: formation of a new city. It is a credit to the leadership of each group that rather than being leery of the other's motives or fearful that their addition would jeopardize the coalition's overall status, they banded together because they understood that they needed one another to achieve self-determination and self-governance. The person who brought the groups together was Ron Stone, an openly gay man. In the fall of 1983, he formed the West Hollywood Incorporation Committee, an organization that eventually included the Coalition for Economic Survival (CES) and the Harvey Milk Club and the Stonewall Democratic Club, two gay and lesbian organizations.

CES is a countywide community action group that works in low-income and minority neighborhoods in Los Angeles. It led the fight for the rent control ordinance that was adopted by the supervisors in 1979. In 1983, CES believed that the only way to strengthen the existing rent control ordinance was through a countywide referendum. Voters rejected the ballot measure, even though it passed by more than five to one in West Hollywood, signaling the widespread electoral support residents had for the issue. Because of their grassroots work in the campaign, CES had the seasoned organizers and the political expertise to help conduct the cityhood campaign.

One of the first people to join the West Hollywood Incorporation Committee was a twenty-five-year-old attorney named John Heilman. Heilman was raised in Cleveland, Ohio, and attended Northwestern University. He did not consider himself a typical Northwestern student, whom he described as upper class and preppy. "I was visibly strange," he said, "always wearing outrageous clothes." The six-foot, brown-haired, blue-eyed Heilman took African History and American Studies courses and joined the school's gay and lesbian alliance. After graduating with a degree in journalism, Heilman came west to attend USC Law School and to be in warmer weather.

In 1973, while attending USC, Heilman moved to West Hollywood because he felt it was a physically safer place for gay people to live than Los Angeles. He got involved in politics, becoming cochair of the ACLU's gay and lesbian club and active in the Harvey Milk Club. In 1983, when the idea of cityhood was discussed, Heilman immediately was interested and served on the steering committee.

The State of California has a four-step process that must be followed before an unincorporated area such as West Hollywood can become a city. The first step is gathering the signatures of 25 percent of the registered voters who support cityhood. CES's organizing skills were critical in this effort, with its members helping to obtain 6,573 signatures, 2,000 more than needed. Next, a county agency called the Local Agency Formation Committee conducted an economic feasibility study to determine if the area could support itself. The report came back affirmative: West Hollywood was paying $15 million per year in county taxes but getting only $10 million in services. Thus, the area had a $5 million operating surplus, more than enough to finance the cost of running a city. Third, the County Board of Supervisors had to give its approval to cityhood and set a date for an election. This was done, with the election scheduled for November 1984. The last step was the election itself, in which a majority of the voters had to approve.

The campaign became rather heated at times, with the opposition led by the group Keep West Hollywood United. Composed mainly of landlords and realtors, the opponents touched on antigay and antiwelfare issues in their arguments to have the area remain under county control. But they were simply overwhelmed by the momentum in support of cityhood. Incorporation won by a better than two-to-one margin—10,248 to 5,017.

In addition to voting on incorporation, voters elected a five-member city council. There were forty candidates, seventeen of whom were openly gay. Various groups endorsed slates of candidates, but the organization with the most clout was CES. According to Heilman, who was one of the endorsed candidates, CES made a conscious decision to include people from all demographic groups— gays, lesbians, women, Jews, seniors, and renters. Along with Heilman, their recommended candidates included an eighty-three-year-old grandmother, a twenty-two-year-old male orthodox Jewish urban planner, and Valerie Terrigno, a lesbian, who was president of the Stonewall Democratic Club. These four candidates, along with Steve Schulte, who was best known as a pinup model for Colt Studios, were elected, with Terrigno as top vote-getter.

At the first council meeting, held in a West Hollywood park under the bright lights of television cameras and attended by 1,000 people ready for a party, the council chose Terrigno as mayor, making her the first openly lesbian mayor in the country. (As with most smaller cities in California, in West Hollywood the post of mayor rotates yearly among the council members.) Their first legis-

lative actions were to order a moratorium on development, tempo-
rarily freeze all rent increases, and pass an ordinance banning antigay discrimination in employment and housing. In subsequent
months, the council voted to allow gay and lesbian couples to
register with the city, provide domestic partnership benefits to city
employees, outlaw the practice of bars requiring three pieces of
identification as a means to discriminate against certain customers,
refuse to do business with companies with ties to South Africa, and
adopt one of the country's strongest rent control ordinances.

The city council also endorsed an aggressive social service agenda.
Whereas such services are usually the responsibility of county government, West Hollywood spends millions for services through contracts
with nonprofit groups. Part of the reason for this commitment was a
reflection of Heilman's and other council members' philosophy that
cities must do more to care for their citizens. The other reason had to
do with external political and economic events. When the city was
incorporated, federal and state social services were being cut because
of a recession and because of the low priority given to such services by
the Reagan administration. This occurred at a time when a majority of
West Hollywood residents—gay men and seniors, in particular—
needed more, not fewer, services. Any financial surplus the city had
was spent on extensive programs and in-home services for AIDS
patients and seniors. Today, the city spends more per capita on services
for seniors and people with AIDS than any other U.S. city. In addition,
a long list of other programs are funded that deal with affordable
housing, child care, women's health, drug and alcohol abuse, and gay
and lesbian youth, to name just a few.

*   *   *

As the media attention died down, the council started the hard
work of running a city. While council members in other cities have
to contend with an entrenched bureaucracy and time-bound procedures, in West Hollywood the five newly elected officers had the
rare opportunity to create a city in their own image. Said Heilman,
"We all started with an initial feeling of panic as we assumed office.
Suddenly after a grueling campaign, we were faced with the tre-
mendous responsibility of setting up our new city. We soon realized
that we had no resources to carry out our duties. We had no city

manager, no city attorney upon which to build our government. We essentially had to start from scratch."

Heilman stated that the council was committed to creating a first-class city and hiring innovative administrators who could take the city where few had gone before. "When we advertised for positions, we got many qualified people to apply, but we still struggled in the beginning as a city. Now we get awards on how well the city is run."

Behind all the jubilation and groundbreaking legislation, though, a scandal was brewing. Shortly after the election, rumors began to circulate about possible financial wrongdoing by Terrigno. In 1985, accusations were made that she had embezzled money from a federal job referral agency that she administered before her council election. Although she at first denied it, in 1986 she was convicted and sentenced to sixty days in a halfway house and had to repay $7,000. She also resigned from the council. Her conviction took some of the air out of the city's high-flying spirits. "The city was still new, we had gotten all this media attention, and then we had something like this happen," Heilman reflected. "But we did not let it deter us. We kept moving forward, and my colleagues—even though we had been divided in certain respects—came together. It was a difficult period for everyone, but I think we handled it the appropriate way." With Terrigno's departure, gays lost their three-member majority. Although it was a symbolic loss, it did not change the city's progay and prolesbian stance. In its fourteen-year history, the council has never had an antigay member or taken an antigay position. It is Heilman's opinion that no one who is openly antigay would ever be elected in West Hollywood.

Because the original five members were elected simultaneously in 1984, terms had to be staggered thereafter. The council drew straws to see who would serve two-year and four-year terms. Heilman picked a two-year term. He was reelected in 1986, and again in 1990 and 1994. His present term does not expire until 1999 because of a change in the date of the city's elections. In 1990, Schulte chose not to seek reelection, so for the next four years, Heilman was the only gay member. He viewed this period as a fluke. "It just happened," he stated. But Heilman does not think that gays and lesbians vote as a bloc to ensure that only gays are elected. "There's too much diversity and disagreement within our community for that," he laughed.

In 1994, Heilman was joined on the council by gay attorney Steve Martin. Born in 1954 in the San Fernando Valley town of Pacoima, Martin first set foot in West Hollywood while a student at UCLA. "I was twenty-two and some college friends said we should go over to The Odyssey, a gay disco. I mentioned that I had never been to West Hollywood before, and they just laughed and said I should go to the corner of Santa Monica and San Vicente. The next Saturday afternoon we drove there, and I was completely blown away by what was happening. The rest is history. I was coming here for a few years before I moved into an apartment."

Martin was involved in the cityhood campaign, and later served on the city's Rent Stabilization Commission. When Schulte decided not to run for another term, he asked Martin to be his successor. "I was honored by that," Martin stated. He lost by 200 votes. Like many first-time candidates everywhere, Martin had to pay his dues a little longer. Over the next four years, he was involved in a number of city issues, including a ballot measure to oppose building the new civic center in West Hollywood Park, a project supported by Heilman. Martin also served two years as president of the Stonewall Democratic Club, where he helped elect a number of candidates. In 1994, he ran again, this time receiving the most votes.

Heilman and Martin occasionally take different positions on issues, but Martin downplayed any talk of a feud. "We have a normal political relationship," he said. "Just because someone is gay doesn't mean that you're always going to agree with him. When it comes to gay and lesbian issues, we obviously work very closely, and we work on other issues where we have common ground. But it wouldn't be truthful to say there is no rivalry. But there's nothing wrong with that, either."

Martin, who is Filipino, Chinese, and Mexican on his mother's side, described West Hollywood as a "bizarre community" demographically because approximately 86 percent of its citizens are Caucasian. With only 8 percent of its population Hispanic, it has the lowest percentage of Latinos of any city in L.A. County, which has an overall total of 37 percent. "It's a little odd living in West Hollywood," he grinned. "It doesn't feel like the rest of L.A. at all."

Many people who live or travel through West Hollywood probably feel the same way. Along with constant partying that seems to occur on sections of Santa Monica Boulevard, there are a number of demographic differences between West Hollywood and the rest of the world. With its high number of apartment buildings, it is the most densely populated city west of the Mississippi. Also, 56 percent of the residents live alone. Only 4 percent of the residents are under seventeen years of age, compared to twenty-six percent statewide. Half of the residents are between the ages of twenty-five and forty-four.

The city has the highest per capita rate of AIDS in Los Angeles County. As of July 1998, approximately 650 residents have died of AIDS, 350 are living with AIDS, and an estimated 2,700 are infected with HIV. Ninety-eight percent of the AIDS cases are gay or bisexual men, compared to 86 percent in the county. Only 1 percent of the cases are women, whereas it is 6 percent countywide.

But the statistic which receives most of the attention and which makes West Hollywood unlike any other town is the fact that between 35 and 40 percent of its 37,000 residents are gay or lesbian. The story of one gay man's migration to West Hollywood is perhaps illustrative of the arrival of thousands in Southern California.

Jeff Prang was born in 1962 in a blue-collar suburb of Detroit where almost everyone worked in the auto industry. His father was a Ford engineer, and his mother built M-1 tanks for Chrysler. He attended Michigan State University, majoring in international relations.

It was on a cold March morning in 1985 that Prang scraped off the ice on his Ford Escort so he could drive to the airport to catch a plane to Los Angeles. "I landed at LAX. It was one of those particularly clear days where everything was green; it was just amazing. I drove to West Hollywood and saw all these men wearing tank tops and shorts. In fact, I saw more attractive men in that one thirty-minute drive than I had seen in Michigan over several years. It was very captivating." After traveling back and forth between Detroit and Los Angeles on business for two years, he quit his job in August 1987, packed his car, and drove to West Hollywood.

Prang, who was always interested in politics and government, worked on Martin's 1990 campaign, and later joined the West Hollywood Democratic Club, where he was chosen vice president at his second meeting. As he had done in Michigan, he became involved in Democratic Party politics, being elected to a seat on the Los Angeles County Democratic Central Committee. Like Martin, he served on the Rent Stabilization Commission, a necessary stop on the road to electoral office to demonstrate protenant credentials. In addition, he worked for a number of candidates and elected officeholders, among them Kenneth Hahn, the openly gay Los Angeles County assessor. In 1997, Martin asked Prang if he was interested in running for council. He was. Prang ended up spending $48,000 to win his race, a sum he considered high for a town with only 25,000 registered voters, most of whom are Democrats. With his victory, a gay majority was reestablished.

Heilman, Martin, and Prang all attest to the need to run a grassroots campaign in West Hollywood. This involves walking door to door and participating in the numerous forums and debates. Coalition-building was what West Hollywood was founded on, and it remains the key ingredient to electoral success. Martin believes that being gay is not, in and of itself, enough to be elected. Nor is having gay activist credentials enough either, although they are a prerequisite. "You need to have the support of many groups," he said. For instance, Prang received the endorsement of the Sierra Club, the County Federation of Labor, the Peace Officers Association, the

Deputy Sheriffs Association, the Stonewall Democratic Club, and a long list of elected officials.

Lesbians are noticeably absent in West Hollywood governance. Although several women have served on the council since cityhood, Terrigno was the only lesbian. Nancy G. Cohen, cochair of the city's Lesbian and Gay Advisory Council and board member of the Victory Fund Foundation, believes this too is a fluke and that one day another lesbian will win election. "In my opinion, the city council has done what it can to keep the doors open to the lesbian community," she stated. One of the more well-known programs that the city sponsors is Lesbian Visibility Week, a time when the city celebrates lesbian contributions to society and sponsors numerous activities for lesbians. In 1998, the period of lesbian visibility was expanded to a month.

Not only are there fewer lesbians in positions of power than gay men, but lesbians are not as visible on West Hollywood streets. Cohen explained that lesbians tend to hide away and be in their own world. "Many women don't go to bars nor feel a need to be out in a crowd," she said. Cohen also commented that many lesbians view West Hollywood as more of a town for gay men to play in.

All in all, Cohen is proud of what the city has accomplished for lesbians as well as gay men. As for the future, Cohen remarked, "My dream is to have a city where it's neither Boys' Town nor Girls' Town, but it's everybody's town where the bars are mixed with gays, lesbians, and bisexuals. If the bars were mixed, then perhaps we'd all be more united."

*   *   *

Over its fourteen years of incorporation, West Hollywood has been known for innovative—if not controversial—ordinances. Along with protections for gays and lesbians and renters, the city has been on the forefront of many social and political causes. One example is West Hollywood's landmark smoking ordinance that required restaurants to set aside 40 percent of their seating in nonsmoking sections. As more California cities adopted similar policies, the state legislature eventually passed a law prohibiting smoking in all restaurants and businesses. Another example is the city's ban of sales of cheap handguns by commercial dealers. The city spent $250,000 in legal costs defending its gun ordinance. When the courts ruled the measure constitutional, other cities proceeded to enact similar ordinances.

The council is well known for delving into foreign policy. In keeping with its ban on trade with South Africa during apartheid, West Hollywood voted not to do business with companies that conduct business with Myanmar (formerly Burma) because of that country's human rights violations. No such business is known to exist in West Hollywood, but the council believed it was important to take a stand.

The council also serves as a watchdog for antigay sentiments. In 1997, a local television station aired a story about gays and lesbians who turned straight. Many gay and lesbian leaders viewed the story as biased, leading the city council to pass a resolution condemning the station for unbalanced reporting.

Defending the city for taking such positions, Prang remarked, "Our basic job is the delivery of municipal services. That is our primary job. But there are several aspects of my job as well. One is local; the other is to be part of a greater civil rights movement."

Prang stated that some straight people in West Hollywood get frustrated because the council seems to get too involved in gay and lesbian issues. Prang's response to the criticism was, "Yeah, you probably get a bigger dose here than in other parts of the world, but we do it here because they can't do it in other places. What we do here provides inspiration; it provides leadership for others."

Law enforcement is another key area where the city has had an impact beyond its borders. After incorporation, the city took over the contract from the county for police services, despite worries that deputies were not sensitive to gay and lesbian concerns. There was an initial movement to have the city operate its own police force, but economically it made little sense because of the high costs of starting up and running a department. Contracting out remained the best way to proceed. Many other cities in the county arrived at the same conclusion, which explains why the Sheriff's Department's jurisdiction covers one-third more people than the Los Angeles Police Department and more than forty cities.

Because of complaints by citizens over insensitivity and lack of responsiveness to gay concerns, in 1988 the city's Lesbian and Gay

Task Force recommended to the city council that a committee be formed to improve relations between the gay community and the Sheriff's Department. Few thought the department would consent to participate, but the gods must have been watching over West Hollywood because at that moment the captain of the West Hollywood Sheriff's Station was Rachel Burgess, an African-American woman whom many people credit for initiating many of the changes that later took place. According to Nancy Greenstein, the city's Public Safety Administrator during this critical period, the West Hollywood station was where captains who did not quite fit into the system were sent, a situation that applied to Burgess because of her race and gender. It was Burgess who agreed to the department's involvement in the joint city/sheriff committee and who issued the unprecedented directive that any deputy caught making homophobic remarks would receive a three-day suspension.

Through hard work and long hours, the ten-member committee composed of five gay community members and five deputies made monumental changes, although, as Greenstein admitted, "everything was a battle." These changes included instituting gay and lesbian sensitivity training at the Sheriff's Academy and in regular patrol training; changing the wording in psychological tests so gays and lesbians were not automatically "tested out"; screening applicants for antigay bias; adding sexual orientation to the nondiscrimination clause of the contracts the Sheriff's Department signs with all cities; recruiting at gay and lesbian events; and having Sheriff Sherman Block issue a letter saying that his department has a policy against discriminating against lesbians and gays in employment. As a sign of how far the department has progressed, several years ago Sheriff Block began riding in the Gay Pride Parade. These policies, Greenstein pointed out, improved the department's attitudes toward gays and lesbians in all cities, not just West Hollywood.

Because of problems with gay bashing, the Sheriff's Department worked with the city to go into gay bars and distribute brochures informing patrons how to better protect themselves against hate crimes. "The first time we did this people wondered what was happening because they were used to sheriffs coming into the bars to go look into the bathrooms," Greenstein said. "When the deputies said they were there out of concern for the community's safety, 90 percent of the people greeted them warmly."

Another program is a "reverse sting" operation in which male deputies dress in stereotypical gay garb to attract potential gay bashers. "At first deputies said, 'You want us to do what?' but it was actually kind of cute," recalled Greenstein. "One guy went through his mother's jewelry box and used her earrings. Some really got into it. The whole process has been great for community relations because the deputies know what it's like to be called 'fag' and to feel a sense of vulnerability. And gays saw that the deputies' jobs aren't that easy." Because of these and other proactive efforts, hate crimes in West Hollywood have dropped substantially to only ten in 1997, while the number has risen throughout L.A. County.

Where there was once great animosity toward the Sheriff's Department, there is now much support. In the last community survey taken by the city, one of the highest-rated services was law enforcement. This is a remarkable turnaround from 1992 when a referendum to establish a separate police force was narrowly defeated by the voters. Community leaders give much of the credit for the change in attitudes to community activists, the deputies themselves, and to Heilman, who tracked progress on the issue over the years.

Another distinction that West Hollywood has is that it is the only city with an openly gay city manager. Like almost all cities in California and the western states, West Hollywood has what is called a city manager form of government. This means that the council members—who receive a monthly stipend of only $550—are supposed to be part-time policymakers. It is the city manager's responsibility to carry out the policies and to run the day-to-day operations of the city. The city manager is one of the few administrators hired directly by the council, and he or she serves at the will of the council.

Charles Makinney came to West Hollywood as the assistant city manager in 1994 and was named manager in 1996. Previously, he was director of management services for the Portland, Oregon, Police Department. He was interested in the post because he was at the top of his field in Portland and was excited about the innovative programs initiated by West Hollywood. There was another draw as well: the weather.

One of the main differences that the fifty-three-year-old Makinney found between West Hollywood and other cities is that West Hollywood is more hands-on. "My number is listed in the city's directory and people can call me directly. And they don't hesitate to do that," he said, smiling. "This gives West Hollywood a completely different atmosphere. People feel they can call the city manager and get my attention, which is great. It is pretty unusual that in the megatropolis of Los Angeles people can have that kind of contact with their local officials."

Makinney estimated that 30 to 40 percent of the 200 city employees are gay or lesbian. He also stated that it is easy to recruit highly qualified people to fill vacant positions. "Every time we recruit, we get large numbers of gay and lesbian applicants, often from bigger cities such as Chicago and New York, where it might be considered a step down professionally to come here." This view was echoed by Heilman, who said, "Applicants view this as a place where they can work and be open about their lives and not fear retaliation."

One of the most daunting and delicate tasks that confronted Makinney when he arrived was creating a more professional atmosphere within city hall. "When I got here, there was a lot of friendly banter and sexually loaded comments between people. It was fun; it was very gay, very light, and great, but we had to come to the realization that this kind of conduct is not acceptable to everybody," he said. "Also, there were pictures of naked men in people's work stations, and I came from an environment where we wouldn't let male police officers put up pictures of naked women, even on the inside of their lockers. For it to be so different down here, I thought, my God, what is this?"

Makinney soon learned there was a price to pay for the overly relaxed atmosphere. A complaint was lodged from a constituent about being sexually harassed by a gay employee, which resulted in the employee being terminated for cause. The arbitration proceedings that followed split the staff, with about half supporting the employee, the other half favoring management. In the end, the city's actions were upheld by the arbitrator. "After that," explained Makinney, "we did a lot of diversity training and team-building so people understood they had to be more respectful of one another.

The casual comment that maybe ten years ago was okay really isn't anymore. You have as many gay and straight employees who are offended by the traditional gay humor as not, which can be acceptable in a social setting, but this is not a social setting. This is work, and you have to be on a different standard of behavior here. This was a telling moment in the change of the culture of the city." Given the complexities of the problem, it is likely that only a gay manager could have walked the thin line between appreciating gay sensibilities and placing boundaries on it in the workplace.

As for how it has been to be gay and to work for the city, Makinney responded, "It's been terrific. Being gay is so accepted that you just take it for granted that it's part of life. In that sense, it's almost like an ivory tower. But then you go somewhere else and you get the rude awakening that maybe this is not the standard by which others live."

Helen Goss, the city's Public Information Officer, expressed similar sentiments when she said, "I am very spoiled from working here. Several years ago I was invited to speak at Cal Poly Pomona, my alma mater. The kids seemed so suburban, so to the right of all the issues we care about. I remember getting back on the freeway and thinking that I couldn't wait to get back to West Hollywood. I just wanted to breathe in the air there."

Goss stated that she is a better person because of the years she has been employed by the city, mainly because the atmosphere allows for the acceptance of differences among people. She explained that the reasons she went ahead and became a single parent were the policies in place that allowed her to have a child and continue working. Nor did she have to worry about her co-workers being judgmental. "I've seen intolerance and prejudice at other places," said Goss, who is African American. "This organization is very consistent with my value system."

It is Goss's job to guarantee that citizens are part of the decision-making process. "Before they can do that," she stated, "people need to have information. We do a lot of public outreach so citizens can begin to see the intricacies and complexities of the issues."

As to whether the city has been making the right decisions over the past fourteen years, particularly as it applies to allocating an unprecedented amount of money toward social services and in ensuring that government is inclusive and responsive to citizens' concerns, the results from a city-commissioned needs assessment are telling. Consultants were hired to determine how residents rated the importance of various services and to understand how residents viewed their city. The April 1998 findings showed a government remarkably in sync with its inhabitants.

For example, respondents felt that the city was very safe and that governmental services were very good. They complimented the accessibility of city staff and the progressive attitude of city employees. There was a sense of community in West Hollywood, expressed by such phrases as "small town atmosphere" and "community spirit." Many residents appreciated the acceptance of gay or bisexual men, saying that they felt welcome, safe, and free in a gay-friendly city. They believed the city was clean and well kept. Traffic and parking were cited as the two areas that needed the most improvement.

As to the rating of importance of city services, the top five rated services were HIV prevention and transmission information (78 percent); in-home services to assist seniors and people living with AIDS or other disabilities (77 percent); library services (75 percent); programs for at-risk youth (69 percent); and domestic violence services (69 percent).

* * *

The three gay council members were asked if they felt West Hollywood had lived up to its promise and what the lessons were to be learned from cityhood.

Steve Martin: "One of the promises for gays and lesbians in West Hollywood is to have a safe haven and an opportunity to have power within their own community. In that regard, we have definitely lived up to or exceeded expectations. As for being a city for everybody, I think we are on the cutting edge as to how urban government should be. We are showing that we can have a smaller governmental unit that responds to the needs of residents. Governments are not held in high regard these days, and if someone says that West Hollywood is a city that works, then I can't think of a higher compliment."

Jeff Prang: "One of the challenges that all gay and lesbian officials have is to demonstrate that we can do the job well. If we can show that we can run a prosperous, livable city under a gay majority, it should give comfort to everybody who is wondering whether we are going to be just gay council members or council members for everyone. And I think we are demonstrating very clearly that we are council members for everyone."

John Heilman: "This is a small progressive community that took its own destiny in its hands and made a difference. We are a symbol of the gay and lesbian community, but we are also a symbol of what anyone can do if they get involved at the local level. I think we showed people that you can initiate things locally and see them come to fruition. Most people don't get to start a city. We did. It's been exciting to watch our vision become a reality."

Chapter 12

With Each Election Comes a New Spring: Victory Fund Founder William Waybourn

As cofounder and executive director of the Gay and Lesbian Victory Fund from 1991 to 1995, William Waybourn helped elect openly gay and lesbian candidates to public office across America. He did this largely by offering them what they needed most: access to money.

The work of the Victory Fund is critical because elected office is one of the remaining public service areas still closed to lesbians and gays. Out of the 497,155 elected officials nationwide, only 124 are openly gay or lesbian, a statistic that exemplifies the meager electoral inroads gay people have made almost thirty years after Stonewall.

"The next step in the maturity of our movement is to have our own people represent us," said Waybourn. "Blacks, women, and other minorities weren't able to create change until they elected their own people."

Waybourn believes it is essential to have gay and lesbian politicians in office to introduce legislation and develop strategies for civil rights laws that straight politicians cannot or will not sponsor. "In Texas, the Dallas Gay and Lesbian Alliance helped elect a straight woman, but she never wanted to put any gay and lesbian issues to a vote because she was afraid she'd lose," recalled Waybourn, who cut his teeth on Texas politics. "Well, you have to lose some before you win some. If you can't get something on the table for discussion, then you can't engineer any passion on either side of the issue. Only when it's on the table and becomes a controversy can you inflame passions and get people motivated. You may not win the first time, but at least you have the opportunity to mobilize people to get involved."

Waybourn's goal while director was to elect 2,000 gay and lesbian politicians by the year 2000. The 6-foot, blue-eyed fifty-year-old crusader missed his mark, but the gay community has come far since 1991 when there were only fifty-five documented openly gay officials.

*   *   *

When individuals join the Victory Fund, they pledge to contribute $300 annually. Of that amount, $100 goes to cover the cost of operations and $100 to at least two recommended candidates. Members receive periodic mailings that contain information about candidates seeking office. These detailed profiles describe each candidate's background, the demographics of the district, and the odds of winning. Checks are made payable to the individual candidate's campaign and mailed to the Victory Fund. The Victory Fund records the checks and forwards the contributions to candidates.

Oregon State Representative Gail Shibley told the following story about the Victory Fund's support: "After a day of extremely difficult campaigning, I would go home and open my mail. There would be the envelope from the Victory Fund, full of individual checks from people I had never met, many from people in cities where I had never been. These contributions of faith, hope, and financial assistance amounted to more than $20,000. Their support not only sustained me through some of the hardest days of my race, but each one strengthened my resolve to win. And I did."

Shibley's election in Oregon in 1992 helped make it possible to have openly gay George Eighmey appointed to a vacant seat in the Oregon House of Representatives. But perhaps most stunning is that two other state representatives, Cynthia Wooten and Hedy Rijken, came out as openly lesbian. This was a big turnaround for a state that nearly voted to ban legal protections for gays and lesbians. It is also indicative of the dramatic changes that occur when a legislative body has its own openly gay or lesbian member.

Glen Maxey, who ran for the Texas state House of Representatives and to whom the Victory Fund channeled $20,800 in 1992, is another example of the impact a single individual can make in politics. "In Texas, they prefile bills," explained Waybourn. "Before Glen took a seat in the legislature, there were seventy-six bills that were prefiled that were seen as adverse to gays and lesbians. When Glen finished his first term, all seventy-six had been defeated or deferred. During his term, Glen introduced twenty-six bills that were passed or promoted. The difference was not where these legislators stood on gay and lesbian issues; the difference was that they needed Glen's vote. Glen sat on committees that put him in an important position to be able to trade his vote. As head of a committee, Glen could tell his colleagues that if they helped him with his constituents, he'd help them with theirs. This was how he was able to get sodomy out of the Texas penal code, although another legislator put it back in at the last minute."

Getting the nod from the Victory Fund for recommendation is not easy. In addition to being openly gay and supporting several key principles, candidates must demonstrate electoral viability. Candidates are required to answer a long list of questions dealing with their campaign, demographics of the district, polling results, previous campaign experience, consultants, expense and income budgets, fund-raising plan, media strategy, and endorsements. Based on this information, the board of directors decides who will be endorsed.

One Victory Fund rule that has ruffled more than one set of political feathers is that incumbents can be recommended, although they usually are not. In Waybourn's opinion, if someone has already been elected to office, they should know how to raise money. Moreover, incumbents overwhelmingly win reelection. "I don't doubt they need the money," said a pragmatic Waybourn, "and we try to help them as much as we can. But being gay is not much of a factor anymore because they've already won an election as a gay person. We want to increase the number of gay elected officials, not keep it static."

As a sign that Waybourn has had more than one shouting match with incumbent officeholders over this policy, he joked half-seriously, "I'm not saying that incumbents aren't worthy of our support, it's just that there should be an organization to help incumbents."

There are exceptions. If a candidate is targeted by the radical right, comes out as publicly gay after being elected, or runs for another office, then the Victory Fund will recommend him or her to their members. When openly gay Congressman Gerry Studds lost 40 percent of his district due to reapportionment in 1992 and was opposed in the Democratic primary by two millionaires, he was recommended and received $53,000. Likewise, after Rhode Island State Senator Will Fitzpatrick came out publicly after his election, he was recommended for his reelection in 1994 when he was targeted by the radical right.

Waybourn uses Jackie Goldberg, a successful candidate for the Los Angeles City Council in 1993, as a good example of how the Victory Fund enables candidates to be less beholden to special interest groups. "Victory Fund members gave Jackie a little over $17,000, and the *L.A. Times* decided that there had to be something to this, so they called and asked what members expect to get from Jackie and I said 'nothing.' They couldn't believe that, so they took it upon themselves to call, at random, members who had written her checks. The first question was, 'I'm calling about your contribution to Jackie Goldberg,' and almost everyone said, 'Who is she?' They explained, 'She is running for office in Los Angeles and you sent her a check for $100,' and they said, 'I did?' And then they would say, 'You may remember that you gave the money through the Victory Fund,' and they'd reply, 'Oh yes, I gave money through the Victory Fund.'

"The *L.A. Times* couldn't believe that some milk producer in Wisconsin would send a candidate a check in Los Angeles and not expect anything. In fact, most people didn't know who she was, and when the *Times* did its story on raising money for political office, they talked about how this could be the new way of giving; that small donors could have an impact on major elections."

Although Waybourn's focus was on electing more gays and lesbians to office, his eyes were also on training the next generation of gay leaders. To accomplish this, the Victory Fund continues to conduct seminars around the country to teach potential candidates and managers about campaigns. "Why are we waiting for people to walk through the door?" he asked. "We should be out recruiting people. If something happens to a state legislator, we don't have time to get some novice to run for office. We are always being accused of recruiting, so we should do it."

The Victory Fund also published a book, *Out for Office*, edited by Victory Fund staffer Kathleen DeBold. The book covers a range of topics from raising money to fighting homophobia on the campaign trail. Each chapter is written by either a political consultant or an openly gay or lesbian elected official.

*   *   *

Washington, DC, is a long way from Waybourn's West Texas hometown of Matador. He is the youngest of three children, the only son. His parents owned a restaurant where the local buses stopped for meals. They lost the contract in the early 1950s because they refused to require black passengers to eat in the back of the restaurant. The drugstore, which had water fountains marked "colored" and "white," got the new contract. "I learned at an early age not to discriminate against anyone," he said. Waybourn's sexual orientation was not an issue for him when he was growing up. It wasn't until he went to college that he realized he was different. "It just didn't work with women," he said, laughing.

He attended South Plains College from 1965 to 1967. He then transferred to Texas Tech in Lubbock and graduated in 1969 with a BA in communications. While attending Texas Tech, Waybourn began working for the *Lubbock Avalanche Journal* as a sports writer but soon advanced to news editor. In 1972, he was hired by *The Dallas Times Herald* as a business writer. From there, he was promoted to managing editor of the Sunday magazine.

In August 1973, he was going up the stairs in the office with a friend when he passed another employee walking down. He asked his friend if she knew him. She had the complete rundown: His name was Craig Spaulding, recently hired as an artist, married, one daughter. As fate would have it, several months later Spaulding was transferred into Waybourn's department. A romance began. Three years later, Spaulding got divorced and moved in with Waybourn.

Waybourn's start in gay politics began through his friend John Thomas. Thomas, who was involved with the Dallas Gay and Lesbian Alliance, convinced him to volunteer with the organization. Later he was asked to serve on the board. From his work with the Alliance and the gay community center that it operates, Waybourn began to understand the depth of discrimination suffered by lesbians and gays. "It's hard for white gay men to understand discrimination, but I saw firsthand what was happening. I saw lesbians lose custody of their children because they happened to be lesbians. I saw men discriminated against because they were gay. I saw people with AIDS lose their homes. I think that if everyone had to witness that, everything would change tomorrow. It's devastating."

Waybourn also served as a volunteer suicide crisis counselor and learned about the experiences faced by many gay youth. He asked why gays and lesbians were at a high risk of killing themselves, only to learn that there is no support from churches, family, or school to help troubled kids when they consider killing themselves. This results in higher suicide rates for gay and lesbian youth than nongay teenagers.

Over time, Waybourn became president of the Alliance. During his tenure, he helped start the Dallas Gay and Lesbian Alliance Credit Union, which, according to Waybourn, was the first gay credit union in the country. It also issued its own gay credit card, another first.

Waybourn was instrumental in coordinating the national boycott of Philip Morris Corporation and its subsidiary Miller Beer because of a political contribution they made to South Carolina Senator Jesse Helms, an arch enemy of the gay community because of his homophobic politics. A settlement was reached in 1991 when Philip Morris agreed to give $3.68 million to gay and lesbian groups around the country to atone for its sins. Miller Beer is now a large supporter of gay and lesbian organizations, including the Victory Fund.

Waybourn's inspiration for the Victory Fund occurred in November 1990 after Ann Richards was elected governor of Texas against Clayton Williams. Williams had raised $20 million to Richards's $10.5 million. Waybourn was perplexed by the disparity in fundraising until he read that Williams had loaned himself $10 million, meaning Ann Richards had out-raised her millionaire opponent by $500,000. Waybourn then learned that a group called EMILY's List, an acronym for Early Money Is Like Yeast (it makes the dough rise) had given her $500,000 early in the campaign. It became apparent to him that the money had leveraged more money.

In many ways, the Victory Fund is a carbon copy of EMILY's List, whose donors contribute to Democratic, prochoice women candidates for governor, House, and Senate. In the 1992 elections, EMILY's List members contributed $6.2 million to fifty-five candidates, helping to elect four new senators and twenty-one new members of Congress. "We were lucky because the experience of EMILY's List was very useful to us, and we basically just ripped them off. We used information that they had developed over the years," explained Waybourn.

When he learned the importance of EMILY's List in Richards's victory, he called up Vic Basile, who was the former executive director of the Human Rights Campaign Fund (HRCF), a Washington-based gay and lesbian political action committee that donates funds to candidates running for Congress who support gay rights. Basile was intrigued by Waybourn's idea of creating an organization that raised money for gay candidates. Said Waybourn, "I'd helped start up a lot of organizations, and I thought I was just going to help start another one. In fact, I just assumed that the Campaign Fund would run it."

In December 1990, Waybourn bought a ticket to Washington and met with people involved with HRCF. People agreed that a gay organization like EMILY's List was needed, but no one wanted to take on the project. In January, he and Basile went to New York to speak with other gay leaders, where they received the same positive reaction. "These were politically savvy people who understood that the real issue in campaigns is money, not stuffing envelopes," said Waybourn.

The next step came in May when Waybourn and Basile invited twenty-four people to a meeting in Washington to see if they would serve on the board. Twelve agreed. One of the apostles was David Mixner, arguably the most well-known and influential gay leader in America at the time. Mixner was semiretired due to the death of his long-time business partner Peter Scott and was living in Connecticut. People who agreed to serve on the board told Waybourn, "This is your idea. You have the vision, and although we support you, you have to do it."

When Waybourn moved to DC in 1991, he worked out of Basile's Washington home. In July the Victory Fund officially opened for business. "We set out to build a base of support across the country. We asked board members for their mailing lists so we could mail a letter saying what we wanted to do. The letter wasn't very professional because we didn't have a logo. I was surprised at the immediate response. That's where our first 200 members came from. Then we got some major donors to make contributions. That was the first year. We really didn't anticipate doing anything until 1992, but then Sherry Harris came to our attention."

Harris, who was running for Seattle city council, was known to Portland, Oregon, Victory Fund board member Terry Bean. Bean thought that the Victory Fund might be able to help her financially. Waybourn decided to set the Victory Fund's wheels in motion earlier than scheduled. Was he nervous about the results? "Nervous? I was a wreck."

"We had 181 members when we did our mailing for her," he recalled, "and I had a lot of concern because being from Texas and knowing how many people have certain prejudices, I thought, 'A lot of these people are my friends. Would they actually contribute to a black woman running for office in the Northwest?' Forty-one people sent checks in immediately and we immediately gave her $4,000. Then we thought, my God, what if she doesn't win? In this particular case, we were jumping hurdles and could trip at any time. At any time in an organization's infancy, there exists a high infant mortality rate, and little things can be magnified that will kill it."

To the relief of Waybourn, Harris won a slot in the primary and beat a twenty-four-year incumbent in the November runoff. "We ended up giving her $11,000, but the point is that those forty-one people responded immediately. It was the first time I realized that it was going to work.

"Her victory was like a stamp of approval because although we were actually endorsing her, her victory in effect endorsed us. Then suddenly our phone started ringing. People heard about the Victory Fund and it began to grow."

Besides Harris, Shibley, Maxey, Fitzpatrick, and Goldberg, a few other politicians that the Victory Fund helped elect in the early 1990s include Tammy Baldwin to the Wisconsin State Assembly, Sheila Kuehl to the California Assembly, Susan Leal to the San Francisco Board of Supervisors, Ken Cheuvrant to the Arizona House of Representatives, Tim Van Zandt to the Missouri House of Representatives. Craig McDaniel to the Dallas City Council, Tom Roberts to the Santa Monica City Council, Chris Kehoe to the San Diego City Council, Michael Nelson to the Carrboro, North Carolina, City Council, Wally Swan to the Minneapolis Board of Estimate and Taxation, Tom Chiola to the Cook County, Illinois, Circuit Court, Marilyn Shafer to the Manhattan Civil Court, Bonnie Dumanis to the San Diego Municipal Court, and Shelley Gaylord to the Madison, Wisconsin, Municipal Court.

*   *   *

The election of Bill Clinton in November 1992 played a crucial role in the organization's early success. Because of his relationship with Mixner, who was a major fund-raiser for Clinton, Waybourn bet on the right presidential horse. "The gay community was pretty much headed in Massachusetts Senator Paul Tsongas's presidential camp due to his historical representation of our issues. I don't want to belittle what he had done, but it was clear to a lot of people that Tsongas wasn't going to win. Then Clinton come along. No one knew Bill Clinton except David Mixner. David went around the country pulling people into that campaign. I'm a good example. I probably never would have gotten involved with Clinton if it hadn't been for David. David literally got people off their butts and got them involved in a very positive manner for our community."

Waybourn tells the story of Midge Costanza, who, as a Carter advisor, was the highest-ranking gay person in his administration. Although gays played an important role in electing Carter, Costanza was never a strong advocate for gay rights. Waybourn believes that the reason that Carter did so little for the gay community is that he only received input from Costanza.

Mixner, on the other hand, wanted as many gay men and lesbians as possible working in the administration because he believed it was important for Clinton to hear a wide range of views. That is why Mixner supported the Victory Fund's Coalition '93, an organization formed to get qualified gays and lesbians named to administration posts. Coalition '93 was instrumental in the appointment of twenty-two openly gay men and women. "David Mixner could have been the gatekeeper for gay issues, but he chose to open the gate and let in as many people as possible," said Waybourn. "That's why Mixner is so powerful. People owe their jobs to him."

Waybourn believes that Mixner is one of the smartest people in politics. "He has no organization, no constituency, no responsibility, yet you'd be shocked at the influence he has in Washington."

As a sign of the respect that Waybourn earned in Washington, when Clinton issued his now-famous letter stating that human rights should not be determined at the ballot box, he addressed it to Waybourn. The letter, which was widely reprinted in the press, was written to combat the radical right's strategy of placing initiatives on ballots that banned laws protecting gays and lesbians.

A section of the letter read, "Those who would legalize discrimination on the basis of sexual orientation or any other grounds are gravely mistaken about the values that make our nation strong. The essential right to equality must not be denied by a ballot initiative or otherwise." The letter concluded that this was not an issue of "special rights but a battle to protect the human rights of every individual." This wording, said Waybourn, was to call attention to the radical right's big lie about special rights.

The idea for the letter had been Mixner's, who had originally discussed the issue with Clinton. Waybourn, on behalf of other national gay organizations, sent a follow-up letter to President Clinton restating Mixner's request. When the White House called Waybourn to say that the letter was ready, he came to the White House to pick it up.

"When I got there, I had to wait. Whenever a letter goes out under the president's signature, George Stephanopolous or another top aide had to sign a cover sheet that folds over the letter. So, I had to cool my heels outside of George's office because he was on the phone. So, George signed off on it, then the president signed it, and then I got it." What happened next is a good example of the complications that can arise unexpectedly in politics.

As Waybourn was rushing out the door in the West Wing, he glanced at the letter and saw to his surprise that it was written to him. Waybourn, who knows a land mine when he sees one, turned around and told a presidential aide that the letter needed to be changed by having it addressed to all groups. The aide looked at him as if he were crazy, adding, "You got to be kidding!" Waybourn said that addressing the letter to the Victory Fund and not to any other gay organization might cause jealousy. "I told him that I wasn't happy, that he wasn't doing me any favors. He said that if I wanted the letter I had better walk out of there." So he left, feeling uncomfortable about how the other groups would react to the letter being addressed to him only. When he got back to his office, he called the other groups and told them what had happened. None of the groups seemed upset. They said they understood how the confusion could have happened.

The issue that erupted when Clinton first took office and which was still festering while Waybourn was at the Victory Fund was that of gays in the military. Waybourn believes that one reason it was such a disaster for all parties is that there was no preparation to handle the crisis. "The whole issue was very costly. Basically, it took a new administration and dropped it on its head for three months. It was on the national news for months about gays in the showers. Horrible things, like when Senator Sam Nunn took the below-the-deck tour. It was a bunch of crap. And what did we have? Nothing. I'm going crazy because every night on television we are getting this continual battering about what gays and lesbians do in the Navy, Air Force, on planes, lavatories. Awful stuff. I personally went to all the networks and said you have to stop this, and everyone of them said, 'Look, give us something to show.' So, we started

holding press conferences." Waybourn's background in media consulting and journalism proved vital as the controversy grabbed the
nation's attention. Because of his efforts, the advocates of lifting the
ban began to receive their thirty seconds of air time along with the
opponents.

*   *   *

Waybourn, who continues to work in Washington for his own
public relations and marketing firm, has seen how the trappings of
power have compromised some gay and lesbian activists. This is
usually manifested by not being openly critical of administration
policies. Waybourn calls it "passing"—letting issues pass instead of
being confrontational because people want to be seen as team players who can be relied upon. Recounting the time when he and David
Mixner got arrested in front of the White House to protest the policy
on gays in the military, Waybourn commented, "Some said we
would never be invited back, but we were back the following
week."

An example of someone who didn't follow the party line was
Clinton aide Bob Hattoy. In a frank discussion with *Poz Magazine*
in 1994,[1] Hattoy, who is a longtime friend of the Clintons and a
self-identified person with HIV, criticized Clinton and then Health
and Human Services Secretary Donna Shalala for not developing an
overall AIDS strategy. It was not the first time he voiced his frustration in the press. In the interview, Hattoy made it clear what a price
he has paid for speaking out. Although he was not banned from the
kingdom, he had fallen from grace and was shifted to the Department of Interior to rewrite regulations affecting grazing fees and
mining laws. However, Hattoy's strategy paid off in the end because
AIDS Czar Kris Gebbie—whom he often criticized for being ineffectual—was later fired.

Just as Hattoy saw Clinton as an ally, so does Waybourn. The
problem often is with Clinton's advisors. "The thing I tell people is
that Bill Clinton understands, he gets it, he has no problem with
gays and lesbians," said Waybourn. "What happens is you have
people in staff positions who say to him, 'Well, you really ought not
to do that. That's rocking the boat.' The problem is that the aides are

people who are already in the boat. Gays and lesbians will never be in the boat."

The comment was the only note of pessimism Waybourn expressed about the future. Like most activists who endure year after year, Waybourn, by his nature, must be optimistic about where the movement is headed or else he would have tired of the fight long ago. For him and the Victory Fund, each election is like a new spring, a time when the movement is reborn and hope fills the air. His remark about gays and lesbians never being in the boat must have rung false to him because after saying it he paused. "But who knows," he continued. "Maybe some day we will be."

Chapter 13

The Making of a Candidate: A Personal Memoir

My interest in politics began at an early age. Two weeks after starting the seventh grade, I ran for class president and won. I do not know what possessed me to run or, to be more accurate, what possessed my mother to encourage me to run. Surely it was her idea, since I had never been so much as a room monitor in elementary school. I remember sitting around the kitchen table with my family making campaign buttons out of construction paper and writing clever political slogans that Mom made up as we went along. Holding office gave me a great deal of confidence and helped me establish my own identity.

My mother, while never a political activist, always had a sense of fairness and high moral standards. It was from her that I inherited my interest in politics. She was against war, poverty, bigotry, and racism, and by the time I was a teenager, I was against these things, too. After joining the school newspaper staff in the eighth grade, I wrote editorials against the Vietnam war and in support of the student protests. In the ninth grade, I was named editor and elected student body president. Looking back, I have no idea where I found the wherewithal to do either, much less both. As a teenager, I was on automatic pilot, full of energy and free of the self-doubts that plague me as an adult.

From my father I inherited my work habits and work ethic. He runs a heavy construction company in our hometown of Riverside, California, which is sixty miles southeast of Los Angeles. He is highly competent and successful at what he does. Throughout my childhood, I would see him leave for work in the morning and come home late in the day, six days a week. He never complained, seldom was cross, and was practically never home. Observing him, I learned that for any endeavor to succeed you must devote a large amount of time and energy to it. That is why by the time I was twelve I was willing to put in extra hours on school projects like student government and the newspaper.

Ever since I can remember, I knew I was gay. I also knew that I could never be openly gay in my hometown, and that I would have to leave as soon as I could. That is why on one hot, smoggy day after I graduated from high school I left Riverside for good, driving 400 miles to San Jose State University. Friends assumed I would major in political science, but I knew the conflict between the intensity of my political beliefs and the realities of what I could accomplish in the world would cause me too much anguish. Instead, I decided to major in English, with the intent of becoming a journalist.

Looking back on why I had to leave and what I missed out on, I wonder if the radical right realizes how their lies about gay people separate families, for we gay and lesbian youth leave our hometowns in greater numbers than nongay teenagers. Our absence means we do not have the opportunity to get to know our parents, siblings, and nieces and nephews as well as we would had the climate allowed us to stay.

*   *   *

It was my good fortune that San Jose State University had (and still does have) an excellent political science department, particularly when it comes to the study of local government. When I was a junior, I did an internship at San Jose City Hall with a councilwoman with whom I would have a long association, Susanne Wilson. I remember planting myself in her office, almost demanding that she give me as much work as was available in order to prove myself.

During my final semester, I worked on Councilwoman Wilson's reelection campaign as her precinct coordinator. It was an overwhelming job for a twenty-two-year-old who had never worked on a political campaign before, but I lived and breathed the campaign, barely attending my classes. Through the job, I met people with whom I still have contact nearly two decades later, many of whom helped me when I decided to run for public office.

The years between college graduation in 1976 and when I came out publicly as a gay man were filled with politics. Throughout this period, I was resolved to be a behind-the-scenes person. It never once occurred to me that I would run for public office. How could I run? I was gay. Except for Harvey Milk, there were no gay politicians that I was aware of. Also, there was an antigay backlash sweeping the country. In the late 1970s and early 1980s, gay civil rights laws were being repealed across the country, starting in Dade County, Florida. In this homophobic atmosphere, the best I could do was to be in the background. In most cases, I worked for women candidates because I felt that having women in leadership roles would begin to change the rigid roles that society dictated for men and women. The ability to break down barriers—be they for women, gays and lesbians, or any minority group member—is why I am involved in politics.

In 1982, I was hired to run the reelection campaign for San Jose Congressman Don Edwards. After the campaign, he asked if I wanted to work in his DC office. After telling him I was gay (something he had no problem with), I said yes, under the condition that I would be his press secretary. He agreed, and off I went to Washington, believing my rapid ascent in national politics had begun.

After a year, I decided Washington wasn't for me. I figured if I worked like a dog for years, I might one day be able to rise to a position of moderate authority. Even then, I knew my being gay would always restrict how high I could move in the government. Believing that I could bring about greater change from the bottom up rather than from the top down, I came back to San Jose, knowing that if I wanted to live the same fast-paced life I had had in Washington then I would have to create it for myself.

When I returned in 1984, San Jose was still reeling from the 1980 repeal of city and county ordinances that would have given gays and lesbians protection in housing and employment. In a mean-spirited and homophobic campaign, the fundamentalists defeated us badly at the voting booth by a three-to-one margin.

It was in this political and moral devastation that a local state assemblyman declared in a *San Jose Mercury* editorial that a new state bill forbidding discrimination against gays and lesbians should not be signed by the governor because it would give the "wrong-ful" practice of homosexuality legal, social, and political legitima-cy.[1] So prevalent was the antigay rhetoric that it probably never occurred to him that there would be any outcry against his views.

I was angry that an elected official thought I had forfeited my civil rights simply because I was gay. I realized that if I was to have any rights in San Jose, I would have to fight for them. I decided to challenge the assemblyman, using his weapon of choice: an edito-rial in the *Mercury*.

There was one small glitch. I wasn't completely out. My byline in the *Mercury* meant I would come out to the newspaper's entire Bay Area readership. I knew that the publicity might cause me problems. I wondered if my political friends would distance them-selves because I was too out, or if I would ever be hired to manage another political campaign.

I told Congressman Edwards of my plans, realizing he might not think it a plus to have a press secretary who was openly gay. To my knowledge, there was only one openly gay legislative aide in the entire county. But he didn't bat an eye. He said, "Do it." And I did.

The day my editorial appeared in 1984 was a momentous one for me.[2] Personally, I no longer had to keep two identities, one straight, one gay. I could start meeting more gays and lesbians. I even hoped I would become well adjusted, even happy. Politically, I would be free to resurrect the gay movement in San Jose. Inspired by the success of David Mixner with a group called MECLA—Municipal Elections Committee of Los Angeles—I cofounded the Bay Area Municipal Elections Committee (BAYMEC) with Wiggsy Sivert-sen, a professor and counselor at San Jose State University.

At first, Wiggsy and I thought of operating only in Santa Clara County where San Jose is located, but Mixner had a vision of a statewide network of political action groups, so we added San Mateo and Santa Cruz counties to our sphere of influence. Two of the original BAYMEC board members were John Laird, an openly gay council member in Santa Cruz, and Rich Gordon, who later was elected to the San Mateo County Board of Supervisors.

It was important from the outset that BAYMEC be professional. Wiggsy, who is one of the most dynamic and articulate people I have ever met, did the speaking, helped plan strategy, and used her impressive network of friends to open doors and raise money. Moreover, she made sure that lesbians were welcomed into BAYMEC, an accomplishment of which not all gay organizations can boast.

My role was more behind the scenes, doing all the work that keeps an organization going. I am a much better writer than speaker, so I wrote the brochures and newsletters, as well as doing the media work. I also brought my campaign and fund-raising skills to the group, which I used when I managed the local Stop LaRouche/AIDS Quarantine campaigns. Together, Wiggsy and I walked the corridors of city halls, county buildings, and boards of education, lobbying our elected officials on numerous issues and serving on a variety of task forces and committees.

For six years, I served as BAYMEC's treasurer. I remember the contributions we received from the first solicitation, and the second, and the third. I remember the names of the people to whom I wrote notes thanking them for their support. I recall the first candidate endorsements, the first fund-raiser, the first speaker's forum. It was an exhilarating time.

Wiggsy and I made a good team. Each of us brought something to the relationship that the other lacked. I believe I provided Wiggsy more discipline and organization, and she gave me more confidence and assertiveness. We often joke that we should have gotten married, given how much time we spend with each other. It is remarkable to us both that after all these years we have never grown bored or impatient with each other.

To me, the access BAYMEC has to all South Bay elected officials indicates to our contributors that their donations over the years have paid high dividends. Many PACs give money to politicians, but few are on a first-name basis with all the recipients. We have an excellent working relationship with almost all locally elected officials and can count on them to support fairness and equity for gays and lesbians.

BAYMEC did more than satisfy my need to do gay politics; it fulfilled an emotional need to connect to people. BAYMEC provided me a conduit to the gay community that I could never get through gay bars. As BAYMEC grew, I was like a proud parent who became more outwardly focused once a reason to exist beyond himself was found. The more I became involved with my city, the more my sense of alienation began to fade. John Gardner, the former secretary of health, education, and welfare under President Johnson and writer of several books on leadership, explained this occurrence best when he wrote, "Young people run around searching for identity, but it isn't handed out free, not in this transient, rootless, pluralistic society. You have to build meaning into your life, and you build it through your commitments. Your identity is what you've committed yourself to."

By 1985, I had grown tired of being a congressional aide. I did not want to wake up one day and find myself being an unemployed political hack. I was always interested in education, and I knew Stanford's School of Education had a well-regarded education studies department. I applied and was accepted. When I finished my master's degree, I was accepted into the PhD program with a full scholarship.

The years of graduate school were hectic. First there was school: going to class, doing research, and studying. Second, I was as busy as ever with politics, running BAYMEC, chairing the county's AIDS task force, and managing two regional campaigns against Lyndon LaRouche's AIDS quarantine initiatives.

In November 1990 after I turned in my dissertation, I traveled to Atlanta with a friend, Ira Greene, a dermatologist. He was attending a conference, and he invited me to go along. In the hotel room, he noticed a blemish on the back of my right upper arm and asked how long I had had it. I said I was not sure, but that I thought it was a big freckle. He expressed concern and said that I should have a biopsy done as soon as we returned.

As he suspected, I had a form of skin cancer called malignant melanoma, which is believed to be caused when a cell is damaged by ultraviolet rays, usually when a person is a child. For reasons oncologists do not fully understand, this genetically altered cell can then evolve, often many years later, into melanoma. If removed early, the cancer is not fatal, but it is deadly if allowed to spread. In December 1990, I had the operation to remove the tumor. Since then, there has not been a reoccurrence, and my doctor is optimistic that the melanoma will not reappear.

This episode with melanoma was not my first confrontation with a health crisis. I had taken the HIV antibody test in 1986 when a friend of mine learned he was HIV positive. I thought that if he could have the virus, then I could too. While waiting two weeks for the results, I could think of little else except my own mortality. My days were full of anxiety and soul searching. Although the trauma ended when I learned I was HIV negative, I know my psyche was altered in immeasurable ways by coming face-to-face with my own death for the first time. Perhaps this is why I was not as paralyzed by the melanoma diagnosis as I would have been otherwise.

This is not to say the cancer had no effect on me. It did. If I was going to die, I reasoned, I wanted to do two things. First, because I had started long-distance running in 1989 when I stopped smoking, I wanted to run a marathon. Second, I wanted to run for public office. Over the next two years, I accomplished both.

Would I have run for office without the cloud of death over me? I do not know. I might have put it off, waiting for a better time that never would have come.

*   *   *

In San Jose, as in many cities in Western states, there is a multitude of school districts. Many of these are separate K-8 and 9-12, each with their own independently elected school board. The elementary school district in which I lived had severe problems, and I contemplated running for the board. Although I knew I could do a good job, there were political liabilities that could not be ignored, such as the fact that I did not have kids. Also, I knew it would be difficult to be an advocate for gay issues at the elementary school level. I envisioned friends and voters thinking to themselves, "It makes no sense that he is running for this office"—an observation that too many candidates miss. The irony was that at Stanford I studied children and family issues, and wrote my dissertation on the politics of child care. In this respect, I was as much an expert on educational issues as anyone in the community.

A political office that is often overlooked by candidates locally and throughout the state is that of community college trustee. In California, community college trustees have real power, making policy on issues dealing with curriculum, vocational education, academic standards, collective bargaining, and so on. In the community college district where I live—the San Jose/Evergreen Community College District—there are two colleges with a combined student population of 25,000 and an operating budget of $70 million.

As soon as I had the idea of running for college board, I knew the position was the right office at the right time. There were five reasons why it was a good fit.

First, I had paid my dues. For almost twenty years, I helped elect scores of people to office. I donated hundreds of dollars of my own money to candidates, political organizations, and minority groups. Through my work with BAYMEC, I helped hundreds of other candidates with endorsements and contributions. I joined marches and testified at hearings in support of other groups' causes. I worked to build coalitions with women's groups, unions, Democratic Party groups, Hispanic groups, Asian groups, and African-American groups. I knew the political players, and they knew me.

Second, I was a good match for the district. In my college board district, trustees run in specific geographical areas rather than at-large, making the campaign less costly and easier to manage. This allowed me, as a gay candidate, to run a competitive campaign. Although my area contained 110,000 people, 42,000 of whom were registered voters, within its boundaries was the older section of San Jose. This is where I had lived for most of my adult life and which had a high concentration of liberal Democrats and gay people. Also, there was no incumbent, which meant I could spend my time establishing my credibility rather than attacking a sitting politician.

Third, I had the credentials, both academically and professionally. Because of my PhD in education and my MA in sociology, I knew a great deal about educational policy and educational organizations. Professionally, I was teaching at San Jose State University, where I was hired after I finished my dissertation. This gave me classroom experience at the college level and added to my credibility as a candidate. It also provided me with an image that I could use in my literature. The main photo was of me lecturing to students in a classroom, reinforcing the message that I was an educator and knowledgeable about higher education. I never allowed myself to be defined as the "gay" candidate, which could have happened if I had not promoted myself as the candidate who was a San Jose State University professor.

Fourth, I knew how to run campaigns. I had worked for a national campaign consulting firm that was located in San Jose. Through managing school bond campaigns and overseeing the production of mail pieces for congressional candidates across the country, I learned the latest techniques in campaign management. I used much of this knowledge in my own campaign.

Fifth, I would be the first openly gay person ever elected to public office in Santa Clara County, a relatively liberal area with a population of two million people. I knew it was important for qualified gays and lesbians to run for office so voters would know that gays and lesbians can represent the interests of the entire community. Given my skills, connections, and resolve, I believed I would be a strong candidate.

For all these reasons, I felt confident about my decision to run for the college board. My main concern was whether I would be a good candidate and how well I would interact with voters. From past experience, I knew I was a good campaign manager, but I was unsure if I had what it took to be the person on center stage.

I was aware that it would be difficult to know how to balance my gayness and my qualifications for the job. It was fortunate that anybody who knew me in San Jose was aware I was gay because of how often I was quoted in the newspaper and appeared on local television. Setting aside the gay issue, I was a candidate like anybody else. When my consultants and I were designing my brochure, we saw my being gay as a nonissue because I was already out. Thus, we assumed my gayness would either be a big problem or no problem. If it was a big problem, then we would deal with it when it came up; otherwise it was to be downplayed.

When the filing period closed, there were six of us running, all men. It was fortunate for me that no women had entered the race because women candidates were expected to do well in the 1992 election. One candidate had a Spanish surname, which would help him in Hispanic neighborhoods. Only one of my opponents had strong community ties, and he proved to be my main competitor. He was a lawyer and a former ESL teacher at the community colleges.

After consulting with my political friends, I finalized the campaign strategy and budget. Once I was able to form a mental picture of the entire campaign from start to finish, my stress level went down. No longer was the campaign a nebulous concept, but a series of tasks that needed to be completed, one by one, day by day.

The budget was set at $15,000, although I had no idea if I would be able to raise that amount. I loaned the campaign $500 to do initial printing of literature. Fortunately, money came in steadily, mostly from people I had known over the years. Without these prior contacts, I never would have found 200 people to donate between $25 and $100. At first, it was hard to ask for money, but I knew that if I didn't have the grit to do it, then I was no good to myself or the issues I represented. Furthermore, as my campaign coordinator kept telling me, people will not give what they do not have. Amazingly, the more I asked for money, the easier it became.

Endorsements from elected officials and community leaders are crucial in any race, but even more so in low-profile ones where voters have not heard of the candidates. Because of the work I had done with many politicians on a variety of issues, securing endorsements was not hard. All I did was pick up the phone and talk to the person or his or her top aide. I usually got an answer the same day. My long list of endorsements helped to establish my credibility early, to raise funds, to get volunteers, and to win the support of other organizations.

The main strategy for the campaign was to contact voters through the mail. There were a total of three mailings: a four-page brochure, a personalized letter, and a jumbo postcard, all of which were to be mailed the final week. Selection of which voters would receive the pieces was determined by a longtime friend who owns a political database management company that handles lists of registered voters.

The second way that voters would be contacted was through a field and volunteer operation. The field operation included walking precincts, putting up signs on supporters' lawns, and passing out literature. The volunteer operation mainly consisted of addressing envelopes. All the work was run out of my garage, which the previous homeowner had turned into a recreation room, complete with astroturf, telephone, toilet, and sink. Volunteers were there Monday through Friday from 6 to 10 p.m. and all day Saturday and Sunday writing names of voters on envelopes. On average there were five people working in the garage each day. One regular volunteer would bring her fourteen-year-old daughter because she felt it was part of her responsibility as a parent to teach her how government worked. Most of the volunteers were people I had known from my work with BAYMEC.

The volunteer operation was the aspect of the campaign with which I had the least involvement. For one thing, I was too busy raising money and meeting people, and for another I was not good at handling volunteers. I was blessed to have my good friend Leslee Hamilton as my campaign coordinator. She had worked for many years as the canvass supervisor for a political organization and knew how to deal with different personality types. Throughout the campaign I never once had to worry about whether the volunteers were happy or had enough to do. There was no sniping, no back-stabbing, no rebellions, a feat which many political campaigns—gay or straight—cannot claim.

One of the primary volunteer efforts was to do neighbor-to-neighbor letters. These were one-page letters that detailed my qualifications and goals targeted by neighborhood. I broke down my area into sixteen different neighborhoods, then asked a friend living in each one if I could use his or her name. Next, our computer programmer printed the person's name and address on a letterhead. Each letter was the same except that the first line differed by neighborhood. Then, volunteers hand-addressed the envelopes. One glorious night, the last of 12,000 letters was folded, sealed, stamped, and ready to go. They were mailed six days before the election and arrived in people's mailboxes the next day.

As it turned out, the neighbor-to-neighbor letters were enormously effective, mainly because they looked like personalized mail from a neighbor, not campaign literature. People must have read them because when I was walking precincts many people said, "I got a letter from someone down the street telling me about you."

Another successful aspect of the campaign was the lawn and street signs. The colors we chose were lavender and white—lavender being the color identified with gay pride. About 150 people agreed to put signs on their lawns, which was a high number for any campaign. Even the mayor of San Jose, Susan Hammer, put out a sign in front of her house. In addition, I put up 500 street signs on telephone poles, fences, and atop traffic signs. Every now and then I would be driving and see a wave of lavender with my name on it and think, "You're really out there with being gay, Ken." Sometimes this would make me nervous, believing I could be a victim of a hate crime. Only once since I was elected was my house a target, in a poorly executed toilet paper and egg attack.

The campaign was a three-month endurance race, not unlike a marathon. In the afternoons when I came back from teaching, I would either walk a precinct, write thank-you letters, or answer a group's questionnaire. There were always two or three events to attend in the evenings. Late at night, I would grade papers or prepare my lectures for the next day.

As a child, I had a severe stuttering problem and I didn't talk much until I began to overcome the speech impediment in the fourth grade. As I grew older, I became more comfortable with writing than with speaking. As a consequence, I was never a good public speaker. However, giving speeches is part of the job description for a politician, so I had to learn how to give an effective political speech. By asking friends what they thought of my talks, I learned what I needed to include, such as information on the community colleges, duties of a trustee, and my work in the gay community. People told me that I needed to say more about who I was, so I included personal background. Through this process I discovered what most politicians already know: A good speaker is not born; he or she is made. It was not until well into the second month of the campaign that I got the stump speech memorized so I would not have to panic when I stood in front of a group.

Even though I became physically exhausted near the end of the campaign, I was never emotionally drained. As the candidate, I was the center of attention. People were putting on fund-raisers for me, donating money, and singing my praises. These activities would always revive my spirits.

Throughout the campaign I was continually inspired by the actions of others. I know it took courage for some people to put up a lawn sign for a candidate who neighbors might know was gay. Often these were older men who led closeted lives and whom I met only because friends invited them to fund-raising parties at their homes. Sometimes one person in a couple wanted to put up a sign but the other one did not, fearing what people might say. Eventually the sign went up because they were willing to do their small part to help me win. I am sure there were other acts of bravery that involved people coming out, most of which I will never know about.

One disappointment I experienced in the campaign was the failure of the progressive community to see the value in electing a qualified gay candidate. Because my main opponent had been involved in union politics, several organizations and individuals endorsed us both. From my perspective, they failed to see the importance of doing a single endorsement of an openly gay man over a liberal heterosexual male. All things being equal, it was time that the gay community had representation, much as women and other minority groups now do.

One group that failed to understand this was a local women's group. As I mentioned at their candidates' forum, for almost twenty years I had worked to get women candidates elected to office, and I had attended many of their events over the years. In my role with BAYMEC, I made sure that we built coalitions with women's groups and that we endorsed women candidates because it increased diversity among elected officials. Moreover, my efforts helped a group of women that is often overlooked: lesbians. I added that I had done considerable research on women and family issues at Stanford. Despite this, the group dual-endorsed one of my opponents and me, because they said that he was good on women's issues too.

Finally election day came. In the morning, there was nothing more to write, deliver, stamp, or seal, so I went jogging. Later, I heard on the radio that George Bush also went running. I laughed, amused that election-day jogging was the only thing that Bush and I had in common. I then went to vote.

The first results that came in were the absentee voters. I had sent all absentee voters a special mailing that they received prior to getting their absentee ballots. I assumed that none of the other candidates had thought of this, so I was not surprised that I did well with these voters. It was not until after midnight that I learned I had won, racking up 40 percent of the vote—a phenomenal percentage given that six people were in the race. Everyone was flabbergasted. One explanation for the landslide was that many people knew me from two decades of community work. Because it was a low-profile race, the opinion of these people carried much weight with their spouses and friends. The lawn signs, the three pieces of mail, and the precinct walking all helped me to win with an impressive total.

I was not ready for all the attention I received afterward. As the first openly gay elected person in Santa Clara County, I was interviewed by radio and television stations, although not by the local newspaper, which I thought would be the only coverage I would get. I received many calls and letters from friends congratulating me. One friend in the East called to say he heard about my victory on CNN. Flowers arrived. The only time since then that I was happier was a month later when I was sworn in as a trustee. A picture taken of me at the ceremony captured the widest smile physically possible.

*   *   *

My first six months as a trustee of the San Jose/Evergreen Community College District were a whirlwind of activity. I put in many extra hours, just as I had done with all my activities beginning with junior high school. It seemed that every other day there was a meeting to attend. I viewed these meetings as opportunities because the more people I got to know, the more information I gained about the district, and the better able I was to bring about meaningful change through understanding the issues and building coalitions with groups and board members.

As a result of my efforts, I believe significant progress was made in a relatively short time, demonstrating why it is important to elect lesbians and gays to office. Achievements continue to happen, but here is a brief record of my first term.

My top campaign issue was to raise standards so students get the quality education needed to compete for well-paying jobs. As chair of the Committee on Academic Excellence and Comprehensiveness, I believe we have made great strides in improving academic standards.

Another of my campaign issues was to have the college district work with high schools and San Jose State University to create a unified educational system. The district now has joint programs with K-12 districts and San Jose State University.

The current library system was inadequate and inefficient. I successfully advocated for the board to allocate monies to install a library automation system similar to the one at San Jose State University, bringing the libraries into the modern age.

The district had no recycling program. Today, our district makes a concerted effort to recycle whenever possible.

I convinced the Board of Trustees to vote to have the district divest nearly $2 million from Bank of America because of its financial support of the Boy Scouts of America, an organization that openly discriminates against gays.

I directed the personnel department to research the cost of offering domestic partnership benefits to employees. After a report showed that the cost would be minimal, the board approved the benefits, making us the second public agency in the county to do so.

At my request, the Santa Clara County Public Health Department is doing free HIV testing on the campuses.

*   *   *

Four years after my election, I ran for state assembly. Because of term limits, the incumbent could not run, creating a vacancy in the heavily Democratic, multiethnic Twenty-Third Assembly District. It was an ideal seat for me because my community college district was wholly contained in the assembly district. I knew the area well and many of the residents had already voted for me. There were three others in the March 1996 Democratic primary: Mike Honda, a Santa Clara County Supervisor; David Cortese, son of the incumbent assemblyman; and Patricia Martinez Roach, a school trustee.

I ran on a platform of education reform. This was an important issue for residents of the district because of the high education levels needed for employment in Silicon Valley. Of all the candidates, I was the only one who had a vision and a plan to improve preschools, elementary and secondary schools, community colleges, and four-year universities.

It was a perfectly executed campaign, built upon the foundation of my first one. I was able to raise the $250,000 needed to run a viable campaign. This was achieved by holding numerous large fund-raisers over a year's time, having forty people sponsor house parties, and receiving checks from over 1,500 individuals.

I was blessed with an army of 400 dedicated and talented volunteers. These friends walked 100 precincts, phoned thousands of voters, addressed 30,000 envelopes, stuffed tens of thousands of letters, registered hundreds of voters, hung hundreds of doorhangers on election eve, and stood on the streets election morning with banners blaring "Yeager for Assembly." I could not have asked for a finer group of volunteers.

I received most of the endorsements, including that of the *San Jose Mercury.* The officeholders who supported me included two members of Congress, numerous council members, state assembly members, county supervisors, school superintendents, and school trustees. Some of the groups that endorsed me were the Sierra Club, the South Bay AFL-CIO, California Federation of Teachers, National Women's Political Caucus, National Organization of Women, and the San Jose Firefighters.

All along, I knew that Supervisor Honda's name recognition was formidable. For me to win, the other two candidates had to take a sizable bloc of support away from him, particularly in East San Jose, which was their base of support. If my three opponents could divide up East San Jose, I could win by outdistancing them elsewhere.

Until the last week of the campaign, this scenario was playing itself out. All four of us had the finances to stay competitive. While we each had different strategies, we all were running viable campaigns. Then things turned ugly. Cortese mailed out a classic hit piece against me. It was vicious, distorted my record, and arrived in the campaign's final week. Moreover, it explicitly fed into society's view that gay men were antifamily.

Most hit pieces are quickly forgotten after the election. Not so in this case. Because the piece was so homophobic, its repercussions continue to haunt Cortese, Phil Giarrizzo, the consultant who designed it, and David Binder, his pollster.

On one side of the 8½ x 11 flyer were three photographs. Under a photo of a policeman read the sentence, "Cut funding for police." Under an anguished-looking woman read, "Oppose rights for rape victims." Under a young boy in a Scout uniform read, "Outlaw the Boy Scouts." On the opposite side in large bold letters it read, "These are Ken Yeager's positions. Are they yours?" Then, "If you put your family first, watch out for Ken Yeager. He's an ultraliberal who fights for his agenda, not yours." After a brief discussion of the accusations, the piece ended with, "Put San Jose Families First. Vote No on Ken Yeager."

The facts were distorted, of course. The piece said that I wanted to outlaw the Boy Scouts from San Jose schools. However, the issue was never one of outlawing the Scouts from school facilities. Rather, because the Scouts discriminate based on sexual orientation, I fought against public funding of a Scouts' program in a school district.

Cortese stated that I opposed mandatory AIDS testing for rape suspects. In fact, I took a stand against an emotionally charged 1987 bill to require such testing because it was a political ploy by Republicans to find cracks in California's AIDS confidentiality laws. The bill was not about health or about medical or emotional needs of women who are victims of rape. Health officials opposed the bill for this reason.

Lastly, the statement that I voted to cut police protection at the San Jose/Evergreen College District was false. To offset budget cuts at the state level, I supported the chancellor's proposal to eliminate an administrative staff person in the police department office. The issue was never one of cutting police officers.

Cortese and his consultant initially said that they did not engage in gay bashing. I disagreed, as did most people who saw the piece. For me, the message of the mailer was obvious: people who fight for the rights of lesbians and gays are a threat to families. Although I was not being personally attacked for being gay, my record had been distorted to confirm people's prejudices that gay people were a menace because they put their own agenda before the concerns of rape victims, children, and ultimately society. My "agenda" over two decades of community work had been education, good neighborhoods, and many other issues beneficial to families of all sorts.

I agreed with my veteran consultants, Carol Beddo and Joy Alexiou, that the less media focus on the piece the better. We knew that each time the voters heard the allegations that I lost votes. Our main response was to quickly send out a mailer criticizing several votes Cortese had made while on the school board.

To my mind, the *Mercury* reporter who had been assigned to cover the campaign, De Tran, played right into the hands of Cortese's consultant. It was the front-page story in the local section, complete with a sidebar restating the charges. The local TV station ran a full story. All told, more people heard about the piece from the media than had received it in the mail.

The last week of any campaign is pure hell anyway, but it was made even more so by the hit piece. With twenty years of fighting in the political trenches, I consider myself a veteran campaigner. But as I walked door-to-door, I knew the piece had distorted my position and that some voters were now viewing me (and perhaps other gay people) in a negative light. My years of working to make San Jose a better place to live seemed to have been overshadowed.

I came in second place. Cortese, with his well-known family name, finished third, barely outdistancing the last-place finisher. Word on the street was that the hit piece probably turned voters away from Cortese and me and gave them to Supervisor Honda, who led in the polls going into the final week.

In the months following the campaign, I came to know the personal trauma that Giarrizzo, Binder, and Cortese have experienced because of the piece. Each deeply regrets his involvement in it. It is their story that I want to tell.

*   *   *

Shortly after the campaign, Phil Giarrizzo asked to come before the Harvey Milk Gay and Lesbian Democratic Club in San Francisco to explain his position on the piece. The president of the Milk Club then called me and asked if I would attend.

Perhaps Giarrizzo had asked to speak because gay Democratic leaders had been circulating a resolution to hold accountable candidates and their consultants who had used homophobic tactics against their opponents. Perhaps he just needed to ask for forgiveness. In any case, the man I saw at the meeting looked as if he was carrying a heavy weight on his shoulders.

Giarrizzo began by saying that for the last three months he had felt like (in his own words) shit. He admitted that he had committed the major sin of campaign politics by showing poor judgment. He said the piece clearly went over the line, that he accepted full responsibility, and that he wanted to personally apologize to me.

He then proceeded to rationalize his actions. He stated that as a consultant it was his job to win at any cost. He also said that the campaign's gay pollster had reviewed the piece and had not criticized it. Several times he said that although there is a line in campaigns that should not be crossed, he was unsure where that line is.

I then gave my interpretation of the piece, pointing out its misrepresentations and its homophobic message. As an aside, I mentioned that I was uncomfortable with him partially blaming the gay pollster, as if a gay man's complicity somehow justified mailing out the piece.

Several audience members made insightful comments. One person commented that most people learn at an early age where the line between right and wrong is drawn, be it from family, church, or synagogue. What concerned her most about his talk was that he lacked that internal gauge.

Another speaker talked about the high rate of suicide among gay and lesbian youth. In poignant terms, he explained how a troubled teenager might have seen the hit piece on his family's kitchen table, sending him another negative signal that gay people are depraved. It could be one more piece of evidence for the teen that he was inherently amoral and should not keep living.

Giarrizzo seemed shaken by the speaker's words. After revealing that he had a gay sister living in San Jose who had not spoken to him since the piece was mailed, he concluded somberly that it would not be easy for him to live with the fact that he might be responsible for someone's suicide.

David Binder, Cortese's pollster, is a well-known San Francisco consultant who has worked for numerous gay and straight candidates. I was told of Binder's role in the campaign by Cortese in the first conversation we had shortly after the campaign. Cortese, too,

228 Trailblazers: Profiles of America's Gay and Lesbian Elected Officials

had tried throwing blame on Binder by saying that a gay man had not objected to the piece. Because Binder is an acquaintance of mine, I felt comfortable calling him to find out if what Cortese had said was true. Binder confirmed that it was.

Binder's complicity seems hardest to explain. As a gay activist, he should have known better. Over the phone, he told me that he saw his role in the campaign strictly as a consultant. He did not think it was his place to judge whether the piece should be sent but only if it accurately reflected the data from the polls. Although disturbed about the piece, he had kept silent. Binder has done much soul-searching since the piece went out, and he regrets his actions. Next time, he says, he will not stay quiet.

Five months after the election, I received a second call from Cortese asking if we could get together. I could tell from the tone of his voice that this would be an altogether different conversation from the first, when he was still defending the overall intent of the piece.

Over lunch, Cortese apologized profusely for the piece and confided that he would always carry the burden of his actions with him. He had been taught by the Jesuits at Bellarmine High School in San Jose that there exists a window of opportunity for a person to make the right moral choice. When he first saw the piece, he knew it was wrong but did not speak out. It was a decision he would always regret.

Although he didn't initially consider the piece as gay-bashing, he had come to understand from conversations with several people that it was. It was wrong, Cortese said, to accuse someone of being antifamily solely because he is gay.

Cortese revealed that on the day the piece arrived he did not want to walk precincts. He was ashamed of himself for sending the piece and expected to be reprimanded as he went door-to-door. In addition, his wife, who was unaware of the piece before it was sent, did not approve of it.

In talks with close friends after the election Cortese realized that people were beginning to view him differently. In fact, Cortese's best friend asked for an explanation. A counselor who works with gay and lesbian youth at the East Side Union School District where Cortese serves as an elected trustee asked if he now was going to oppose the program. Cortese began to think of the many cousins he has in his large extended family. He realized the likelihood that some could be gay or lesbian. He wondered if they changed their view of him, too.

His eyes welling with tears, Cortese said he wished he could apologize to everyone who had seen the piece and say how sorry he was. He worried that in some way the piece could contribute to the antigay climate that was fueling the religious right's attempt to overturn a domestic partner registry recently passed by the Board of Supervisors. He asked if there was anything he could do to show his support of the gay and lesbian community.

I could tell his remorse was genuine. Although I am not a religious person, I do believe in the healing power of personal redemption. I also know that he will be able to fight homophobia in his circle of influence more effectively than anyone in the gay movement could ever do.

*   *   *

To better understand how I could have better responded to the piece, I called Dave Fleischer, coordinator of training for the Gay and Lesbian Victory Fund. I had met Fleischer in 1995 when he led a two-day candidate workshop that I attended.

Fleischer explained how hit pieces against gays and lesbians fall into three categories. The first is the overt homophobic piece which states that the opponent is unfit to hold office because he or she is gay. The second is an explicit homophobic attack. It reinforces the belief that gays have bad character. Most often the message is to protect our children. It is the hardest piece to respond to because it plays on internalized homophobia. The third is an implicit homophobic attack. These pieces say that the heterosexual candidate is more like the voter than the gay candidate. One candidate even sent out mailings titled "Straight Talk" just to be sure that everyone understood his point.

Fleischer said that Cortese's piece fit into the second category because there was little I could say by way of a direct defense. Discussing the particulars would have been useless. The charge was that the candidate is a bad person. Therefore, the only response is to show that the candidate has good character.

Fleischer gave two suggestions for a strategy. The first is to ask the local paper to write an editorial condemning the piece, calling it sleazy and unethical. This could be reprinted and sent to voters identified as undecided. The second is to send a piece with three testimonials: A Boy Scout or Scout leader could vouch for my support of youth programs; a husband of a rape victim or a rape victim counselor could detail my work in support of women and social service issues; and a police officer could discuss my platform on crime prevention.

Fleischer added that one reason why antigay attacks can be so effective is that voters have not yet become as desensitized to them as they are about candidates' immoral or unethical behavior. It is not such a big story the second time around. In that sense, Bill Clinton is the beneficiary of the intense media coverage given to Gary Hart's infidelities. Likewise, the next time a homophobic piece is mailed in San Jose it will have less effect.

Hit pieces will always be a part of a candidate's arsenal. Despite their dislike from all quarters, they are enormously effective, which is why they will continue to be used. However, as Cortese and his consultant and pollster realized, there are lines that should not be crossed when it comes to personal attacks based on race, gender, or sexual orientation.

In ways that political insiders and journalists have never explored, there can be a long-term psychological price to pay for waging such attacks. These hit pieces reinforce society's worst stereotypes and can do untold harm to members of the assaulted group. The stakes are higher than just the outcome of a single election. In this regard, the knowledge that one has done irreparable harm will live on long after the campaign is over.

* * *

My assembly race did not preclude me from running for a second term on the community college board. I was unopposed in the November 1996 election. This allowed me to serve for another four years without having to again ask my friends for their money and time. For this, they were as eternally thankful as I was.

Chapter 14

Campaign Checklist
for Gay and Lesbian Candidates

Gay men and lesbians need to be elected to all levels of government—federal, state, city, and school—but the fact is most gay people will not be running for high-profile seats such as mayor or state assembly. Rather, they will run in low-profile races in cities that have never before elected an openly gay person. This does not mean the stakes are not as high—they are. It is just that these candidates will have fewer resources available to them.

One consequence of running a campaign with limited resources is that there is not enough money to hire a campaign consulting firm or a full-time manager. This means candidates must either know about campaigns or know where to get the information directly. If they expect people to come to their rescue, their campaigns will never leave the starting gate.

The following is a checklist of campaign activities that low-profile candidates need a basic understanding of if they expect to run a viable campaign. Candidates need not excel in all areas, but the list does provide a reality check that will help in deciding if this is the year they should run.

- **Money.** A high name identification is essential for winning public office, and the only way to increase name ID is through the mail or the airwaves, both of which are costly. That is why it takes a lot of money to get elected.

    One way to get a handle on fund-raising goals is to determine a budget and then figure how many donors are needed. Let's say the budget is $10,000. Estimate that 100 people must give $25, 50 people must give $50, and 50 people must give

$100. Put names of people after these dollar amounts and begin making phone calls. If the candidate cannot determine who will give the money, chances are fund-raising will not go well.

- **In-kind contributions.** Almost as good as money (which is saying quite a lot) are in-kind contributions. Often individuals and businesses who are reluctant to write checks are willing to donate goods and services at a reduced rate or free. When this is done, it is called an in-kind contribution because the campaign is benefiting from not having to pay for a service or product.

  There is a wide range of in-kind contributions that candidates should pursue. One is reduced or free consulting services. Others include free office space, reduced rates for printing, and discounts on stationery items. Do not overlook having food and beverages donated, especially from gay restaurants and bars. Chips and soft drinks for volunteers can be very costly over the course of a campaign, and funds should be going for mailings, not food.

  In-kind contributions must be reported just like monetary contributions. Be sure to get a receipt from the business for the market value of the product or service and include that amount in the report.

- **Endorsements.** Endorsements by elected officials and community leaders are crucial in any race, but even more so in low-profile ones in which voters have not heard of the candidates. If there is no political party designation on the ballot (which is true in many local races, especially in Western states), then the main way for a voter to determine a candidate's politics is to see who endorses him or her. Early endorsements are especially critical because they help to establish a candidate's credibility.

  Candidates should assess how many big-name endorsements they can get and whether they can personally contact community leaders or if must they go through an intermediary, or worse, send a letter. If candidates do not know the person well enough to phone, then the odds decrease that an endorsement will be given because politicians are not likely to endorse people they do not know.

- **Volunteers.** If a candidate thinks that friends, ex-lovers, and potential lovers have nothing else to do but work on the campaign, think again. Volunteers are needed, however, especially in low-financed campaigns. If the campaign strategy calls for the use of volunteers, candidates need to assess if they can get four or five people a night, six times a week, for three or four months. Make a list of the people who might volunteer, then call them. It is not a good sign if the candidate hears a lot of hemming and hawing.

- **Qualifications.** Good credentials in the gay community might qualify people for some things, but being elected to public office probably is not one of them. Voters want reassurances that the candidates they support are credible and have knowledge about mainstream issues. They look carefully at a candidate's experience and qualifications, especially academic degrees, business titles, and community work. A list of five or more solid qualifications in a candidate's brochure looks impressive. If the list is too short, perhaps it would be wise to hold off running and get appointed to several governmental committees.

- **A nongay label.** People will vote for someone who is gay, but not for someone they think will represent only gay interests. That is why it is important not to be classified as a gay candidate. Political consultants Roger Lee and Carol Beddo advise that candidates should look in the mirror and say, "I'm the one who. . . . " Candidates must fill in the blank before voters or the opponent do. If not, the "gay" candidate label will stick.

  In my first campaign, Lee and Beddo knew that I should own the title of the "educator candidate." Because I was running for college board, we emphasized my PhD in education and my faculty job at San Jose State University. Even though I have been involved in gay politics for years, it was my educator image that was reinforced in my literature. As a result, when I was walking precincts people did not say, "You're the gay candidate," but, "You're the professor at San Jose State."

- **Issues.** Candidates are not expected to be aware of all the issues at the beginning of the campaign, but it is essential that they know people they can turn to for assistance. Candidates need to know people from various ethnic, racial, political, and social groups who will assist them in responding to questionnaires and preparing them for candidate forums. This help will increase the odds of winning endorsements and forming coalitions with other minority groups, something that gay and lesbian candidates must do.

- **Campaign literature.** Production of direct mail should not be left to amateurs; if it is, it will look amateurish, and voters don't want to be represented by amateurs. Each mail piece should have one overall message or purpose, with three subareas to help make the message clear. The most common copy error is trying to tell too many different things. The rule is that there should be only one message for each mail piece.

  Many components go into a quality mail piece: photographs that capture the essence of the candidate, effective writing, a creative design, and a good layout. One reason why direct mail consultants are expensive is the hours involved in production. To help keep costs down, candidates need to be familiar with aspects of direct mail or know people who will provide their services at reasonable rates.

- **Graphics.** Good, crisp graphics will send a message that a candidate is competent and experienced. That is why it is important for the campaign to have a professional look. If possible, ask several graphic artists to come up with potential logos. Look them over and discuss the pros and cons of each design. Make sure that this process is started early because once a logo is chosen it should not be changed mid-campaign.

- **Voter lists.** It makes little economic sense to mail to every voter in the district since only about 60 percent or fewer go to the polls in general elections. The percentage is much smaller for cities with off-year elections. A vendor who works with voter files can determine which voters should receive the candidate's mail by using a variety of criteria: voter history, age, political party, gender, etc. These are strategic decisions, and candidates must work with someone they trust. Good targeting is even more important in low-budget campaigns because money cannot be wasted on people who do not vote.

- **Campaign coordinator.** A candidate should be meeting voters, not spending time with volunteers. Even if there is no money to pay a staff person, the candidate needs to have a friend who can coordinate activities and be responsible for volunteer efforts. This person must be very good with people, because nothing will sidetrack a campaign faster than unhappy, sniping volunteers.
- **Treasurer.** States and most cities have laws governing campaign financing and reporting. Missing filing deadlines or filling out the reports incorrectly can create unnecessary bad press and may result in fines, even when errors were unintentional and innocent. If the candidate does not know how to complete the reports, then he or she needs to find someone who can.
- **Computer programmer.** A good database can make or break a campaign. That is why it is important for the candidate to have someone who will create a database, continuously put in new names, send thank-you letters, and generate mailing lists. If the candidate is computer illiterate, it is all the more important that a computer genius be found.
- **Campaign headquarters.** Renting a campaign headquarters can be very expensive. Candidates on a low budget need to find an alternative. One option is to find a business owner who will donate the space. A second is to share space with some organization at no charge. A third is to run the campaign out of someone's garage. Any of the three are better than watching the money go down the drain in the form of rent checks.
- **Printing.** Seasoned candidates know that as goes the printing, so goes the campaign. A candidate can have the best looking, best written literature in the world, but if it cannot be printed in time, then no one will see it. Printing schedules fill up fast during campaign season, so it is important to establish a good relationship with several printers by taking business-related work to them prior to the campaign.
- **Postage.** To save postage costs, it is important to learn the latest postal regulations, including what is considered oversize mail, how large to make the label area, and where to put the address return and indicia. Knowing this information ahead of time will

prevent candidates from having thousands of pieces of mail rejected at the post office three days before the election.

- **Flexible work hours.** There are never enough hours in a day
  to do the work required in a political campaign. That is why it
  is critical that candidates have a flexible work schedule. If the
  boss requires the candidate to be at his or her desk from 9 to 5,
  then it will be difficult to run errands, attend meetings, and
  make countless phone calls. Remember, in low-budget campaigns there is no staff, so the person doing most of the work is
  the candidate. If the candidate does not have time for campaigning, then there is not much of a campaign.

*   *   *

This assessment is not meant to discourage anyone from running.
Rather, its purpose is to help candidates avoid jumping into a campaign without forethought, only to raise false hopes for themselves
and the gay and lesbian community.

If candidates with limited resources don't know enough about
campaigns, there are two options. The first—and best—option is to
volunteer on someone's campaign to learn how it is done. The
second option (and one I do not often recommend) is to enter the
race in order to gain experience, knowing the groundwork is being
done for another run. Nothing is wrong with this as long as the
candidate does not lose sight of the objective.

Candidates need to be able to assess their chances realistically. If
they think there is a good chance they can win, they should run.
However, sometimes it pays to be patient and run later when everything is in place.

Appendix A

A Selected Chronology of Openly Gay and Lesbian Elected Officials

(Year designates when elected, not necessarily when came out publicly)

1972

Allan Spear
Elected to the Minnesota State Senate

Gerry Studds
Elected to Congress from Massachusetts

1974

Elaine Noble
Elected to the Massachusetts House of Representatives—first openly gay person elected to public office

Kathy Kozachenko
Elected to the Ann Arbor (MI) City Council

1977

Harvey Milk
Elected to the San Francisco Board of Supervisors

Steve Camara
Elected to the Fall River (MA) School Committee Office; elected
to the Fall River City Council in 1981

1978

William Chambers
Elected Morristown (NJ) Town Clerk

Abby Soven
Appointed to the Los Angeles Municipal Court; elected to the Los
Angeles Superior Court in 1982

1979

Harry Britt
Appointed to the San Francisco Board of Supervisors

Stephen Lachs
Appointed to the Los Angeles Superior Court

1980

Gene Ulrich
Elected mayor of Bunceton (MI)

Karen Clark
Elected to the Minnesota House of Representatives

Steve Gunderson
Elected to Congress from Wisconsin

Richard Wagner
Elected Dane County (WI) Supervisor

Tim Wolfred
Elected to the San Francisco Community College Board

1981

Barney Frank
Elected to Congress from Massachusetts

John Laird
Elected to the Santa Cruz (CA) City Council; appointed to Cabrillo
Community College Board in 1994

1982

Robert Gentry
Elected to the Laguna Beach City Council

1983

Bryan Coyle
Elected to the Minneapolis City Council

Jerold Krieger
Appointee to the Los Angeles Superior Court

Al Oertwig
Elected to the St. Paul Board of Education

David Scondras
Elected to Boston City Council

1984

John Heilman
Elected to the West Hollywood City Council

Jim Kolbe
Elected to Congress from Arizona

Valerie Terrigno
Elected to the West Hollywood City Council

1985

Bill Crews
Appointed mayor of Melbourne (IA)

Roslyn Garfield
Elected Provincetown (MA) Town Moderator

Tim Mains
Elected to the Rochester (NY) City Council

Tom Nolan
Elected to the San Mateo County (CA) Board of Supervisors

1986

Tammy Baldwin
Elected to the Dane County (WI) Board of Supervisors;
elected to the Wisconsin House of Representatives in 1992;
elected to Congress from Wisconsin in 1998

1987

Tom Brougham
Elected to the Peralta (CA) Community College Board

Joe Herzenberg
Elected to the Chapel Hill (NC) Town Council

Gary Miller
Elected to the Robla (CA) School Board

1988

Judy Abdo
Elected to the Santa Monica (CA) City Council

Cal Anderson
Elected to the Washington House of Representatives; elected to the
Washington State Senate in 1994

Earl Bricker
Elected to the Dane County (WI) Board of Supervisors

John Fiore
Elected to the Wilton Manors (FL) City Council

1989

Ricardo Gonzalez
Elected to the Madison (WI) Common Council

Joseph Grabarz
Elected to the Connecticut House of Representatives

John Neese
Elected to the Shorewood Hills (WI) Board of Trustees

Ken Reeves
Elected to the Cambridge (MA) City Council

Keith St. John
Elected to the Albany (NY) Common Council

1990

Roberta Achtenberg
Elected to the San Francisco Board of Supervisors

Tom Ammiano
Elected to the San Francisco School Board; elected to the San
Francisco Board of Supervisors in 1994

Deborah Glick
Elected to the New York State Assembly

Neil Guiliano
Elected to the Tempe (AZ) City Council; elected mayor in 1994

Kenneth Hahn
Elected Los Angeles City Assessor

Donna Hitchens
Elected to the San Francisco Superior Court

Dale McCormick
Elected to the Maine State Senate

Carole Migden
Elected to the San Francisco Board of Supervisors; elected to the
California State Assembly in 1996

Ronald Squires
Elected to the Vermont State Legislature

1991

Kate Brown
Elected to the Oregon House of Representatives; elected to the
Oregon State Senate in 1996

Thomas Duane
Elected to the New York City Council;
elected to the New York State Senate in 1998

Sherry Harris
Elected to the Seattle City Council

Jeff Horton
Elected to the Los Angeles Board of Education

Glen Maxey
Elected to the Texas House of Representatives

Antonio Pagan
Elected to the New York City Council

Joe Pais
Elected to the Key West City Commission

Mark Pocan
Elected to the Dane County (WI) Board of Supervisors

Irene Rabinowitz
Elected to the Provincetown (MA) Board of Selectmen

Janice Wilson
Appointed to Multnomah County (OR) District Court

1992

Angie Fa
Elected to the San Francisco School Board

Susan Farnsworth
Elected to the Maine House of Representatives

Will Fitzpatrick
Elected to the Rhode Island State Senate

Ed Flanagan
Elected Vermont State Auditor

Tom Fleury
Elected to the Vermont State Assembly

Rich Gordon
Elected to the San Mateo County (CA) Board of Education;
elected to the San Mateo County Board of Supervisors in 1997

Wayne Peterson
Elected to the Laguna Beach (CA) City Council

Gail Shibley
Appointed to the Oregon House of Representatives

Liz Stefanics
Elected to the New Mexico State Assembly

Ken Yeager
Elected to the San Jose/Evergreen (CA) Community College Board

1993

George Eighmey
Appointed to the Oregon House of Representatives

Shelley Gaylord
Elected to the Madison (WI) Municipal Court

David Gernant
Appointed Portland Trial Judge

Jackie Goldberg
Elected to the Los Angeles City Council

Jill Harris
Elected to the Brooklyn School Board

Susan Hyde
Elected to the Hartford (CT) City Council

Christine Kehoe
Elected to the San Diego City Council

Susan Leal
Appointed to the San Francisco Board of Supervisors; elected San
Francisco Treasurer in 1996

Linda Leslie
Elected Village Trustee of Douglas (MI)

Ann Manthei
Elected to the Castle Rock (WA) City Council

Craig McDaniel
Elected to the Dallas City Council

James McGill
Elected to the Wilkinsburg (PA) Borough Council

Michael Nelson
Elected to the Carrboro (NC) Board of Aldermen; elected mayor
in 1995

Marya Ryan
Elected to the Urbana (IL) City Council

Tom Roberts
Elected to the Santa Barbara City Council

Marilyn Shafer
Elected to the Manhattan Civil Court

Dan Stewart
Elected to the Plattsburgh (NY) City Council

Wallace Swan
Elected to the Minneapolis Board of Estimate and Taxation

Roey Thorpe
Elected to the Ithaca (NY) City Council

Katherine Triantafillou
Elected to the Cambridge (MA) City Council

Bruce Williams
Elected to the Takoma Park (MD) City Council

Chris Wilson
Elected to the Oakland Park (FL) City Council

1994

Patti Bushee
Appointed to the Santa Fe City Council

Tom Chiola
Elected to the Chicago Circuit Court

Leslie Katz
Elected to the San Francisco Community College Board; appointed
to the San Francisco Board of Supervisors in 1996

Sheila Kuehl
Elected to the California State Assembly

Bill Lippert
Appointed to the Vermont House of Representatives

Scott McCormick
Elected to the Dane County (WI) Board of Supervisors

Steve Martin
Elected to the West Hollywood City Council

Gregory Pettis
Appointed to the Cathedral City (CA) City Council

Edward Ryan
Elected to the Champaign (IL) City Council

Victoria Sigler
Elected to the Dade County (FL) Court

David Stevens
Appointed to the Northampton (MA) County Commission

Kathryn Turner
Elected to the Laguna Beach (CA) Board of Education

Tim Van Zandt
Elected to the Missouri House of Representatives

Lawrence Wong
Elected to the San Francisco Community College Board

1995

Donavan Hannis
Elected Erie (IL) Village Trustee; elected Village President in 1997

Mark Leban
Appointed to the Dade County (FL) County Court

Martine Meijerling
Elected to the Mashpee (MA) Planning Board; elected to the
Barnstable County Assembly of Delegates in 1996

Jim Moeller
Elected to the Vancouver (WA) City Council

Sebastian Patti
Appointed to the Chicago Circuit Court

José Plata
Elected to the Dallas Board of Education

Tina Podlodowski
Elected to the Seattle City Council

Debra Simone
Elected to the West Haven (CT) Board of Education

Zeke Zeidler
Elected to the Redondo Beach (CA) School Board

Stephen Zemo
Elected to the Ridgefield (CT) Board of Selectmen

1996

Ken Cheuvront
Elected to the Arizona House of Representatives

Libby Cowan
Elected to the Costa Mesa (CA) City Council

Scott Cowger
Elected to the Maine House of Representatives

Art Feltman
Elected to the Connecticut House of Representatives

Paul Feinman
Elected to the New York Civil Court

Margo Fraiser
Elected Sheriff of Austin, Texas

Barbra Kavanaugh
Elected to the Buffalo (NY) City Council

Kevin McCarthy
Elected to the San Francisco Superior Court

Larry McKeon
Elected to the Illinois House of Representatives

Jane Moore
Elected to the New York Community School Board

Edward Murray
Appointed to the Washington House of Representatives

John Nalley
Elected to the New York Community School Board

Michael Pisaturo
Elected to the Rhode Island House of Representatives

Judy Powers
Elected to the Maine House of Representatives

Michael Quint
Elected to the Maine House of Representatives

Tom Radulovich
Elected to the California Bay Area Rapid Transit Board

Diane Sands
Appointed to the Montana House of Representatives

Larry Sauer
Elected to the New York Community School Board

Andrea Shorter
Appointed to the San Francisco Community College Board

Sabrina Sojourner
Elected Washington, DC Shadow Representative

Kay Tsenin
Elected to the San Francisco Municipal Court

Dennis Van Avery
Elected to the Minneapolis School Board

1997

David Catania
Elected to the Washington, DC, City Council

Jay Frisette
Elected to the Arlington (VA) County Board

Bryan Knedler
Elected to the Mt. Rainier (MD) City Council

Rod Krueger
Elected to the Minneapolis Library Board

Margarita Lopez
Elected to the New York City Council

John Loza
Elected to the Dallas City Council

Annise Parker
Elected to the Houston City Council

Phil Reed
Elected to the New York City Council

Linda Siegle
Elected to the Santa Fe (NM) Community College Board

Deborah Silber
Elected to the Brooklyn Civil Court

Joanne Trapani
Elected to the Oak Park (IL) School Board

Susan Weinstein
Elected Wayland (MA) Board of Selectman

Mary Wiseman
Elected to the Dayton (OH) City Commission

1998

David Atkinson
Elected to the Provincetown (MA) Board of Selectman

Jarrett Tomas Barrios
Elected to the Massachusetts State House of Representatives

Scott Bernstein
Elected to the Dade County (FL) Court

Jackie Biskupski
Elected to the Utah State House of Representatives

Kevin Dowling
Elected to the Hayward (CA) City Council

Janet Garrow
Elected to the Bellevue (WA) Court

Jim Graham
Elected to the Washington DC City Council

Mary Ann Guggenheim
Elected to the Montana State House of Representatives

Mark Leno
Elected to the San Francisco Board of Supervisors

Liz Malia
Elected to the Massachusetts State House of Representatives

Evelyn Mantilla
Elected to the Connecticut State House of Representatives

Steve May
Elected to the Arizona State House of Representatives

Kim Painter
Elected Johnson County (IA) Recorder and Registrar

David Parks
Elected to the Nevada State Assembly

Mark Pocan
Elected to the Wisconsin State Assembly

Gary Resnick
Elected to the Wilton Manors (FL) City Council

Jean Rietschel
Elected to the Seattle (WA) Court

John Schultz
Elected to the Atlantic City (NJ) City Council

Jim Splaine
Elected to the New Hampshire State House of Representatives

Anne Strasdauskas
Elected Sheriff of Baltimore County (MD)

Rick Trombly
Elected to the New Hampshire State Senate

Kriss Worthington
Elected to the Berkeley (CA) City Council

1999

Dan Baker
Elected to the Long Beach (CA) City Council

Brian Ellner
Elected to the Manhattan (NY) School Board

Christine Quinn
Elected to the New York City Council

Doug Robinson
Elected to the New York City School Board

Matt Sloan
Elected to the Madison (WI) City Council

Appendix B

Listing of Gay and Lesbian Elected Officials

Tom Ammiano
Supervisor
401 Van Ness, Room 235
San Francisco, CA 94102

Tammy Baldwin
State Representative
P.O. Box 8952
Madison, WI 53704

Tom Brougham
Community College Trustee
1725 Berkeley Way, #B
Berkeley, CA 94703

Kate Brown
State Representative
State Capitol, H-288
Portland, OR 97310

Patti Bushee
Council Member
124B Mesa Verde St.
Santa Fe, NM 87501

David Catania
Council Member
1333 New Hampshire Ave.,
    NW, Suite 400
Washington, DC 20036

Ken Cheuvront
State Representative
P.O. Box 17043
Phoenix, AZ 85012

Tom Chiola
Judge
5812 North Magnolia Ave.
Chicago, IL 60660

Karen Clark
State Representative
2633 18th Ave. South
Minneapolis, MN 55407

Libby Cowan
Council Member
3007 Fernheath Lane
Costa Mesa, CA 92626

Scott Cowger
State Representative
RR1 Box 1145, Outlet Road
Hallowell, ME 04347

Bill Crews
Mayor
P.O. Box 1997
Melbourne, IA 50162

Tom Duane
Council Member
275 7th Ave., 12th Fl
New York, NY 10011

George Eighmey
State Representative
1423 SE Hawthorne St.
Portland, OR 97214

Paul Feinman
Judge
111 Centre St.
New York, NY 10013

Art Feltman
State Representative
596 Broadview Terrace
Hartford, CT 06106

John Fiore
Council Member
2450 NE 15th Ave., No. 210
Wilton Manors, FL 33305

Jay Fisette
Commissioner
311 N. Jackson St.
Arlington, VA 22201

Ed Flanagan
State Auditor
132 State St.
Montpelier, VT 05602

Barney Frank
Congress Member
2210 Rayburn Office Building
Washington, DC 20515

David Gernant
Judge
P.O. Box 5573
Portland, OR 97228

Neil Giuliano
Mayor
P.O. Box 5002
Tempe, AZ 85280

Rich Gordon
Supervisor
401 Marshall St.
Redwood City, CA 94063

Kenneth Hahn
Assessor
771 Crane Blvd.
Los Angeles, CA 90065

Donovan Hannis
Village President
925 5th St.
Erie, IL 61250

Jill Harris
School Trustee
376 Pacific St., Apt. 2
Brooklyn, NY 11217

John Heilman
Council Member
8300 Santa Monica Boulevard
West Hollywood, CA 90069

Donna Hitchens
Judge
633 Folsom St., Dept. 11
San Francisco, CA 94107

Jeff Horton
School Trustee
450 N. Grand Ave., A201
Los Angeles, CA 90012

Leslie Katz
Supervisor
401 Van Ness Ave. Room 308
San Francisco, CA 94110

Barbra Kavanaugh
Council Member
City Hall, Room 1412
Buffalo, NY 14202

Christine Kehoe
Council Member
2515 Meade Ave.
San Diego, CA 92116

Bryan Knedler
Council Member
3807 31st St.
Mt. Rainier, MD 20712

Jerold Krieger
Judge
111 North Hill St.
Los Angeles, CA 90012

Rod Krueger
Library Board Member
4420 Nokomis Ave. South
Minneapolis, MN 55406

Sheila Kuehl
Assembly Member
Capitol Building #2141
Sacramento, CA 95814

Stephen Lachs
Judge
111 North Hill Drive
Los Angeles, CA 90012

John Laird
Community College Trustee
1214 King St.
Santa Cruz, CA 95060

Mark King Leban
Judge
1351 NW 12th St., Room 500
Miami, FL 33125

Bill Lippert
State Representative
Rural Route 1, Box 830
Hinesberg, VT 05461

Margarita Lopez
Council Member
237 E. 14th St., 4th Fl
New York, NY 10009

John Loza
Council Member
1500 Marilla, Room 5FN
Dallas, TX 75201

Tim Mains
Council Member
6 Highland Heights
Rochester, NY 14618

Ann Manthei
Council Member
P.O. Box 545
Castle Rock, WA 98611

Steve Martin
Council Member
8300 Santa Monica Boulevard
West Hollywood, CA 90069

Scott McCormick
Supervisor
509 N. Lake #503
Madison, WI 53703

Jim McGill
Council Member
800 Ross Ave., No.1
Pittsburgh, PA 15221

Lawrence McKeon
State Representative
1967 W. Montrose
Chicago, IL 60613

Martine Meijering
Planning Board Member
P.O. Box 2647
Mashpee, MA 02649

Carole Migden
Assembly Member
State Capitol, Room 2114
Sacramento, CA 95814

Gary Miller
School Trustee
213 Peachleaf Way
Sacramento, CA 95838

Jim Moeller
Council Member
4600 Harney St.
Vancouver, WA 98663

Jane Moore
School Trustee
317 East 5th St.
New York, NY 10003

Ed Murray
State Representative
303 Harvard Ave. East, No. 304
Seattle, WA 98102

Jon Nalley
School Trustee
344 W. 17th St. #2D
New York, NY 10011

Michael Nelson
Mayor
105 Fidelity St., #A-22
Carrboro, NC 27510

Annise Parker
Council Member
P.O. Box 1562
Houston, TX 77251

Sebastian Patti
Judge
552 W. Belden Ave.
Chicago, IL 60614

Gregory Pettis
Council Member
38-073 Chris Dr.
Cathedral City, CA 92234

Mike Pisaturo
State Representative
6 Winthrop St.
Cranston, RI 02910

José Plata
School Trustee
303 South Edgefield Dr.
Dallas, TX 75203

Tina Podlodowski
Council Member
600 Fourth Ave.,
    1100 Muni Bldg.
Seattle, WA 98104

Judy Powers
State Representative
50 Spring Lane
Rockport, ME 04856

Jeff Prang
Council Member
8300 Santa Monica Blvd.
West Hollywood, CA 90069

Michael Quint
State Representative
32 Grant St.
Portland, ME 04101

Tom Radulovich
BART Director
4173 17th St.
San Francisco, CA 94114

Kenneth Reeves
Mayor
City Hall
Cambridge, MA 02139

Tom Roberts
Council Member
1726 San Pascual
Santa Barbara, CA 93101

Diane Sands
State Representative
1733 Phillips
Missoula, MT 59802

Larry Sauer
School Trustee
23 West 73rd St., No. 302
New York, NY 10023

Marilyn Shafer
Judge
100 W. 12th St.
New York, NY 10011

Andrea Shorter
Community College Trustee
50 Phelan Ave.
San Francisco, CA 94112

Linda Siegle
Community College Trustee
P.O. Box 8602
Santa Fe, NM 87504

Victoria Sigler
Judge
821 NE 107th St.
Biscayne Park, FL 33161

Debra Silber
Judge
100 Centre St.
New York, NY 10007

Debra Simone
School Trustee
207 Fresh Meadow
West Haven, CT 06516

Allan Spear
President of the Senate
27 State Capitol
St. Paul, MN 55155

Keith St. John
Alderman
135 Green St.
Albany, NY 12202

David Stevens
Commissioner
1378 Westhampton Rd.
Northampton, MA 01062

Dan Stewart
Council Member
P.O. Box 1142
Plattsburgh, NY 12901

Wallace Swan
Board of Estimate
15 S. 1st St., Towers, A-420
Minneapolis, MN 55401

Joanne Trapani
School Trustee
1014 North Hayes
Oak Park, IL 60302

Katherine Triantafillou
Council Member
90 Reed St.
Cambridge, MA 02140

Kay Tsenin
Judge
850 Bryant St., Rm 201
San Francisco, CA 94103

Kathryn Turner
School Trustee
780 Balboa Ave.
Laguna Beach, CA 92651

Gerald Ulrich
Mayor
104 Olive St., Box 200
Bunceton, MO 65237

Dennis Van Avery
School Trustee
88 West Minnehaha Parkway
Minneapolis, MN 55419

Tim Van Zandt
State Representative
P.O. Box 10216
Kansas City, MO 64171

Bruce Williams
Council Member
326 Lincoln Ave.
Takoma Park, MD 20912

Janice Wilson
Judge
1021 SW Fourth Ave.
Portland, OR 97204

Mary Wiseman
City Commissioner
P.O. Box 4460
Dayton, OH 45401

Lawrence Wong
Community College Trustee
50 Phelan Ave., Box E200
San Francisco, CA 94112

Ken Yeager
Community College Trustee
1925 Cleveland Ave.
San José, CA 95126

Zeke Zeidler
Trustee
419 South Juanita Ave.
Redondo Beach, CA 90277

Notes

Chapter 1

1. Howell, Deborah, "State Sen. Allan Spear Declares He's Homosexual." *Minneapolis Star.* December 9, 1974.

Chapter 2

1. Altman, Lawrence. "Rare Cancer Seen in 41 Homosexuals." *The New York Times.* July 3, 1981.
2. Freiberg, Peter. "Miami Grapples with the Legacy of Anita Bryant's Victory." *Washington Blade.* May 23, 1997.
3. Patron, Eugene. "How Will Dade Remember Campaign Over Gay Rights?" *Miami Herald.* January 12, 1997.
4. Branch, Karen. "Dade Kills Gay-Rights Ordinance." *Miami Herald.* June 18, 1997.
5. Branch, Karen. "How Gay-Rights Ordinance Met Quick End." *Miami Herald.* June 19, 1997.
6. Hiaasen, Carl. "Old-Fashioned Discrimination Back in Vogue." *Miami Herald.* June 19, 1997.

Chapter 3

1. Crews, Bill. "The Face of Gay America." *Des Moines Register.* April 25, 1993.
2. Offenburger, Chuck. "For Iowa Gays, a 'Matter of Justice.' " *Des Moines Register.* April 26, 1993.
3. "After the March Is Over." *Time.* May 10, 1993.
4. Santiago, Frank and Kelley, Matt. "Gay Mayor's House Vandalized." *Des Moines Register.* April 28, 1993.
5. Ibid.
6. Letters to the Editor. *Des Moines Register.* May 2, 1993.
7. Letters to the Editor. *Marshalltown Times-Republican.* May 15, 1993.
8. Letters to the Editor. *Des Moines Register.* May 2, 1993.
9. Letters to the Editor. *Marshalltown Times-Republican.* May 26, 1993.
10. *Newsweek.* September 4, 1972.
11. "Incumbent and Challenger Contest for Mayor's Seat in Melbourne." *Enterprise-Record.* November 2, 1995.
12. Letters of the Editor. *Marshalltown Times-Republican.* June 15, 1993.

Chapter 4

1. *Seattle Post-Intelligencer.* "City Council Recommendations." October 23, 1995.
2. Reis, Beth. "Fostering Safety and a Sense of Belonging." *Seattle Times.* May 23, 1997.

Chapter 5

1. Collins, Andrew. *Fodor's Gay Guide to the USA.* Fodor's Travel Publications: New York. 1996.

Chapter 6

1. Massa, Robert. "The HIV Closet." *Village Voice.* August 27, 1991.

Chapter 7

1. Lopez, Nora. "Data Show Blacks Hold 50% of Top DISD Jobs." *Dallas Morning News.* June 30, 1996.
2. Ibid.
3. Lopez, Nora. "DISD Board Meeting May Be Moved Up." *Dallas Morning News.* December 6, 1996.
4. Hendrie, Caroline. "Dallas Board Is Buffeted by Racial Unrest." *Education Week.* February 26, 1996.
5. "Vote Today." *Dallas Morning News.* January 21, 1995.
6. Garcia, Joseph and Puente, Veronica. "Plata's Remarks Draw Fire." *Dallas Morning News.* January 24, 1995. 13A.
7. Cropper, Carol Marie. "New Turn in Power Struggle Over Dallas School System. *The New York Times.* October 12, 1997.
8. Tatum, Henry. "Schools Continue Racial Juggling Act." *Dallas Morning News.* October 9, 1996.
9. Bleiberg, Larry. "Gays, Lesbians Included in DISD Policy." *Dallas Morning News.* March 28,m 1996.

Chapter 9

1. "Our Choices in Tempe." *Phoenix Gazette.* May 6, 1994.
2. Yantis, John. "Giuliano Says He's Gay; Feared 'Inquisition.' " *The Tribune.* August 29, 1996.
3. Ibid.
4. Lewis, Michael. *Trail Fever.* New York: Knopf. 1997.

Chapter 10

1. Sojourner, Sabrina. "I Think I Was Nine When It Started." *Psychic Scars and Other Mad Thoughts.* : Washington, DC: Soitgoz Press. 1995.
2. Ibid.

3. Sojourner, Sabrina. "Black People Do Not Commit Suicide." *Psychic Scars and Other Mad Thoughts.* Washington, DC: Soitgoz Press. 1995.

4. Sojourner, Sabrina. "Loving Us Both." *Psychic Scars and Other Mad Thoughts.* Washington, DC: Soitgoz Press. 1995.

Chapter 12

1. Minkowitz, Donna. "Bob Hattoy: On the Record." *Poz.* April/May 1994.

Chapter 13

1. McAlister, Alister. "Deukmejian Should Veto the Gay Employment Bill." *San Jose Mercury News.* March 9, 1984.

2. Yeager, Ken. "Tolerance Will Allow Gays to Help 'Build Our Land.' " *San Jose Mercury News.* March 18, 1984.

Index

Order Your Own Copy of
This Important Book for Your Personal Library!

TRAILBLAZERS
Profiles of America's Gay and Lesbian Elected Officials

_____ in hardbound at $29.95 (ISBN: 0-7890-0299-X)

_____ in softbound at $19.95 (ISBN: 1-56023-920-4)

COST OF BOOKS_____

OUTSIDE USA/CANADA/
MEXICO: ADD 20%_____

POSTAGE & HANDLING_____
*(US: $3.00 for first book & $1.25
for each additional book)
Outside US: $4.75 for first book
& $1.75 for each additional book)*

SUBTOTAL_____

IN CANADA: ADD 7% GST_____

STATE TAX_____
*(NY, OH & MN residents, please
add appropriate local sales tax)*

FINAL TOTAL_____
*(If paying in Canadian funds,
convert using the current
exchange rate. UNESCO
coupons welcome.)*

☐ **BILL ME LATER:** ($5 service charge will be added)
(Bill-me option is good on US/Canada/Mexico orders only;
not good to jobbers, wholesalers, or subscription agencies.)

☐ Check here if billing address is different from
shipping address and attach purchase order and
billing address information.

Signature_____

☐ **PAYMENT ENCLOSED: $**_____

☐ **PLEASE CHARGE TO MY CREDIT CARD.**

☐ Visa   ☐ MasterCard   ☐ AmEx   ☐ Discover
☐ Diner's Club

Account #_____

Exp. Date_____

Signature_____

Prices in US dollars and subject to change without notice.

NAME _____

INSTITUTION _____

ADDRESS _____

CITY _____

STATE/ZIP _____

COUNTRY _____ COUNTY (NY residents only) _____

TEL _____ FAX _____

E-MAIL_____
May we use your e-mail address for confirmations and other types of information? ☐ Yes   ☐ No

Order From Your Local Bookstore or Directly From
The Haworth Press, Inc.
10 Alice Street, Binghamton, New York 13904-1580 • USA
TELEPHONE: 1-800-HAWORTH (1-800-429-6784) / Outside US/Canada: (607) 722-5857
FAX: 1-800-895-0582 / Outside US/Canada: (607) 772-6362
E-mail: getinfo@haworthpressinc.com
PLEASE PHOTOCOPY THIS FORM FOR YOUR PERSONAL USE.

BOF96